THE
COMMANDER-IN-CHIEF'S GUARD

REVOLUTIONARY WAR

BY

CARLOS E. GODFREY, M. D.

Washington, D. C.

ILLUSTRATED

JANAWAY PUBLISHING, INC.
Santa Maria, California

Notice

In many older books, foxing (or discoloration) occurs and, in some instances, print lightens with wear and age. Reprinted books, such as this, often duplicate these flaws, notwithstanding efforts to reduce or eliminate them. The pages of this reprint have been digitally enhanced and, where possible, the flaws eliminated in order to provide clarity of content and a pleasant reading experience.

Copyright © 1904, Carlos E. Godfrey

Originally published
Washington, D. C.
1904

Reprinted by:

Janaway Publishing, Inc.
732 Kelsey Ct.
Santa Maria, California 93454
(805) 925-1038
www.janawaygenealogy.com

2014

ISBN: 978-1-59641-317-7

Made in the United States of America

CONTENTS.

	Page
INTRODUCTION	9
HISTORY OF THE GUARD	19
ROSTER OF THE INFANTRY GUARD	105
ROSTER OF THE CAVALRY GUARD	110
RECORDS OF THE OFFICERS AND MEN	113
ELIJAH FISHER'S DIARY	275
CALENDAR FOR YEARS 1776 TO 1783	293
REFERENCES TO THE INTRODUCTION	295
REFERENCES TO THE HISTORY OF THE GUARD	295
REFERENCES TO THE RECORDS OF THE OFFICERS AND MEN	300

LIST OF ILLUSTRATIONS.

GENERAL GEORGE WASHINGTON . . Frontispiece
    From an engraving (after Trumbull's painting) by Thomas Cheesman, under the personal supervision of Colonel John Trumbull, London, 1796.

                                             Opposite Page

CAPTAIN GEORGE LEWIS . . . 21
    Silhouette, belonging to Miss Attaway M. Lewis, Washington, D. C.

FIRST PAY ROLL OF THE CAVALRY GUARD . 39
    Reproduced in fac-simile for the first time from the original in the possession of Mrs. Lucy L. Funsten, of White Post, Va., a great-grand-daughter of Major George Lewis.

THE HUTS OF THE GUARD AT VALLEY FORGE 52
    A sectional engraving, by David G. Smith, now in the Congressional Library.

DR. SAMUEL HANSON . . 54
    From the hitherto unpublished portrait painted by Hesselyus, now owned by Mrs. H. Rieman Duval, of New York.

DR. EBENEZER CROSBY . . 70
    From an engraving after an original miniature, by permission of General James Grant Wilson, of New York.

LIEUTENANT WILLIAM COLFAX . 76
    From the original painting in the possession of Richard S. Colfax, Pompton, N. J.

LIEUTENANT LEVI HOLDEN . . . 81
    From a painting, by permission, now in the New Jersey Historical Society.

MUSTER ROLL OF THE INFANTRY GUARD . 88
    Reproduced in fac-simile from the original in the National Museum.

FLAG OF THE GUARD 98
    Reproduced from Benson J. Lossing's sketch of the original.

CAPTAIN BEZALEEL HOWE 99
    From an artotype by E. Bierstadt of the original miniature painted about 1782.

CAPTAIN BEZALEEL HOWE'S INSTRUCTIONS . . 100
    From the original document belonging to the Howe collection in the New Jersey Historical Society.

SIGNATURES OF THE OFFICERS AND OF THE MEN 104
    Fac-simile of the originals.

INTRODUCTION.

At this late day the possibility of elucidating the obscurity surrounding such a distinguished command as the Commander-in-Chief's Guard, composed as it was of the flower and pick of the American army, would ordinarily be considered too remote and unpromising; particularly when such an eminent authority as Dr. Benson J. Lossing, the foremost investigator of the period culminating in our National birth (who gave particular attention to this corps), substantially states that the silent and unwritten records of the organization are buried in the oblivion of the grave[1].

However, I entered vigorously on such a research as I believe has hitherto never been excelled in the preparation of the history of any military organization. The pension and land warrant lists of the Government and the States, the minutes and correspondence of the Continental Congress, and the orderly books, diaries, journals and correspondence of Washington, were carefully examined. Original manuscripts, muster and pay rolls, published and unpublished diaries and memoirs of officers and men, inspection and State returns, and military maps, found among the various archives of the Government and of the States, historical societies, libraries and private individuals, were faithfully compared. And the published military works, historical magazines, and official notices contained in the current newspapers of the day, were likewise fully investigated. The result of all this research, after the lapse of a century and a quarter of time, has been most gratifying and successful. Not asserting that it is complete or without error, I do affirm that no record has been made hastily or without what seemed to me to be well verified.

It is a source of much regret that, after a most thorough and diligent search, the descriptive[2] and other rolls of the Commander-in-Chief's Guard for the year 1776 cannot be found. They were undoubtedly destroyed, among other valuable papers of the Guard, during the fire which occurred at the Charlestown Navy Yard in 1815, where they had been carefully preserved by Major Caleb Gibbs while naval-storekeeper at that station[3]. However, through various returns and claims, it is believed that seventy-five per cent of the men composing the command during that period have been accounted for. The subsequent service of all the officers and men while in the Guard, from its reorganization under the special order of April 30, 1777, to June 6, 1783, are full and complete, except the identity of some of those who were either killed, wounded or missing at the skirmish of King's Bridge, July 3, 1781, for which period the roll is unfortunately missing. Thereafter, no further rolls appear; and the three year's men who were detailed from the New Hampshire Line to form the new and final reorganization of the Guard on June 16, 1783, were doubtless carried on the rolls of their organization as being "On command".

Revolutionary War.

The *personnel* and rank of the men comprising the corps is shown by a Return dated Rocky Hill, October 22, 1783, but unfortunately their christian names do not appear thereon, and whenever they could be positively identified by rolls, returns, or claims, the given name was added to the record.

The principal features of the work have been arranged and prepared upon the following lines:

First: The history of the Commander-in-Chief's Guard, commencing from its formation under the general order of March 11, 1776, until its dissolution on December 20, 1783, is designed to contain all official orders, returns, court-martial proceedings, sentences, death warrants and casualties occurring ad interim; and the uniforms, duties and pay of its officers and men. As the corps was *always* attached to the Head-quarters of the Commander-in-Chief[4], its specific movements are traced through the orders contained in Washington's orderly books, and from other authentic sources; all of which is interwoven with such well known historical and pertinent facts as become material to preserve a continuous chronological history of the command.

Second: In the preparation of the individual service records of the officers and enlisted men diligent care and attention was exercised in ascertaining when and where they entered the service—rank, company and regiment, and when and where they were transferred to the Guard, as well as any subsequent service. This continuity of service, and the battles and skirmishes in which they were engaged, and the casualties incidental thereto, is based entirely upon rolls,

State records and returns, and from evidence adduced in their individual and adjudicated claims. In a few instances no connecting service could be established; and the prior or connecting service of some of the men belonging to Captain Lewis's Troop of Cavalry Guards, most of whom were undoubtedly in the Commander-in-Chief's Guard during the campaign of 1776, could not be clearly identified. While it has been my purpose to make these records as full and comprehensive as possible, particularly while they were in the Guard, they are abbreviated to the extent that no repetition of rank is made by reason of any transfers or re-enlistments, unless otherwise promoted or reduced; and for the same reason the term "regiment" is used throughout the work which Congress was otherwise pleased to designate "battalion" on the establishments prior to 1781. The thirty-eight regiments of infantry that were raised in the colonies for the eight months' service in 1775 were shortly after recognized and designated numerically as Continental Troops. This plan has been adhered to in the preparation of the records, notwithstanding they are otherwise designated numerically by States and by the names of their colonels.

Third: The family records of the officers and men of the Guard form this important branch of the work. In my examination of the various claims filed by the officers and men, their widows or legal representatives, with the General Government and the States, much original data was found relative to their personality and immediate families. So

Revolutionary War.

general was this information that I determined to make a departure from the main subject of the work by incorporating these family records (to the extent of their immediate families) with their individual military record, which will not only serve to identify the soldier more definitely, but may be of inestimable value to their descendants in tracing pedigree, if any of them should desire to apply for membership in the Revolutionary Societies, or otherwise. Every effort was exercised in perfecting these records, and in the gathering of others where no claims had been filed, through the descendants of these illustrious heroes—many of whom responded with promptness, some with willingness, others with indifference, while some could not be found.

The Commander-in-Chief's Guard, sometimes otherwise officially designated as "His Excellency's Guard" and "The General's Guard," was popularly and synonymously known by the soldiers as "Washington's Life Guard" and "Washington's Body Guard;" by which misnomers they continue today to be erroneously recognized in historical works[5] and in the official military records of many States[6], notwithstanding Congress resolved as early as April 15, 1777 that these appellations were improper, and admonished the officers that these practices must cease. Also, it has been inadvertently stated by distinguished authors that the Guard was organized at New York shortly after the siege of Boston,[7] on May 13, 1776,[8] and that the corps consisted of a major's command of one hundred and eighty men,[9] all of which has been successfully controverted in the history of the command by unquestionable authority.

The Commander-in-Chief's Guard.

In the course of my research my attention has frequently been directed to numerous men alleged to have had service in the Commander-in-Chief's Guard. In every instance their military records were inquired into with the possibility of perfecting the rolls of the Guard in the campaign of 1776. Almost invariably these allegations could not be verified. It is true, however, that after Captain Lewis's Troop of Cavalry Guards[10] rejoined their regiment September 26, 1778, small squads of cavalrymen were thereafter occasionally detailed for brief periods to escort Washington upon long journeys, or to serve as an auxiliary guard of his person in times of action, though while in the performance of these special duties they were in *nowise whatever* considered a part of his regular Guard.

I can readily understand the motive which prompts the descendants of these Revolutionary sires to connect their ancestor's service with this famous command if possible, but I fail to comprehend why numerous unsupported pretensions should be made unless they are deliberately done with the knowledge that the records of the Guard have heretofore been regarded as a sealed book, or by a perversion of the facts communicated to them by tradition or otherwise. A conspicuous example of the manner in which many of these abuses have arisen is manifested in the case of Uzal Knapp, whose alleged service in this corps is noticed and confirmed as a fact by eminent authors, who have emblazed his portrait and autograph upon the pages of history for all time as the last surviving member of the Commander-

REVOLUTIONARY WAR.

in-Chief's Guard[11]. It is related that Sergeant Knapp was transferred to the Guard at Morristown in the winter of 1780, with which command he continued to serve until his discharge in June, 1783; and after his death, which occurred at New Windsor, New York, January 11, 1856, his body was laid in state in the reception-room of the Hasbrouck House at Newburgh, when it was appropriately interred with military honors the following Wednesday at the foot of the flag-staff in the lawn before the former head-quarters of Washington, which he had previously so faithfully guarded[12]. At an earlier date, nevertheless, Dr. Lossing admits that the narrative of Sergeant Knapp's public life was obtained in the lifetime of the latter through another person[13]. As a matter of fact the records show that Uzal Knapp enlisted for the war at Stamford, Connecticut, May 1, 1777, in Captain Stephen Butts's Company, Second Connecticut Regiment; and after being successively promoted a corporal and a sergeant, was honorably discharged from his regiment June 8, 1783; and subsequently died at New Windsor, New York, July 10, 1856. In his application for pension he negatives any service in the Commander-in-Chief's Guard, which is supported by the rolls of the organization. Another similar case is that of Moses Long, who is reputed to have been transferred to the Guard, among twelve others, shortly after the battle of Monmouth[14]; whose service in reality was strictly confined to the Ninth Massachusetts Regiment.

References and acknowledgments are made throughout this volume, but it is a pleasure to mention here a more general obligation to the late Major-General William S. Stryker, of Trenton, New Jersey, for valuable suggestions and advice relative to the preparation of the work. It is also a great pleasure for me to acknowledge the generous favor of Brigadier-General M. I. Ludington, Quartermaster-General of the United States Army, for specifying the uniform worn by the Guard during the earlier campaigns. To the Hon. William M. Olin, Secretary of the Commonwealth of Massachusetts, I am greatly indebted for permission to obtain certain advance data from the valuable compilation of Revolutionary records in his department, now in course of publication. They contain many invaluable records relative to the officers and men of the Commander-in-Chief's Guard. My sincere thanks are due to Mr. Aaron A. Plaisted, of Waterville, Maine, for furnishing me the Return[15] of the commissioned and non-commissioned Officers and enlisted Men of the Guard for October 22, 1783 —which I had tried in vain to discover, and for permitting me to use certain valuable extracts from the manuscript reminiscences of his grandfather, Corporal Asa Redington of this command. I also owe many thanks to Mr. George Rowland Howe, of East Orange, New Jersey, for the portrait of Captain Bezaleel Howe, and for his liberality in allowing me to examine and use in the work certain papers of the Guard belonging to the family, now deposited with the New Jersey Historical Society; and for similar courtesies I am likewise indebted to Mr. Richard S. Colfax, of Pompton, New Jersey. The facilities that have been extended to me in my research and the courteous attention that I have received from the custodians of the archives of the Government and the States, the officers in charge of the military departments of the several States, librarians of historical societies and libraries, and from many others, are gratefully remembered. Without the assistance and co-operation of these persons the work would hardly have been possible.

HISTORY OF THE GUARD.

The Commander-in-Chief's Guard was organized precisely at the hour of twelve, noon, March 12, 1776, pursuant to a general order* issued by General Washington the previous day wherein he directed the formation of a corps of sober, intelligent and reliable men, detailed from the various regiments of infantry then assembled at Cambridge, Massachusetts, to be known as the Commander-in-Chief's Guard. He further specified that the men selected should be between five feet eight inches and five feet ten inches in height, well drilled, and to be handsomely and well built. On the following morning Caleb Gibbs, of Massachusetts, and George Lewis—a nephew of General Washington, of Virginia, were commissioned captain and lieutenant, respectively, of the Guard, to whom were intrusted the details of the organization.

"HEAD-QUARTERS, CAMBRIDGE, March 11, 1776.
"The General is desirous of selecting a particular number of men as a guard for himself and baggage. The colonel or commanding officers of each of the established regiments, the artillery and riflemen excepted, will furnish him with four, that the number wanted may be chosen out of them. His Excellency depends upon the colonels for good men, such as they can recommend for their

The Commander-in-Chief's Guard.

The necessity for such a corps was early manifested after Washington had assumed command of the American forces at Cambridge, July 3, 1775, by the rapid accumulation of valuable papers and for the safety of his person from the enemies that abounded in and about the camp; and, during the existence of the organization, it was always esteemed a mark of *particular* distinction by the soldiers to be members of this command[1], and its popularity was early shown by the letter[2] of Captain Seth Harding to Governor Trumbull, dated Fairfield, Connecticut, May 20, 1776, wherein he says: "I am now fitting out another small sloop—privateersman—that was taken from a Tory, that I have called the 'Life Guard', etc."

After the evacuation of Boston by the British, Washington, on Thursday afternoon, April 4, 1776, accompanied by the Guard[3], took his departure for New York, via Providence, Norwich and New London, where he arrived on the thirteenth of the same month[4] and established head-quarters in the spacious brick-mansion situated (in 1860) at 180 Pearl

---

sobriety, honesty and good behavior. He wishes them to be from five feet eight inches to five feet ten inches, handsomely and well made, and, as there is nothing in his eyes more desirable than cleanliness in a soldier, he desires that particular attention may be made in the choice of such men as are clean and spruce. They are all to be at headquarters tomorrow precisely at 12 o'clock at noon, when the number wanted will be fixed upon. The General neither wants them with uniforms nor arms, nor does he desire any man to be sent to him that is not perfectly willing or desirous of being of this Guard—they should be drilled men."

Revolutionary War.

Street, opposite Cedar[5], from whence he issued the following general order*:

"HEAD-QUARTERS, NEW YORK, May 16, 1776.

"Any orders delivered by Caleb Gibbs and George Lewis, Esquires—officers of the General's Guard, are to be attended to in the same manner as if sent by an aide-de-camp."

On the 21st of May, Washington, in pursuance of an invitation, proceeded to Philadelphia to confer with the Continental Congress. Upon his return to New York on the afternoon of June 6 he established head-quarters at the Mortier House, later known as Richmond Hill and the country seat of Colonel Aaron Burr, situated on the spot now known as the south-east corner of Varick and Charlton Streets[6]; which building was appropriated for his use during his absence, near where the Guard took up quarters on the 24th of May*.

No further mention of the Guard is found until the middle of June, 1776, when members of it were suspected of being engaged in an alleged conspiracy to assassinate Washington. At this time the British were anxious to open up a communication between the sea-board and Canada, by taking possession of the city of New York and of the Hudson River, and the establishment of a line of military posts, with a view of separating New England from the rest of the continent, thereby weakening the confederacy of the revolted colonies.

At the time in question, a powerful land and naval armament, under the command of the brothers Howe, were daily expected off Sandy Hook. The town and camp were filled with rumors of a foul conspiracy. It was alleged that, on the arrival of the British fleet, the Tories were to rise, full armed, to co-operate with the ministerial forces; that King's Bridge, at the upper end of the island, was to be destroyed, so as to cut off all communication with the main land; that the magazines were to be fired, and Washington and his staff to be murdered, or seized and given up to the enemy. The finger of rumor also pointed at many residents of the city, and of Long and Staten Islands, as conspirators. Among these were the proprietors of the most prominent taverns of the city; and the tavern of Corbie—situated southeast of Washington's head-quarters, to the westward of Bayard's woods and north of Lispenard's meadows, near the intersection of the present Spring and Wooster Streets— was designated as the general rendezvous of the conspirators. It was further rumored that from this house a correspondence was kept up, through a mulatto, with Governor Tryon, who had prudently taken to the British armed vessel, Duchess of Gordon, lying near Staten Island.[7]

Inasmuch as this alleged conspiracy seriously connected several members of the Guard, as will hereafter appear, it will be proper to state that, shortly after Washington had established head-quarters at New York, certain prominent loyalists formed a secret organization on the 13th of May, wherein they pledged themselves to one another by everything that was solemn and sacred to espouse the cause of their glorious king, George the Third, and seize every opportunity to dissolve the councils of the New York Provincial Congress and defeat, what they termed, "The insidious machinations of an ambitious faction."†

The Star Chamber of the conspiracy appears to have been located at the Sergeant Arms Tavern, situated near the old barracks, which was kept by Alexander Sinclair; where they frequently met in private with the primary object of devising means for the assassination of Washington, the abduction of his staff, and the seduction of the Continental soldiery. William Collier, a waiter at the tavern who usually attended to their refreshments, having become suspicious that these conspirators did not meet for pleasure alone, decided to conceal himself in an adjoining room, where, on several occasions, he caught the drift of their conversation, which he finally and voluntarily communicated to Mr. Joseph Smith, a prominent resident of the city.†

After Mr. Smith had questioned Collier as to the names of these persons who had met at his master's house, and believing the truth of his statement, he presented this intelligence to the Provincial Congress on the twenty-first of June; and after due consideration Congress ordered the arrest of Gilbert Forbes, a gunsmith, the following night. Accordingly, a party of men under the command of Captain John Laboyteaux, proceeded, at two o'clock the following morning, to the house of Forbes, on Broadway, where they placed him under arrest and seized several incriminating papers, including a copy of the constitution of the conspirator's association, and conveyed him to the new jail where he was placed in irons.†

THE COMMANDER-IN-CHIEF'S GUARD.

The same day that Congress ordered the arrest of Forbes, the secret committee appointed on the 17th of June, consisting of Philip Livingston, John Jay and Gouverneur Morris, were directed to cause the arrest of David Matthews, the mayor of the city, who was residing at Flatbush, on Long Island, about a mile and a half from the encampment of General Greene, near Brooklyn. They immediately addressed a note to General Washington requesting the arrest of Matthews and the seizure of all his papers. Washington, on the same afternoon, forwarded this note to General Greene with the indorsement that the arrest should be executed promptly at one o'clock the ensuing morning. In compliance with this order General Greene sent a detachment of his brigade, under the command of Colonel Varnum, to Matthews' house precisely at the hour named, when they seized his person and conveyed him to the city hall in New York, where he was likewise placed in irons[8].

Simultaneously with the arrest of Forbes and Matthews, Washington, with Captain Gibbs of the Guard, and a party of picked men were also out and before six o'clock in the morning had some forty men under arrest at the city hall[9], including Drummer Green, Fifer Johnson, and Private Barnes, of the Commander-in-Chief's Guard†; also the housekeeper of Washington[10], the latter being a daughter of Sam Faunce, a noted innkeeper of the day, from whence it will be remembered Washington took an affectionate farewell of his officers at the close of the war, on December 4, 1783.

On the following day—June 22—Congress, after being

advised of the successful operations of the previous night, appointed a committee of inquiry, whereof Peter R. Livingston was President, with power to sit in judgment in the investigation of the alleged conspiracy. After an examination of many witnesses, in connection with the secret committee appointed June 17, and after receiving numerous reports from the various committees of safety up the Hudson and elsewhere, where testimony of the corrupting agents of the conspiracy was also taken, the Committee was fully satisfied that the entire plot emanated from Governor Tryon, and was developed through the agency of Mayor Matthews, who had given money for the purchase of arms, enlistment of men, and the corruption of the Continental soldiers, chiefly through the instrumentality of Gilbert Forbes, the gunsmith, whose place of business was on Broadway, opposite Hull's Tavern, near Bowling Green.†

However, before the Provincial Congress had taken action relative to the alleged rumors, or upon the intelligence of William Collier communicated by Mr. Smith, the deadly machinations of the conspiracy for the destruction of Washington appears to have been in motion through the arch-traitor, Thomas Hickey, a private in the Commander-in-Chief's Guard. He was a dark complexioned Irishman, who had previously borne a good character at Wethersfield, Connecticut, where he resided after deserting from the British army some few years previous.[11]. He had the confidence of the Commander-in-Chief, and was a favorite at Richmond Hill. Having enlisted in the conspiracy, to him was intrusted the work of destroying Washington. In his resolve to poison him he next approached the housekeeper, with whom he was on good terms, and made her his confidant, who pretended to favor his views.

Washington was very fond of green peas, and it was understood that when a dish was ready for the General's table that he, Hickey, would place the poison in it. It appears that on Saturday, the fifteenth of June, a dish having been so prepared was placed before the Commander-in-Chief, who, being fully cautioned by the housekeeper, made some excuse for sending the dish away[12]; and shortly after, on the same day, Hickey and Private Lynch of the Guard were arrested upon the alleged charge of attempting to pass a counterfeit bill, and were ordered by the Provincial Congress to be confined to the guard in the city hall[13].

On the following Monday the Provincial Congress resolved that, inasmuch as the authority of the courts of the colony was derived from the crown of Great Britain, they were incompetent to furnish a full and impartial trial of Thomas Hickey and Michael Lynch for the offence charged, and directed that they be turned over to the military authorities for trial by court-martial. They further directed that all papers in the case, together with a copy of the resolution, should be transmitted to General Washington[14].

After the Commander-in-Chief had received these papers, and the conclusions of the Committee of Congress, before related, he called a general court-martial to assemble at the head-quarters of the Provost Marshal, at nine o'clock on the morning of the 26th of June, for the trial of Thomas Hickey upon the serious charge "of exciting and joining in a mutiny and sedition, and of treacherously corresponding with, enlisting among, and receiving pay from the enemies of the United American Colonies", where the following proceedings[15] were held:

"Proceedings of a General Court Martial of the Line held at Head Quarters in the City of New York, by Warrant from his Excellency George Washington Esq. General & Commander in Chief of the Forces of the united American Colonies, for the Trial of Thomas Hickey & others, June 26th, A. D. 1776—

"Col. Samuel H. Parsons, Presidt.

"Lt. Colo. William Sheppard	Capt. Warham Parks
Major Levi Wells	Capt. William Reed
Capt. Joseph Hoyt	Capt. Joseph Pettingill
Capt. Abel Pettibone	Capt. David Lyon
Capt. Samuel Warren	Capt. David Sill
Capt. James Mellin	Capt. Timothy Purcival

"Wm. Tudor, Judge Advocate.

"The Warrant being read & the Court first duly sworn, proceeded to the Trial of Thomas Hickey a private Centinel in his Excellency's the Commander in Chiefs Guard commanded by Major (Captain) Gibbs, brought Prisoner before the Court & accused 'of exciting & joining in a Mutiny & Sedition, & of treacherously corresponding with, inlisting among, and receiving Pay from the Enemies of the united American Colonies.'

"The Prisoner being arraign'd on the above Charge pleads not guilty.

"Wm. Green—sworn Deposes: About three Weeks ago I was in Company with one Gilbert Forbes a Gunsmith who lives in Broad Way, & we fell into a Conversation on Politicks. I found Forbes's Pulse beat high in the Tory Scheme. I had repeated Conversations with Forbes afterwards & he was always introducing

Politicks, & hinting at the Impossibility of this Country standing against the Power of Great Britain. He invited me to dine with him one Day, and a Day or two after ask'd me if I would not inlist into the King's service. I ask'd him where the Money was to come from to pay me for the service, Forbes reply'd the Mayor would furnish Money. I was pleased with the notion of getting some Money from the Tories & agreed to the Scheme with a View to cheat the Tories & detect their Scheme. I mentioned the Matter to several & among others to Hickey, the Prisoner. I told him the Principle I went upon & that we had a good opportunity of duping the Tories. Hickey agreed to the Scheme, but did not receive any Money except 2/ which I gave him. Forbes left it with me to inlist & swear the Men. Forbes swore me & one Clark on a Bible to fight for the King. But I swore Hickey to fight for America. After the Prisoner was engaged I proposed to him to reveal the Plot to the General, but Hickey said we had better let it alone till we had made further Discoveries. All that Forbes proposed to me was, that when the King's Forces arriv'd we should cut away King's Bridge & then go on Board a Ship of War which would be in the East River to receive Us. I inlisted ten or a Dozen & told them all my Plan. The Prisoner wrote his Name upon a Peice of Paper with five others, which I gave to Forbes, & this was all the Inlistment that I knew of the Prisoner's signing.

"Gilbert Forbes: A night or two after General Washington arriv'd in New York from Boston, Green fell into Company where I was. We were drinking & Green toasted the King's Health, & I did so too. A Day or two afterwards Green call'd upon me & said that as I had drank his Majesty's Health he supposed I was his Friend, & immediately proposed to inlist some Men into the King's Service, & told me he could procure considerable Numbers to join him. I put him off and declin'd having any Hand in the Business. But on repeated applications from him, I at last fell into the Scheme. Green was to inlist the Men, in which I was not to be concern'd nor have my name mentioned. In a Day or two

Revolutionary War.

Green gave me a List of men who had engaged, among whom was the Prisoner Hickey. Soon after which, Hickey ask'd me to give him a ½ a Dollar, which I did, & this was all the Money Hickey ever receiv'd from me. Green receiv'd eighteen Dollars & was to pay the men who inlisted one Dollar apeice, & we were to allow them ten shillings per Week Subsistence Money. I received upwards of a hundred Pounds from Mr. Mathews the Mayor to pay those who should inlist into the King's Service, Who after inlisting were to go on Board the King's Ships, but if they could not get there were to play their proper Parts when the King's Forces arriv'd.

"Wm. Welch: Between a fortnight & three Weeks ago I met the Prisoner in the Street, he ask'd me to go with him to a Grog Shop. When we got there he told me he had something to tell me of Importance, but insisted on my being sworn before he would communicate it. I accordingly swore on the Bible to keep secret what he should tell me. He then said that this Country was sold, that the Enemy would soon arrive & that it was best for us old Countrymen to make our Peace before they came or they would kill Us all. That we old Countrymen should join together & we would be known by a particular Mark & if I would agree to be one among them, he would carry me to a Man who would let me have a Dollar by Way of Encouragement. I did not relish the Project, & we parted.

"Isaac Ketchum: Last Saturday Week the Prisoner was committed to Goal on suspicion of counterfeiting the Continental Currency, & seeing me in Goal, inquired the Reason of it. I told him because I was a Tory. On this a Conversation ensued upon Politicks. In different Conversations he informed me that the army was become damnably corrupted. That the Fleet was soon expected, & that he & a Number of others were in a Choir to turn against the American Army when the King's Troops should arrive, & ask'd me to be one of them. The Plan he told me was, some were to be sick, & others were to hire Men in their Room. That eight of the General's Guard was concerned, but mentioned only Green by Name. He farther told me that one Forbes a Tavern

Keeper was to be their Captain, but that the Inferior Officers were not yet appointed lest the Scheme should be discovered.

"The Prisoner being here call'd upon to make his Defence produces no Evidence. But says 'He engaged in the Scheme at first for the Sake of cheating the Tories & getting some Money from them; & afterwards consented to have his Name sent on Board the Man of War, in order that if the Enemy should arrive & defeat the Army here, & he should be taken Prisoner, he might be safe.'

"The Court being cleared, after matured Consideration, are unanimously of opinion, that the Prisoner is guilty of the Charge against him, & of a Breach of the 5th & of the 30th Articles of the Rules & Regulations for the Government of the Continental Forces, & the Court unanimously sentence & adjudge that the Prisoner Thomas Hickey, suffer Death for said Crimes, by being hang'd by the Neck till he is dead.

"SAML. H. PARSONS *President*"

At a council of the general officers held at head-quarters on the following day, consisting of Brigadier-Generals Heath, Spencer, Green, Lord Stirling, Mifflin and Scott, General Washington communicated to the council the proceedings of the court-martial on Thomas Hickey, when he was unanimously advised to confirm the sentence, and that it be put in execution the following day at eleven o'clock.[16] In compliance with this advice the following order* appears:

"HEAD-QUARTERS, NEW YORK, June 27, 1776.
"Thomas Hickey, belonging to the General's Guard, having been convicted by a general court-martial, whereof Colonel Parsons was President, of the crimes of sedition and mutiny, and also of holding a treacherous correspondence with the enemy for the most horrible and detestable purposes, is sentenced to suffer death.

Revolutionary War.

The General approves the sentence, and orders that he be hanged tomorrow morning at eleven o'clock.

"All the officers and men off duty belonging to General Spencer's and Lord Stirling's encampment to attend the execution of the above sentence. The Provost Marshal immediately to make the necessary preperations and to attend on that duty tomorrow.

"After Orders: Each of the brigade-majors to furnish the Provost Marshal with twenty men from each brigade, with good arms and bayonets, as a guard of the prisoner to and at the place of execution."

On the following morning Washington issued the following warrant,[17] directed to the Provost Marshal, for the execution of Thomas Hickey:

"By His Excellency George Washington, Esquire, General and Commander-in-Chief of the army of the United American Colonies.

"To the Provost Marshal of the said army:

"Whereas Thomas Hickey, a soldier enlisted in the service of the said united colonies, has been duly convicted by a general court-martial of mutiny and sedition, and also of holding a treacherous correspondence with the enemies of said colonies, contrary to the rules and regulations established for the government of the said troops; and the said Thomas Hickey, being so convicted, has been sentenced to death, by being hanged by the neck till he shall be dead; which sentence, by the unanimous advice of the general officers of the said army, I have thought proper to confirm. These are, therefore, to will and require you to execute the said sentence upon the said Thomas Hickey this day, at eleven o'clock in the forenoon, upon the ground between the encampments of the brigades of Brigadier-General's Spencer and Lord Stirling; and for so doing this shall be your sufficient warrant.

"Given under my hand this twenty-eighth day of June, in the year of our Lord one thousand seven hundred and seventy-six.

"George Washington.

"Head-quarters, New York, June 28, 1776."

The Commander-in-Chief's Guard.

Precisely at ten o'clock on the morning of the twenty-eighth of June, the brigades of Brigadier-Generals Heath, Spencer, Lord Stirling and Scott marched from their respective encampments to the place of execution, where over twenty thousand people had assembled. At quarter of eleven o'clock the prisoner, accompanied by the Provost Marshal and Chaplain, and a guard of eighty men with bayonets fixed, took up the march from the brick guard-house of the Provost Marshal to the place of execution, which was a tree in a field belonging to Colonel Henry Rutger[18], situated a little east of the Bowery Lane, near the intersection of the present Grand and Christie Streets[19]. A letter[20] from Surgeon William Eustis to Dr. David Townsend, of Boston, under date of New York, June 28, 1776, relates the following scene at the gallows: "He (Hickey) appeared unaffected and obstinate to the last, except when the chaplain took him by the hand under the gallows and bade him adieu, a torrent of tears flowed over his face; but with an indignant scornful air he wiped them with his hand from his face, and assumed the confident look; with his last breath the fellow told the spectators that unless General Greene was very cautious the design would yet be executed on him." At eleven o'clock he was hanged, as appears by the return[21] of the Provost Marshal indorsed upon the original warrant:

New York, June 28, 1776.

"By virtue of and in obedience to the forgoing warrant I have this day, at the time and place therein ordered and directed, caused Thomas Hickey, the prisoner within mentioned, to suffer death in the way and manner therein prescribed, and accordingly return this warrant fully executed.

"WILLIAM MORONY,
"*Provost Marshal in the army of the United Colonies.*"

Afterwards, on the same day, the following order* appears:

"HEAD-QUARTERS, NEW YORK, June 28, 1776.
"The unhappy fate of Thomas Hickey, executed this day for mutiny, sedition and treachery, the General hopes will be a warning to every soldier in the army to avoid these crimes, and all others, so disgraceful to the character of a soldier and pernicious to his country, whose pay he receives and bread he eats. And in order to avoid those crimes the most certain method is to keep out of the temptation of them, and particularly to avoid lewd women, who, by the dying confession of this poor criminal, first led him into practices which ended in an untimely and ignominious death."

The fate of Drummer Green, Fifer Johnson, and Privates Lynch and Barnes, of the Guard, is one of conjecture. The testimony of Green, in connection with Forbes's at the court-martial of Hickey, shows conclusively by his own admission that he was not only a principal, but the one who first allured his fellow comrades into this horrible plot. That he was not an unwilling tool of the conspiracy for the destruction of Washington, after Hickey's plans had been foiled, is apparent in the letter[22] of Solomon Drowne to his sister, dated New York, June 24, 1776, wherein he says: "The drummer (Green) of ye Guard was to have stabbed ye General." Inasmuch as neither of these soldiers appear in the list[23] of prisoners of the conspiracy that was sent to Litchfield, Con-

THE COMMANDER-IN-CHIEF'S GUARD.

necticut, and the fact stated in the letter of Surgeon Eustis: "We are hanging them (the conspirators) as fast as we find them out," it is evident that they were not absolved or confined, but that they met the fate of Hickey.[24]

It is uncertain upon what suspicion the housekeeper of Washington was arrested, unless it was by some concocted story of the conspiracy. It is perfectly clear, however, that she not only proved her innocence in the affair, but her patriotism, and was acquitted with honor[25]. Mayor Matthews was convicted and sentenced on the 8th of July, 1776, by the Committee of the Provincial Congress, to suffer death on the twenty-fifth of the following month; which sentence was finally remitted August 1, when he was ordered to be confined at Litchfield, Connecticut,† where Gilbert Forbes was also consigned[26], until further orders.

It is rather remarkable that the *first* soldier of the Continental army to hang should have been a member of the Commander-in-Chief's Guard[27], who were specially selected for their patriotism and fidelity to duty. The ultimate consummation of this sad occurrence in public had a most salutary influence upon the army, particularly so, as far as any further attempt to engage in a conspiracy for the assassination of any general officer. After the removal of this treacherous and obnoxious element from the Guard the rest of the men enjoyed the highest confidence and respect of their immediate officers and the Commander-in-Chief, and most of them thereafter rendered long, honorable and faithful service whereby they became eligible to the Badge of

REVOLUTIONARY WAR.

Merit, a distinction second in rank to the Purple Heart, of which we shall hereafter speak.

At the time of the battle of Long Island, August 27, 1776, no evidence is found of the Guard performing other duty than that at head-quarters, notwithstanding Washington was on Long Island that day viewing the action from a hill crowned by a redoubt, which occupied the block now bounded by Court, Clinton, Atlantic and Pacific Streets, Brooklyn. After the disastrous results of this battle, and immediately previous to the retreat of the American forces from New York, Sergeant Richards of the Guard was court-martialed on the eleventh of September, whereby he was convicted of abusing and striking Captain Gibbs and sentenced to be reduced to the ranks and whipped thirty-nine lashes; which findings were immediately approved by General Washington, who ordered the punishment to be inflicted at eight o'clock the following morning before the head of his company.* These chastisements were invariably performed by the drummers and fifers under the supervision of the drum-major[28]. On September 13 Sergeant Clements of the Guard was also convicted of remission of duty, when he was reduced to the ranks and, by the personal order of Washington, directed to rejoin his regiment*.

On Saturday, September 14, Washington relinquished head-quarters at the Mortier House and established them at the house of Robert Murray, near the corner of the present Thirty-sixth Street and Fourth Avenue, to again take them up the following day—Sunday—at Mott's Tavern, Harlem

Plains. On Monday he again changed them to the house of Roger Morris, situated on a high and commanding ground at Harlem Heights, nearly opposite the intersection of the present Amsterdam Avenue and One Hundred and Sixty-first Street with the King's Bridge Road, where he remained until the twenty-first of October, when he removed to Valentine's Hill, and from there retreated to White Plains, New York, where he arrived October 23 and established head-quarters at the residence of Adjutant Elijah Miller, about a mile north of the village, while the main body of the army was entrenched two miles beyond.[29]

We next find the Guard present at the battle of White Plains, on Chatterton Hill, October 28. At eleven o'clock on the morning of the tenth of November the Guard, with the main army, left White Plains for Peekskill, the entrance to the Highlands. The following day they commenced the memorable retreat of Washington through New Jersey, via Fort Lee, Hackensack, Newark, New Brunswick, Princeton, and arrived at Trenton on the second day of December. Early Sunday morning, December 8, the Guard, with the main army, crossed the Delaware River and encamped near head-quarters established at the Berkley House[30]—situated about a half mile from the river, within the present limits of Morrisville, opposite Trenton, where they remained until the following Saturday, when head-quarters was changed to the farm house of Wiliam Keith[31], on the road from Brownsburg to the Eagle Tavern, within half an hour's ride from Newtown, near McKonkey's Ferry; when Lieuten-

REVOLUTIONARY WAR.

ant Lewis was detached from the Guard with authority from Washington to raise a troop of cavalry.[32]

In the absence of existing documentary evidence it is impossible to state the exact strength of the Guard during this period, but it is certain that the corps was originally composed of fifty enlisted men[33], which was necessarily less at this time. As their term of enlistment was about expiring, Washington, on December 14, gave discharges to some twenty of them upon condition that they would re-enlist for three years in the troop of cavalry then being raised by Lieutenant Lewis, whose rendezvous was at Newtown—close by.[34]

Immediately before midnight on the twenty-fifth of December the Guard, with the main army, crossed the Delaware River at McKonkey's Ferry, now Taylorsville, and surprised the Hessians shortly after sunrise the next morning at Trenton, known as the battle of Trenton. They triumphantly re-crossed the Delaware at McKonkey's Ferry before midnight and encamped the following day at Newtown, five miles west of the river, adjacent to headquarters established in a house occupied by John Harris,[35] situated on the west side of Neshaminy Creek. At the personal request of Washington the remaining men of the Guard, whose term of enlistment expired December 31, 1776, promised to remain six weeks longer to serve a bold move which he secretly had in view[36].

On Monday morning, December 30, Washington, with the Guard, again crossed the Delaware at McKonkey's Ferry and hurried on to Trenton, in advance of the main

THE COMMANDER-IN-CHIEF'S GUARD.

body of troops who later encamped on the south side of Assunpink Creek, where he established head-quarters at the house of John Barnes, situated on Queen Street near the Assunpink Creek Bridge. The following Thursday morning, January 2, 1777, head-quarters was moved to Jonathan Richmond's Tavern, on the south side of the bridge; and late at night, Washington stealthily withdrew the army and eluded the vigilance of the enemy, who had arrived at Trenton in the afternoon, by taking a circuitous route to Princeton, where they arrived before sunrise the following morning and engaged a brigade of British regulars in a brief but decisive action known as the battle of Princeton[87]. In the flight of the enemy Washington pursued them as far as Kingston, beyond the Millstone River, and then filing off to the left, after destroying the bridge, marched to Somerset Court-House, now Millstone, where the army halted for the night, while the Guard encamped near the residence of John Van Doren where Washington was quartered.[88] The next morning the army continued the march to Pluckamin, where they again halted in the afternoon; and, on Monday, January 6, they reached winter-quarters at Morristown, where Washington established head-quarters at the tavern owned and kept by Captain Jacob Arnold, of the New Jersey Militia[89].

There is nothing to indicate the exact date when the men of the Guard were finally discharged at Morristown except the inference which might be drawn from the receipt[40] given by Richard Frothington, conductor of artillery, to Private Samuel Reid for the return of his musket on February 10,

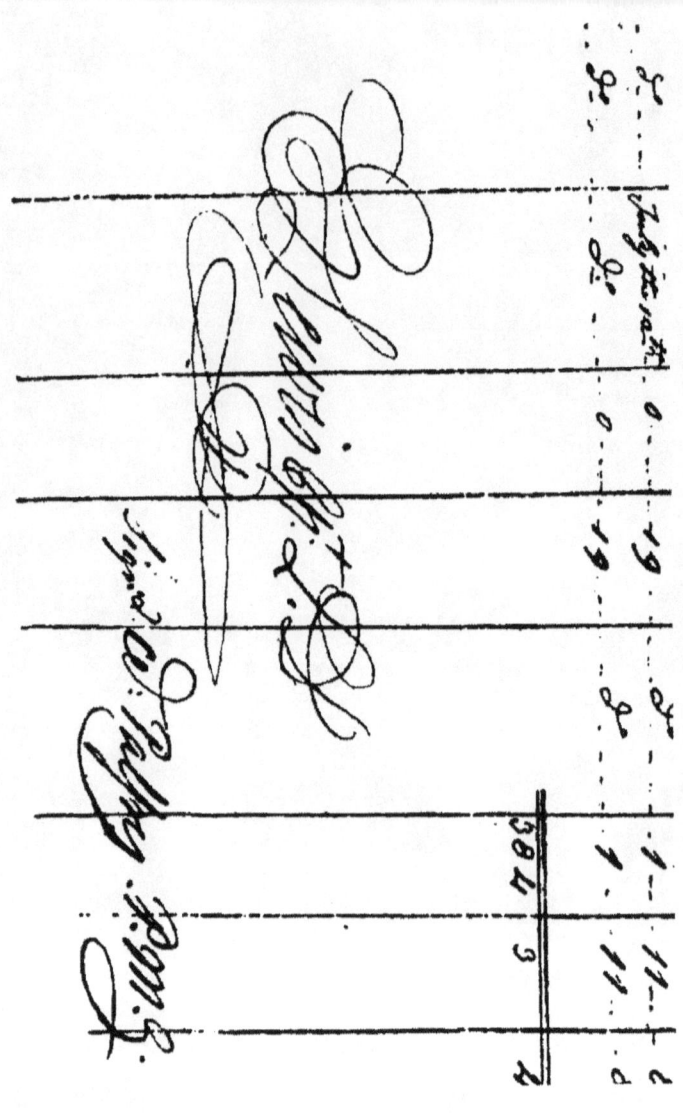

REVOLUTIONARY WAR.

1776. It appears that they were discharged before the fifteenth of February, and no mention is made of them in orders after the eighth of the same month.

Lieutenant Lewis succeeded in raising his troop of fifty men, and was commissioned captain in the Third Regiment, Continental Dragoons, to rank from January 1, 1777, and joined his incompleted regiment at Morristown the following April. On May 1, 1777, part of the troop was transferred to Captain Cadwallader Jones's troop, same regiment, and the remainder, consisting of thirty-eight men under the command of Captain Lewis and Lieutenant Robert Randolph, were detached and assigned as the Cavalry of the Commander-in-Chief's Guard[41].

The adjunct of the Cavalry to the Guard was an innovation in the army, although it was no fixed corps nor incorporated with the rolls of the Guard, and its members were doubtless carried on their regimental rolls as being "On command." They appear to have been attached to the Guard until September 26, 1778, when they were detached and joined their regiment at Tappan[42] two days previous to the date when their regiment was surprised near the last named place, where the colonel, George Baylor, was severely wounded and taken prisoner, while many in the regiment were otherwise inhumanly massacred. They rendered effective service to Washington in his various reconnoiters and as the guard of his person in times of battle, in which they participated at Brandywine, Germantown and Monmouth. At the last named battle Carswell Gardner, of the Cavalry, carried the memorable dispatch from Washington to General Lee, which was disregarded by the latter[43].

The uniform of the Cavalry Guard consisted of a round black felt hat, the sight protected by a flap; around it bound by a broad strip of red cloth, and over it, falling down the neck, a fox-tail for an ornament. The coat was of white cloth, collared, faced, cuffed and lined light blue; two silver buttons on each cuff, and six—arranged two and two—on either breast flap; vest blue, with similar buttons; waist-belt white, with silver buckle; the breeches of yellow leather; black riding boots reaching to the knee, and spurs; black stock and tie for the hair; and the sabre-hilt of steel[44].

The Cavalry Guard was afterwards, from time to time, specially detailed for brief periods from the cavalry regiments of Bland, Sheldon, Moylan, etc., and was on memorable occasions commanded by Henry Lee, Theodoric Bland, Stephen Moylan and Benjamin Tallmadge. As stated before, it was *never* a fixed corps and was thereafter called to the person of the Commander-in-Chief as circumstances might require and always in time of action[45].

Returning to the Infantry or the Commander-in-Chief's Guard proper, we next note the letter of Washington to Captain Gibbs relative to the clothing and arms for the men who are to constitute the new Guard. The letter[46] read:

"MORRISTOWN, April 22, 1777.
"CAPT. CALEB GIBBS,
"Dear Sir:
"I forgot before you left this place to desire you to provide clothing for the men that are to compose my Guard, but now desire

Revolutionary War.

that you will apply to the Clothier-General, and have them forwarded to this place, or headquarters, as soon as possible.

"Provide for four sergeants, four corporals, a drum and fife, and fifty rank and file. If blue and buff can be had, I should prefer that uniform, as it is the one I wear myself. If it cannot, Mr. Mease and you may fix upon any other, red excepted. I shall get men from five feet nine to five feet ten, for the Guard; for such sized men, therefore make your clothing. You may get a small round hat, or a cocked one, as you please.

"In getting these clothes no mention need be made for what purpose they are intended; for though no extraordinary expense will attend it, and the Guard which is absolutely necessary for the security of my baggage and papers, etc., may as well be in uniform; yet the report of making a uniform (or if already made, of providing uniform) for the Guard, creates an idea of expense which I would not wish should go forth.

"That your arms may also be of a piece, I herewith enclose you an order on the commissary of stores for fifty muskets.

"I am, dear sir, your most obed't,

"Geo. Washington."

On April 30, 1777, the Commander-in-Chief issued circular letters to the colonels of the various Virginia regiments of infantry attached to the main army at Morristown, requesting that four men from their respective commands be immediately furnished him for the re-organization of his Guard. Aside from a more uniform height of the men asked than that specified in the general order of March 11, 1776, the letter is particularly noticeable for the reason that Washington had not forgotten his experience with the foreign and treacherous element of his former Guard while at New York in June, 1776, when he expressly insists that none but native born soldiers be furnished him. The circular[47] addressed to Colonel Alexander Spotswood reads thus:

"MORRISTOWN, 30 April, 1777.

"Sir:

"I want to form a company for my Guard. In doing this I wish to be extremely cautious, because it is more than probable that, in the course of the campaign, my baggage, papers, and other matters of great public import may be committed to the sole care of these men. This being premised, in order to impress you with proper attention in the choice, I have to request that you will immediately furnish me with four men of your regiment; and, as it is my farther wish that this company should look well and be nearly of a size, I desire that none of the men may exceed in stature five feet ten inches, nor fall short of five feet nine inches, sober, young, active, and well made. When I recommend care in your choice I would be understood to mean men of good character in the regiment, that possess the pride of appearing clean and soldierlike. I am satisfied there can be no absolute security for the fidelity of this class of people, but yet I think it most likely to be found in those who have family connections in the country. You will therefore send me none but natives, and men of some property, if you have them. I must insist that, in making this choice, you give no intimation of my preference of natives, as I do not want to create any invidious distinction between them and the foreigners.

"I am, yours, &c,

"GO WASHINGTON."

On the following morning, Thursday, May 1, 1777, at guard mounting, the Commander-in-Chief's Guard was again organized (although, from original returns, the command does not appear to have been fully completed until the sixth of May), which consisted of four sergeants, four corporals, one fifer and forty-seven privates, under the command of Captain Caleb Gibbs. On the same day Lieutenant John Nicholas was transferred from the Virginia Line to this corps,[46] where he remained until June 2, 1777, when he was relieved by Lieutenant Henry Philip Livingston, of New York.*

In respect to the pay of the men assigned to the Guard the following general order* appears:

"HEAD-QUARTERS, MORRISTOWN, May 6, 1777.

"The commanding officers of the battalions that furnished the Commander-in-Chief's Guard are not to draw for the men thus furnished after they have left their respective battalions, but are to give each man a certificate of the day on which he was last paid, in order that the captain of the Guard may be enabled to make out their abstract properly."

The Guard, with the main army, remained in winter-quarters, at Morristown, until four o'clock in the morning of the thirty-first of May, when they were moved down to Middlebrook, where head-quarters was established the same day. After their arrival at Middlebrook, when every conceivable plan of the British had been frustrated in their attempt to reach and capture Philadelphia by an overland route, they withdrew their entire force from the soil of New Jersey, and thus began a campaign where the designs of the enemy were never so perplexing, duty so arduous, endurance so great, and the movements of the army so frequent, as that of 1777. Washington was puzzled to know what Howe intended to do next. He first supposed that the English would go around by water to attack Philadelphia,

THE COMMANDER-IN-CHIEF'S GUARD.

but when he heard that General Burgoyne was advancing down the Lakes from Canada, he thought the English general must, in good policy, sail up the Hudson and attack the American forts in the Highlands, preparatory to joining Burgoyne at Albany[49].

However, the Guard, with the main army, broke camp on the third of July and returned to Morristown, where they arrived the following morning. On Friday, July 11, Washington leisurely and cautiously proceeded with the Guard, and a portion of the army, to Smith's Clove, Orange County, New York, via Pompton Plains, where he established headquarters at Suffern's Tavern the following Tuesday[50]. On the twenty-third of the same month, at five in the morning, the army was moved to Ramapo, via Galloway-in-the-Clove, where they arrived the following afternoon. The next day, Thursday, Washington not only received the intercepted and decoyed letter from Lord Howe to General Burgoyne, announcing his intentions to attack Boston, but also received intelligence that the large fleet of the enemy, which left New York July 5, had sailed southward from Sandy Hook on the 23d[51]. He believed that they were bound to Philadelphia by way of the Delaware, possibly destined to Charleston. However, on the 25th of July, at 5 A. M., the army was immediately dispatched southward, via Pompton and Morristown, arriving at Coryell's Ferry, now Lambertville, New Jersey, the evening of the 28th of July. The next morning, Tuesday, they commenced to cross the Delaware, and on Thursday morning took up the march down the Old York

Road and established their camp in the evening of the following day at Roxborough, near the Schuylkill Falls, west of Germantown, where Washington occupied quarters at the house of Henry Hill, now situated in the Twenty-eighth Ward of Philadelphia.[52]

Washington, under the supposition that the British fleet might possibly have gone to the eastward after clearing Sandy Hook, broke camp at Roxborough on Friday afternoon, August 8, at two o'clock, and moved back on the road towards Coryell's Ferry. At nine o'clock the following Sunday evening, while about three miles to the northward of Billet Tavern, now Hatborough, he received an express from the President of Congress informing him of the appearance of the fleet off Sinapuxent Inlet—about fifty miles south of Cape Henlopen—on the 7th instant[58]. The army halted, and head-quarters was established at a house beside the Old York Road near Neshaminy Creek, about half a mile above the present village of Hartsville, then known as the Cross Roads[54].

The sudden withdrawal of the fleet from near the Delaware, and its long voyage, greatly protracted by contrary winds, completely foiled the calculations of Washington as to its ultimate destination. On the 21st of August, Washington submitted the condition of affairs to a council of war, which rendered the unanimous opinion that General Howe had most probably sailed for Charleston. His suspense was soon ended. On the following afternoon, at 1.30 P. M., President Hancock sent an express to Washington announcing the arrival of some two hundred sail of Howe's fleet in the Chesapeake Bay[55].

At four o'clock Saturday morning, August 23, the Guard, with the main army, moved down the Old York Road and encamped for the night near Nicetown, within five miles of Philadelphia, where Washington quartered at the "Stenton," the homestead of the Logan family[56]. At four o'clock the following morning, Sunday, the army proceeded in one column through Philadelphia, going in at and marching down Front Street to Chestnut, up Chestnut to the Commons, and passing out over the Schuylkill at the middle ferry—Market Street—to Darby, where they halted for the night[57]. The next morning, at four o'clock, they advanced towards Wilmington, via Chester and Naaman's Creek, arriving there at six o'clock in the evening, when they learned that the enemy from the British fleet had landed that morning about six miles below the Head of Elk, now Elkton. Washington immediately established head-quarters in a house on Quaker Hill, which stood on the present west side of West Street midway between Third and Fourth Streets[58], where the Guard encamped close by—while the army lodged on the high land west of the town, some going as far as Newport, three miles below.

Before daylight on the 9th of September the Guard, with the main army, moved north from Wilmington, crossing Chad's Ford, and encamped on the east side of the Brandywine, where Washington quartered at the house of Benjamin King, one mile east of the ford[59].

REVOLUTIONARY WAR.

On the morning of the 11th, the British having advanced, the battle of Brandywine opened with vigor and continued all day, when the Americans were repulsed near Birmingham Meeting House and retreated in confusion during the evening to Chester, twelve miles distant. Early the next morning they proceeded to their old encampment on the east side of the Schuylkill Falls, via Darby and the bridge over the Schuylkill[60].

The following Sunday morning, at nine o'clock, they marched up along the Schuylkill and crossed over at Matson's Ford, now Conshohocken. At 3 P. M., the next day they were passing Buck Tavern, up the Old Lancaster Road, and continued thirteen miles to a point near the junction of the Swede's Ford Road, where Washington stopped for the night at the residence of Joseph Malin. The following evening at ten o'clock, after marching through a violent hail-storm, the army encamped at Yellow Springs, three miles from where Washington was quartered at the Red Lion Tavern, now Lionville.[61]

On Friday, September 19, the Guard, with the army, recrossed the Schuylkill at Parker's Ford and continued along the east side of the river—by way of the Trappe, a village on the Reading Road—as far as Perkiomen Creek. On the 21st they moved back within four miles of Pottsgrove, now Pottstown; and on the twenty-sixth, at 9 A. M., the army marched down to Pennybacker's Mills, now Schwenkville, on the Perkiomen, where Washington established head-quarters at the house of Samuel Pennybacker. At eleven o'clock the following Monday morning they proceeded down the Skippack Road to Skippack Creek, within twenty-five miles of Philadelphia, where they remained until the 2d of October; when, at eight o'clock in the morning, they continued five miles further down the road to Methacton Hill, in Worcester Township, where they halted and established headquarters at the house of Peter Wentz[62].

At seven o'clock in the evening of the third of October, the Guard, with the army, left Methacton Hill very stealthily for Germantown. As they emerged from the woods of Chestnut Hill early the following morning Washington's advance surprised the British pickets, who fell back into the main street of Germantown before being re-enforced, when the Americans received the galling fire from the fortified Chew House with disastrous results, although no casualties occurred to the Guard. In the confusion occasioned to both armies by the dense fog which enveloped the country the patriot army withdrew and fell back to Pennybacker's Mills the next morning[68].

On October 8 Washington moved the army to the Baptist Meeting-House, on the Sumneytown Road near Kulpsville, where he took quarters at the farm house of Frederick Wampole, three-quarters of a mile from the meeting-house, on the following day. He rested here until the morning of the sixteenth, when he again established head-quarters at the house of Peter Wentz, on the Skippack Road near Methacton Hill, upon the same grounds upon which they had encamped immediately before the battle of Germantown. The following Monday morning the army marched lower down to Whitpain Township, within fifteen miles of Philadelphia, where Washington occupied quarters at the house of James Morris, between the Skippack and Morris Roads[64].

As a result of a council of war held at head-quarters on the afternoon of October 29, Washington, early the following morning, dispatched Lieutenant-Colonel Alexander Hamilton to Albany, New York, to confer with Major-General Gates, and point out to him in the clearest manner the absolute necessity of his forwarding immediate reinforcements to the support of the main army.[65] The success of this mission was so indispensable to Washington that he also requested Captain Gibbs to accompany the colonel. They arrived at Albany November 5, and by reason of the illness of Colonel Hamilton enroute they did not reach head-quarters at Valley Forge until the nineteenth of the following January[66].

On November 2, at ten o'clock in the morning, another move of the Guard, and the army, was made to Whitemarsh Township, twelve miles from Philadelphia, where Washington established head-quarters at the Emlen Mansion, now standing about half a mile east from Camp Hill Station on the North Pennsylvania Railroad[67]. On Sunday, November 30, a council of war was held to consider a proper place for winter-quarters. No decision being arrived at by the board, Washington determined to form an encampment at Valley Forge, about twenty-one miles from Philadelphia, on the west side of the Schuylkill River.

THE COMMANDER-IN-CHIEF'S GUARD.

At sunrise on the morning of the eleventh of December, the Guard, with the main army, broke camp at Whitemarsh and proceeded towards winter-quarters at Valley Forge. In their efforts to cross the Schuylkill at Matson's Ford they observed a body of the enemy, under the command of Lord Cornwallis, in possession of the heights on both sides of the road leading from the river and the defile called the Gulf, when they were obliged to withdraw and proceed up to Swede's Ford, now Norristown, where they arrived in the evening and encamped in a semi-circle, while a detachment of the army built a bridge of wagons across the Schuylkill, which the Guard, with the army, passed over on the night of December 12, and the following morning marched three miles to the westward and encamped near the Gulf Mill, situated at the intersection of the Gulf Road with Gulf Creek, between six and seven miles from Valley Forge. Tradition points to a house which stood about one mile north of Gulf Mill, and half a mile east of the road, as having been Washington's head-quarters; this was known as "Walnut Grove," the residence of Lieutenant-Colonel Isaac Hughes, of the Pennsylvania Militia[68].

While at Gulf Mill, December 17, Washington, in general orders, complimented the officers and men under his command for the fortitude and patience with which they had sustained the fatigue of the campaign. He reminded them that "while in some respects the campaign has been a failure, upon the whole heaven has smiled upon our arms and crowned them with signal success." After reciting his reasons for wintering at Valley Forge, and pointing out the comforts that might be had from quartering in huts in that locality, he says that "he is persuaded to believe that the officers and soldiers, with one heart and mind, and with a firm and manly perseverance, will resolve to surmount every difficulty and endure the hardships to gain the blessings of Independence, Liberty and Peace against their cruel oppressors." He assures them that "he will personally share with them the hardships and partake of every inconvenience." He closes by reminding them that "the army will remain in their present quarters tomorrow to participate in the solemnities of the day set apart by Congress for public thanksgiving and prayer," and earnestly requests "every officer and soldier to attend divine service with their respective corps in giving grateful acknowledgements to God for their manifold blessings*."

On Thursday morning, December 18, 1777, at seven o'clock, the baggage was ordered to move. At ten o'clock the Guard, with the main army, commenced their sad and dreary march to winter-quarters, where they arrived in the afternoon and erected the tents in which they were to shelter until the log-huts were built according to the specification issued in general orders on the morning before their departure from the Gulf. Washington facilitated the enterprise by ordering the men to be divided into squads of twelve, and a reward of twelve dollars to the party of each corps who would finish their hut in the quickest and most workmanlike manner.* By the end of the month considerable numbers were in their new quarters, and on the 15th of January, 1778, the remaining men were completely sheltered[69]. Washington, good as his word, occupied his marquee until the huts were completed, when he established head-quarters at the small stone-house of Isaac Potts near the mouth of Valley Creek; immediately to the eastward of which the Guard was encamped in their log-cabins.

The American people will ever cherish and remember the hardships, miseries and sufferings of the hungry, bare-footed and half naked soldiers of the patriot army at Valley Forge during the severe winter of 1777 and 1778; a condition largely due to the negligence of Congress, factions in high places, and the intrigues of ambitious men. The British spoke of the army as being "ragged as beggars and hungry as wolves." So desperate was their condition at times for the bare necessities of life, Washington, with great reluctance, was compelled to send officers out to scour the country round, seize supplies wherever they could find them and pay for them in money or scrip. Provisions were likewise scarce at head-quarters, and so grave was the condition that the usual levees and amusements were entirely suspended. It is related by a prominent officer that the men were literally naked; that the officers who had coats, had them of every color and make; and that he saw officers appear on the grand parade in a sort of a dressing-gown made of an old blanket or bed-cover[70]. However the Commander-in-Chief's Guard fared during these months

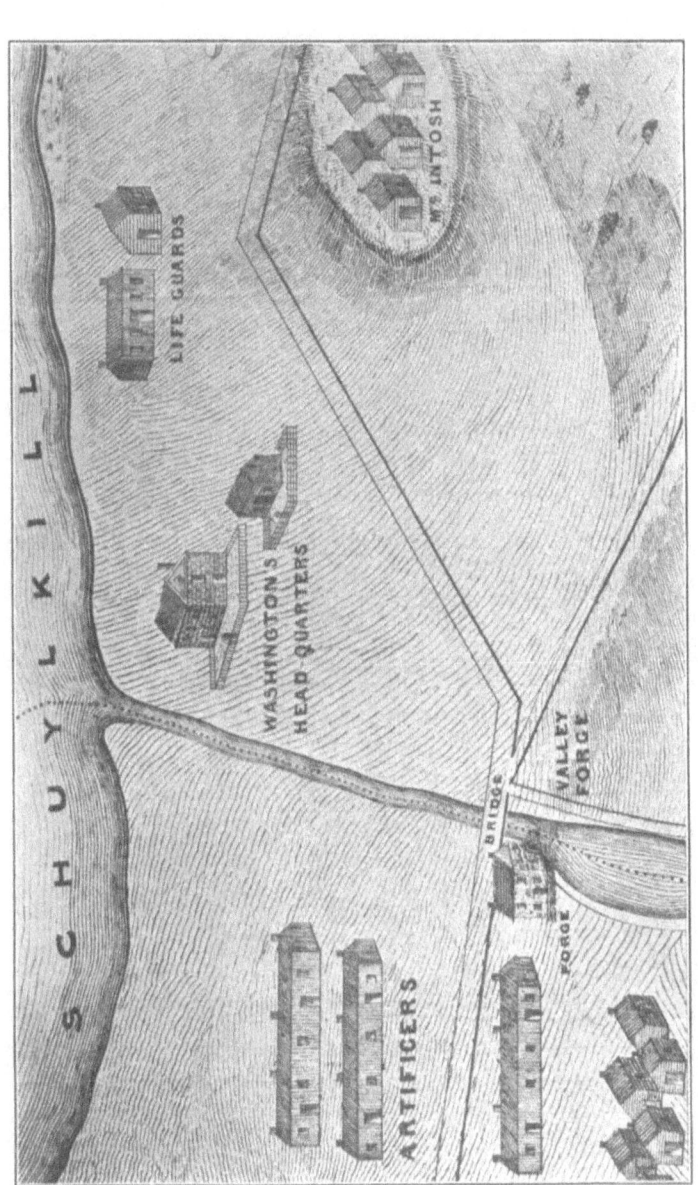

of endurance and perseverance, towards the end of winter the sufferings of the army were effectually alleviated by the approach of spring and the receipt of large quantities of provisions and clothing, which inspired new life among these courageous and patriotic soldiers determined to be free.

The month of March, 1778, marked a new era to the Commander-in-Chief's Guard, not only in its popularity but in its *personnel* and discipline, whereby it became the model for and the pride of the American army, from a military point of view. The reorganization obtained under the special order of April 30, 1777, which consisted of two commissioned officers and fifty-six rank and file, was, on the first of March, 1778, diminished to forty rank and file, and still under the command of Captain Gibbs and Lieutenant Livingston. Baron Frederick de Steuben, a noted disciplinarian in the military circles of Europe, formerly Aide-de-Camp to Frederick-the-Great and Lieutenant-General of the Prussian Army, arrived in this country December 1, 1777, and immediately volunteered his service in the army to Congress; which was accepted by their resolution of January 14, 1778, when he was directed to repair to Washington's head-quarters at Valley Forge, where he arrived February 23, and was shortly after appointed acting, and later, inspector-general of the army. The Baron, upon noticing the deplorable condition of the entire army at this period, without a uniform manual of tactics or regulations in force, suggested to Washington the propriety of increasing the strength of his Guard so that he might drill and instruct them in the tactics and discipline necessary to be introduced for the efficiency of the American arms, and have them serve as a model for the execution of them[71]. The suggestion met with the immediate approval of Washington, who caused the following general order* to issue:

"HEAD-QUARTERS, VALLEY FORGE, March 17, 1778.
"One hundred chosen men are to be annexed to the Guard of the Commander-in-Chief, for the purpose of forming a corps to be instructed in the maneuvers necessary to be introduced in the army and serve as a model for the execution of them. As the General's Guard is composed entirely of Virginians, the one hundred draughts are to be taken from the troops of the other States."

On the ensuing morning the following supplemental order* was promulgated:

"HEAD-QUARTERS, VALLEY FORGE, March 18, 1778.
"The men ordered yesterday for His Excellency's Guard are to parade tomorrow morning at guard mounting on the grand parade."

On the same day First Lieutenant Benjamin Grymes, of Grayson's Continental Regiment, and Second Lieutenant William Colfax, of the First Connecticut Regiment, were detached from their respective regiments and assigned to the Commander-in-Chief's Guard. Surgeon Samuel Hanson —son of President John Hanson of the Continental Congress, of Maryland, who was commissioned March 1, 1778, was also assigned to the Guard at the same time. Upon this reorganization the strength of the command consisted of a captain, three lieutenants, a surgeon, four sergeants,

three corporals, two drummers, a fifer and one hundred and thirty-six privates.

The reorganization being fully completed at guard mounting on the grand parade the morning of the nineteenth of March, the command was temporarily assumed by General Steuben for the purpose of instructing them personally in the tactics which he proposed to establish in the army. As he could not speak a word of English, it is difficult to see how he could bring men into strict subjection and obey the mandates of a master.

At the first parade the men, neither understanding the commands nor how to follow the maneuvers to which they had not been accustomed, even with the instructor at their head, became quickly confused. At this moment Captain Benjamin Walker, of the Second New York Regiment, advanced and volunteered his assistance to the general in interpreting his orders to the Guard. "If," said the Baron, "I had seen an angel from heaven I should not have been more rejoiced."[12] However, through the interposition of Captain Walker the difficulty was entirely eliminated, when the Guard immediately conformed themselves to the maneuvers dictated by the distinguished tactician.

On Monday morning, April 6, 1778, ten men, under the command of a non-commissioned officer, were detailed from the North Carolina Brigade to relieve the Commander-in-Chief's Guard at headquarters from six to eight o'clock, while General Steuben gave an exhibition drill of the latter on the grand parade before all the inspectors, brigade-majors and adjutants of the army, who were specially enjoined to attend.* To use the language of Steuben[78]:

"I commenced operations by drafting one hundred and twenty men from the line, whom I formed into a Guard for the General-in-Chief. I made this Guard my military school. I drilled them myself twice a day; and to remove that English prejudice which some officers entertained, namely, that to drill a recruit was a sergeant's duty and beneath the station of an officer, I often took the musket myself to show the men the manual of exercise which I wished to introduce. All my inspectors were present at each drill. We marched together, and in a fortnight my company knew perfectly how to bear arms, had a military air, knew how to march, to form in column, deploy, and execute some little maneuvers with excellent precision." * * * I had my company of Guards exactly as I wished them to be. They were well dressed, their arms clean and in good order, and their general appearance quite respectable. I paraded them in the presence of all the officers of the army, and gave them an opportunity of exhibiting all they knew. It afforded a new and agreeable sight for the young officers and soldiers. Having gained my point, I dispersed my inspectors, and my new doctrines were eagerly embraced."

After the Guard had attained the distinction and proficiency described by this royal martinet, as he was then familiarly regarded in the army, the following general order* was issued relative to the men recently assigned to the Guard as drawing pay in their respective regiments until the first of April, instead of March 19, when they were actually transferred:

"HEAD-QUARTERS, VALLEY FORGE, April 15, 1778.
"The men who were drafted for the Commander-in-Chief's Guard are to be returned in the pay abstracts of their regiment until the first of April, after which they will draw pay as a distinct corps, although returned 'on command' by their respective regiments."

Revolutionary War.

The armed alliance with the French government, concluded at Paris February 6, 1778, was ratified by Congress on the fourth of the following May. In commemoration of this Glorious event the Commander-in-Chief appointed the sixth of May as a day of thanksgiving and jollification. The day was opened with the liberation of all prisoners, an issue of an extra gill of rum to every man in the army, a proper allowance of blank cartridges, and the suspension of all routine camp duties. The several brigades were assembled at nine o'clock, when their chaplains communicated to them the intelligence contained in the postscript to the Pennsylvania Gazette of the second instant; followed by prayer, and a discourse suitable to the occasion. At 10.30 A. M. a cannon was fired as a signal for the men to be under arms, ready for inspection. At 11.30 o'clock a second cannon was fired for the brigades to march to the stations assigned by the brigade-inspectors. Upon the third signal the *feu de joie,* with thirteen-cannon accompaniment, was opened by the Commander-in-Chief's Guard and taken up by the entire army with much precision and regularity. Three cheers were given: "Long live the King of France!" "Long live the friendly European powers!" and "To the American States!" After which General Washington dined in public with the Commissioners of Congress and with all the officers of the army, attended with a band of music*‡.

At eleven o'clock Tuesday morning, May 12, Captain Gibbs, Lieutenants Livingston, Grymes and Colfax, and

THE COMMANDER-IN-CHIEF'S GUARD.

Surgeon Hunson, of the Guard, together with the general officers of the army, took the oath of allegiance before the Commander-in-Chief at head-quarters, pursuant to and in conformity with the form prescribed by the Resolution of Congress of February 3, 1778[74].

In chapter six of the manual prepared by General Steuben March 30, defining the honors due the Commander-in-Chief and the general officers of the army by their respective corps of guards, approved in general orders May 16, 1778, it was provided that "The Guard of the Commander-in-Chief to pay no honors except to him," which consisted in "parading the corps and presenting arms, the officers saluting and drums beating; except in camp before the enemy, when the drums were not to be beat*."

Early Monday morning, May 18, Major-General Lafayette received written instructions from General Washington to assume command of a detachment of 2,400 men, with five cannon, and proceed immediately towards the enemy's lines; principally to receive intelligence of their motions and designs, besides obstructing the incursions of the enemy and interrupting communication with Philadelphia.[75] At the same time Washington detailed one hundred and two officers and men of his Guard to this duty,‡ undoubtedly to guard and protect the person of the Marquis. With this command Lafayette immediately made a dash towards Barren Hill Church, about midway between Philadelphia and Valley Forge, where he halted and formed a line of battle.

REVOLUTIONARY WAR.

Prompt intelligence of this movement was communicated to General Clinton in Philadelphia. He immediately formed a plan for attacking Lafayette; and, in the night of the nineteenth, three columns, under the command of Generals Clinton, Grant and Grey, respectively, marched with the intent to surround and capture him. At nine o'clock the following morning to Lafayette's surprise he found his army almost entrapped, through the negligence of some of his outer guards composed of Pennsylvania militia-men. In the enemy's attempt to flank his right wing, he instantly withdrew his force by skillful maneuvering and crossed the Schuylkill at Matson's Ford, and took an impregnable position upon the high grounds on the west side of the river in battle array[76]. The following day—Thursday— he recrossed the Schuylkill and occupied the same grounds at Barren Hill that he abandoned the morning before. At four o'clock the next morning Lafayette marched his division directly back to Swede's Ford, crossing it at twelve o'clock, noon, he returned to Valley Forge where the detachment was dismissed late in the afternoon‡.

Lieutenant Livingston, upon learning of the serious illness of his distinguished parent, Philip Livingston, of New York, hastened to the bedside of his dying father at York, Pennsylvania—where he had been attending Congress, and was the only consoling member of his family present at his death, occurring June 12, 1778[77].

On June 18, at half past eleven o'clock in the morning, the camp was startled as George Roberts

THE COMMANDER-IN-CHIEF'S GUARD.

galloped in with the news that the British evacuated Philadelphia early in the morning and had crossed over to New Jersey. Washington, suspecting that the enemy would take a land-route to New York, immediately dispatched General Lee's Division in their pursuit. At five o'clock the ensuing morning the Guard, in company with the main army, broke camp and proceeded to Coryell's Ferry, via Doylestown, where they crossed the Delaware at four o'clock in the afternoon on the twenty-first, and pitched their tents near the residence of Mr. Hayes,‡ where Washington was quartered.

The following Tuesday afternoon Captain Gibbs with eighty rank and file of the Guard was ordered to be attached to Colonel Morgan's Regiment. The rest of the men, under the command of Lieutenant Colfax, were detached and assigned to escort Washington's baggage by a circuitous route. The latter witnessed the battle that subsequently ensued; were present with the main army at the celebration of Independence Day at New Brunswick; and rejoined the Guard some nine miles north of the last named city on the seventh of the following July.‡

The Guard took up the pursuit of the enemy through Hopewell, Kingston, Cranberry, and encamped three miles west of Englishtown on the evening of the twenty-seventh of June. The following morning, at five o'clock, the army was again in motion. Two hours after they advanced on the enemy at Monmouth Court-House, where the general engagement began about noon—a hot and serene Sabbath

REVOLUTIONARY WAR.

day. The Guard participated in the action, known as the battle of Monmouth, where Sergeant John Wilson—the only one who had the honor of being twice transferred to this command—was seriously wounded in the right arm by a musket ball, which resulted in his discharge for disability December 11, 1778, after being confined in the Burlington (N. J.) Hospital for several months. After the royal army had taken their midnight flight, the Guard, with the main army, fell back to Englishtown and leisurely proceeded to King's Ferry, via New Brunswick, Springfield, Acquackanonk, and Paramus. They crossed the Hudson about noon on July 19, and the following afternoon encamped at Wright's Mills, three miles beyond White Plains. When head-quarters was moved into White Plains the following Thursday, the Guard also pitched their tents adjoining the Miller House,‡ where Washington was quartered.

After the Guard had been augmented to one hundred and fifty-two officers and men under the general order of March 17, 1778, Captain Gibbs, on the fourteenth of the following June, communicated in writing to General Washington a desire of obtaining rank commensurate with his increased command;[78] notwithstanding the Commander-in-Chief had theretofore recognized the brilliant service of the captain by offering him an important assignment in one of the sixteen additional regiments of infantry that was raised in the early part of 1777, which he reluctantly declined, preferring to remain in his official family. However, by

THE COMMANDER-IN-CHIEF'S GUARD.

reason of the incidents accompanying the sudden departure of the army from Valley Forge and their arrival at White Plains, Washington was prevented from taking up the matter of the captain's request until the twenty-second of July, when he forwarded his letter to Congress recommending his promotion to the rank of major.[79] The request was referred to and immediately approved by the Board of War on July 28,[80] and confirmed by a resolution of Congress the following day. Upon receiving this advice officially from the President of Congress,[81] Major Gibbs addressed him the following letter[82] of thanks:

"RHODE ISLAND, 8 miles from
"NEWPORT, 13th Augt. 1778.
"Sir:

"I have had the honor of receiving your favor of the 30th July, enclosing a Resolution of Congress promoting me to the rank of major in the army.

"You will please, Sir, accept and return my warmest thanks to that honorable body for the honor they have done me. It shall ever be my study to make my conduct correspond with my rank, that I may be instrumental in establishing the liberties of my country, and ever willing to stand forth in defence of the same; that happy period is not far distant, I trust, when the invaders of this once peaceful country will be totally eradicated, then do I wish to enjoy the sweets of a free citizen.

"I have the honor of receiving the commission you mentioned through the hands of His Excellency General Washington.
"I have the honor to be
"With great respect
"Your most obedn't servant
"THE HON'BLE HENRY LAURENS, Esq'r.   C. GIBBS."

On September 16, at seven in the morning, the army commenced its move to Fredericksburg, then a precinct of

REVOLUTIONARY WAR.

Dutchess County, now a precinct of Putnam County, New York. The Guard took its departure at the same time, and, after encamping at Bedford, New York, finally pitched their tents adjacent to head-quarters at Fredericksburg, now Patterson—a small village near the Connecticut line—on the twenty-fifth of the same month.‡

The marauding and riotous conduct of the soldiers towards the inhabitants, which had prevailed, in a degree, since the establishment of the army, reached alarming proportions while encamped at White Plains, notwithstanding they had time and again been warned in general orders to cease these practices; and, while the army was at Englishtown, June 30, 1778, Washington gave a final warning* "that the detestable crime of marauding will henceforward be invariably punished with instant death." After the army was established at Fredericksburg, Captain Bartholomew Von Heer's Troop, called the "Marechausie Corps" in general orders, received peremptory orders to apprehend and arrest all marauders, rioters, drunkards and deserters, and all soldiers who should be found beyond the limits of the guard of their respective organizations without permission.

In disobedience to the repeated warnings and the precautions instituted for the suppression of these lawless and vicious acts, Fifer Elias Brown and Privates Hurring and Walton, of the Guard, on or about the night of October 3, robbed the residence of Mr. Prince Howland of several spoons, money and clothing. The following Monday night they, in company with Private Herrick of the Guard, also robbed the house of Mr. John Hoag of a quantity of silver spoons, considerable hard money, four hundred and fifty pounds of Continental bills and a large amount of sundry wearing apparel*; for which they were apprehended and arrested on the eighteenth of the same month.‡

In the meanwhile, however, some unknown members of the Guard were taken up in the evening of October 7 for an infraction of some of the regulations that Captain Von Heer was appointed to enforce. Immediately, Privates Desperate, Thompson, Kidder, Cole, Adams, Wortman, Moore, Davis Brown and Wiley, of the Guard, secretly started out of camp with their side arms to avenge their feelings and indignation upon Captain Von Heer's men, when they were detected and placed under arrest. Quickened by these alleged wrongs the revengeful and jealous spirit of their comrades in the Guard was stimulated to further action the following night, resulting in the arrest of Private Timberlake for striking Lieutenant David Zeigler, and the arrest of Sergeant Roach, Corporal Forbes, Privates John Smith, Townsend, Palmer, Flemister, Perry and William Jones for striking Corporal Wingler of Von Heer's Troop and calling him a "Hessian Bugger," and for swearing and unsoldierly conduct when taken up by Captain Von Heer*.

The men arrested on October 7 were acquitted by court-martial on the fifteenth of the same month. The following day Private Timberlake was adjudged guilty of the charge against him, being a breach of article 5, section 18, of the articles of war, and was sentenced to receive one hundred lashes on his bare back. The rest of the men were acquitted by court-martial on the sixteenth, with the exception of Privates Smith and Townsend, which found Private Smith guilty of calling Corporal Wingler a "Hessian Bugger," and Private Townsend of striking him, and both guilty of swearing and unsoldierly behavior after being in the custody of Captain Von Heer; but, in view of the punishment they had received by confinement, the court were of the opinion that they should be released and restored to duty; which opinion was affirmed by the Commander-in-Chief*.

Fifer Brown and Privates Hurring, Walton and Herrick on the twenty-second of October were found guilty of a breach of article 21, section 13, of the articles of war; and, with the exception of Private Herrick, who was sentenced to receive one hundred lashes on his bare back "well laid on," were condemned to suffer death. Washington, in approving these sentences in orders on the twenty-third, says: "Shocked at the frequent horrible villainies of this nature committed by the troops of late, I am determined to make examples which will deter the boldest and most hardened offenders. Men who are called out by their country to defend the rights and property of their fellow citizens, who are abandoned enough to violate those rights and plunder that property, deserve and shall receive no mercy." He directed that Fifer Brown be immediately sent to Major-General McDougall's Division, Private Hurring to Baron

The Commander-in-Chief's Guard.

DeKalb's Division (stationed near New Hackensack, about fourteen miles north-east of Fishkill), and Private Walton to Major-General Gates's Division, and there be executed by hanging as soon as they arrive. He also approved the sentence of Privates Herrick and Timberlake and ordered the punishment to be inflicted the following morning at nine o'clock*.

While Private Hurring was hanged, it is remarkable that Private Walton should have been permitted to escape from the provost-guard, and Fifer Brown from the guard that was conveying him to New Milford for execution.‡ After Fifer Brown escaped he immediately obtained employment as a mechanic in the Continental service, remote from the army, under an assumed name. Upon secretly communicating with his parents at Windsor, Connecticut, his father, Ephraim Brown, on May 15, 1779, addressed a communication[88] to the Commander-in-Chief in behalf of his son's pardon and restoration to duty, which was indorsed by the prominent people of his town. The appeal was so intelligently and manfully put that it unquestionably excited the sympathies of Washington, for he rejoined his regiment and obtained the rank of fife-major before the termination of the war, and was discharged with honor. He afterwards became a prosperous farmer, educated his sons in the prominent colleges of the day, and his descendants to the present generation occupy positions of influence and wealth.

Revolutionary War.

On the fifth of November Lieutenant Livingston forwarded to General Washington the following letter:[84]

"FREDERICKSBURG, Novr. 5: 1778.

"May it please Your Excellency,

"It is with great reluctance that I beg leave to resign my Commission in your Guards, as I feel and shall ever retain a grateful sense of the Honor conferred upon me by your Excellency in that appointment.

"Altho private concerns might justify my leaving the Army, I would by no means do it, could I be reconciled always to hold a subaltern rank, which in my present situation I must, being debarred of all chance of promotion.

"I flatter myself (if) your Excellency will think my reasons compatible with honor and grant me your permission to retire.

"I have the Honor to be
"Your Excellency's
"Most Obed't hum'l Serv't

"HIS EXCELLENCY   "HENRY PH: LIVINGSTON
"GENERAL WASHINGTON.   *Lt. Guards.*"

On November 28, 1778, the Guard left Fredericksburg for their winter-quarters at Middlebrook, New Jersey, via Peekskill, King's Ferry, Ramapo and Morristown, where they arrived on the eighth of the following month and pitched their tents adjacent to the Wallace House—situated about four miles west of Middlebrook, on grounds now in Somerville—where Washington established head-quarters.[85] The following day the Guard began to build their huts, which were completed December 16, when they struck their tents and moved into their new quarters.‡ Before their arrival, however, the ranking lieutenant, Henry Philip Livingston, was promoted captain December 4, 1778, vice Gibbs promoted.[86] On March 16, 1779, Second Lieutenant Colfax was promoted first lieutenant to rank from March 18, 1778.[87] On the twenty-sixth of March, Captain Livingston, Lieutenant Grymes and Surgeon Hanson, after being on furlough since the preceding November, resigned, leaving Major Gibbs and Lieutenant Colfax the only officers in command of the Guard.

It appears that at this date the uniform of the Commander-in-Chief's Guard consisted of a dark-blue coat, collared, faced, cuffed and lined with buff; the bottom cut square and full behind, with a fold on each back skirt; pocket flap on either side at the waist line; ten large gilt buttons on each lapel, four on each cuff, and four below each pocket flap; to button or hook as low as the fourth button on the breast, and to be flaunted at the bottom; vest red, high cut, single breasted with twelve smaller gilt buttons, and pocket flaps with four similar buttons below each; buckskin breeches fitting to the shape, with five small gilt buttons at the ankle, and strapped under black shoes; white bayonet and body belts; black stock and tie for the hair; and a black cocked hat bound with white tape.[88] This was the uniform of the organization from the earliest period.[89] The commissioned officers were clothed with the same uniform, except that they wore knee-breeches with four gilt buttons at the bottom, and black boots reaching to the knee.[90] The major was designated by two epauletts, the captain by one on the right shoulder, and the subalterns by one on the left shoulder; and all officers, commissioned and non-commissioned, wore cockades on their hats, and a small sword upon the left. In the earlier campaigns the sergeants wore an epaulett or stripe of red cloth sewed upon the right shoulder, while the corporals wore one of green; later, the sergeants were designated by worsted shoulder knots upon each shoulder, and the corporals with one upon the right*. At a later and uncertain date it appears that the uniform was modified to the extent that they wore plain cutaway coats faced with buff to the waist line, with six large gilt buttons on each lapel and two on each cuff; buff vest, with similar small buttons; black cocked hat bound with buff; and white chitterlings and ruffles at the wrists.[91]

After passing a remarkably mild and uneventful winter at Middlebrook the Guard, on Thursday, noon, June 4, 1779, leisurely proceeded towards the Highlands, via Morristown. The following Monday they halted in the Clove, Orange County, New York, where head-quarters was at Smith's Tavern. Shortly after Major Gibbs was directed by the Commander-in-Chief to proceed to New Windsor, New York, and inspect the premises of Colonel William Ellison, near where he proposed to advance the army, with the view of making it his head-quarters. Upon his return on the night of June 20, after making his report, he was requested to forward the following letter[92] of acceptance:

"HEAD-QUARTERS, SMITH'S CLOVE, 21st June, 1779.
"His Excellency the Commander-in-Chief thinks proper to accept your house as headquarters from the description I gave him on

my return from thence last night. He with his Guard setts off immediately and the baggage will follow.

"Your most Ob't Humble Servt,

"To COL. ELLISON.   C. GIBBS."

On the same evening the Guard was advanced towards New Windsor, where Washington established head-quarters the following day at the Ellison House—situated on the hill immediately south of the village, when Dr. Ebenezer Crosby of the Flying Hospital, Middle Department, was assigned surgeon to the Guard. Afterwards the following general order* was issued:

"HEAD-QUARTERS, NEW WINDSOR, July 4, 1779.

"The General requests the commanding officers of those regiments who have furnished men for his Guard to send without delay to the adjutant-general certificates of the time of service for which they are respectively engaged."

On July 20, at 4 P. M., the Guard embarked upon a sloop at New Windsor with all their baggage and landed the next morning at West Point, when they camped before the Moore House where Washington was established. They remained here until November 30, when they proceeded to winter-quarters at Morristown.‡

When the Guard left Middlebrook on the fourth of the previous June, however, it is shown by the rolls that Lieutenant Colfax, Sergeant Roach, Corporal Forbes, and Privates William Harris, Samuel Smith, Landon, McIntire, Snow and Jackson were detached and proceeded to Easton, Pennsylvania, accompanied by the Hon. Charles Thomson,

Secretary of the Continental Congress. The purpose of this assignment is not clearly shown, but they undoubtedly conveyed additional instructions from General Washington to Major-General Sullivan relative to the conduct of his campaign against the hostile tribe of the Six Nations of Indians up the Wyoming Valley, and to facilitate the transmission of other important dispatches during the successful operations of that summer. They tarried at Easton until September 20 (the rolls say September 28), when they proceeded as the escort of His Excellency's baggage and rejoined the Guard at West Point the following Thursday.‡

On December 4, 1779, the Guard arrived and pitched their tents in Morristown, while Washington established head-quarters at the residence of Mrs. Ford, widow of Colonel Jacob Ford, Jr., late of the New Jersey Militia. The following Thursday the Guard, after building their huts, moved into their new quarters,‡ situated on the meadows immediately south-east of the Ford Mansion,[93] where they endured the hardships of one of the severest winters theretofore known to the memory of man;[94] and save the frequent alarms caused by British foraging parties, when the Guard would hurry to head-quarters, barricade the doors, take out the windows and stand with musket cocked,[95] the season was an uneventful one aside from the usual levees, and the dancing assemblies towards which Major Gibbs contributed four hundred dollars.[96]

In the spring of 1780 the rank and file of the Guard having been diminished in numbers by discharges, desertions,

THE COMMANDER-IN-CHIEF'S GUARD.

deaths, etc., the following general order* was issued to increase its strength:

"HEAD-QUARTERS, MORRISTOWN, March 19, 1780.

"Two trusty soldiers from each regiment of infantry and a good active sergeant from each brigade, with their arms, accoutrements, blankets, packs, etc., are to assemble on the grand parade tomorrow morning at troop beating. The officers of the day will have them formed into platoons and the brigade-major of the day will march them to headquarters where they are to join His Excellency's Guard 'till further orders."

The following order then appears relative to the pay and clothing of the soldiers assigned to the Guard under the previous order:

"HEAD-QUARTERS, MORRISTOWN, April 12, 1780.

"As the late draught from the line to re-enforce the Commander-in-Chief's Guard is only temporary, the men are to be furnished with pay and clothing from their respective regiments in the same manner as if they had not been drawn out."

On April 27, 1780, George Augustine Washington—a nephew of General Washington, an officer in the Second Virginia Regiment, was ordered to duty in the Guard by direction of the following order,* although the assignment appears to have been temporary inasmuch as his name does not appear upon the rolls of the organization:

"HEAD-QUARTERS, MORRISTOWN, April 27, 1780.

"Congress having been pleased to appoint George Augustine Washington an ensign in the 2d Virginia Regiment, he is to do duty in the Commander-in-Chief's Guard 'till further orders."

Early Wednesday morning, June 7, 1780, Washington received intelligence that a large detachment of the British, commanded by General Knyphausen, had crossed over to Elizabeth, New Jersey, from Staten Island and were advancing towards Connecticut Farms, leaving their path marked by desolation and blood. At seven o'clock he immediately put the army in motion and arrived at Short Hills about noon, near where they met the enemy pushing forward from Connecticut Farms towards Springfield, when they were repulsed and forced to retreat to Elizabeth Point. The Commander-in-Chief's Guard were in the advance and occupied a position in the left wing of the army under the command of General Edward Hand.[97] They gave the Hessian lads a charge just before sunset, followed by about eight rounds after they broke away.[98] In the battle, known as the battle of Connecticut Farms, however, Privates Daley, Hetfield and William Jones of the Guard were slightly wounded, while Private Slocum was shot in the knee by a musket ball, resulting in the amputation of his leg, when he was shortly after transferred to the Invalid Regiment.

Washington remained at Short Hills until Thursday morning, June 22, when, suspecting a design against West Point, the army commenced moving slowly towards the Hudson River, arriving the same day at Rockaway Bridge. On Saturday and Sunday he was at Whippany; on Monday he halted at Ramapo, where he remained until he moved towards Preakness—about five miles north-west of Passaic Falls—the morning of the first of July, when he established head-quarters at the house of Colonel Theunis Dey, of the

THE COMMANDER-IN-CHIEF'S GUARD.

New Jersey Militia,[99] whence the following general order* was issued:

"HEAD-QUARTERS, PREAKNESS, July 21, 1780.
"The men last drafted into the Commander-in-Chief's Guard are to be returned 'on command' in the regiments from which they were drafted, but to draw pay and clothing in the Guard."

Before sunrise in the morning on the 29th day of July the Guard, with the army, left Preakness and encamped the same day at Paramus, fifteen miles distant. On the succeeding morning, at two o'clock, Washington procceeded with the army to King's Ferry, crossed the Hudson, and took quarters in the evening at the house of Beverly Robinson,[100] a little below West Point on the oppositte side of the river. This house has considerable historical interest as having been the head-quarters of Arnold at the time he commanded West Point, and was maturing his plans to surrender that post to the British.

On Monday, July 31, head-quarters was established in Peekskill, New York, at the residence of Daniel Birdsall,[101] opposite the present Westchester Bank. The following Sunday the army left Peekskill for Orangetown, also called Tappan, via Dobbs Ferry, where they arrived the following Tuesday, when Washington established head-quarters at the DeWint House. On the twenty-third, at seven in the morning, the army was moved lower down to Teaneck, a high ridge of land which rises out of the meadows a few miles back of the Palisades. On the morning of the fourth of September the army encamped two miles to the westward at Kinderhamack, west of the Hackensack River, called

REVOLUTIONARY WAR.

"Steenrapie" in general orders, where Washington quartered at the Hopper House.[102]

The army was moved back to Orangetown September 20, at ten A. M., when Washington started for Hartford, Connecticut, accompanied by a small detachment from Captain Von Heer's Troop,[103] to confer with the French officers who arrived off Newport, Rhode Island, the tenth of the preceding July. Upon his return to camp on the twenty-eighth of September he again established headquarters at the DeWint House, where he remained until he proceeded with the army to Paramus at nine o'clock Saturday morning, October 7. The following Monday headquarters was established in the Hogencamp House at Totawa,[104] afterwards called Manchester—a mile or two west of Paterson, New Jersey, while the main army encamped at the foot of Preakness Mountain. On November 17, Major Gibbs received instructions to proceed immediately to New Windsor to arrange suitable head-quarters for the Commander-in-Chief; who went and returned by the way of Pompton and the Clove the following Tuesday night.[105]

Precisely at ten o'clock on the morning of the twenty-seventh of November, 1780, Washington proceeded with the Guard to winter-quarters at New Windsor, via Morristown, where he arrived in the evening of December 6 and occupied his former quarters at the house of William Ellison, while the various brigades of the army cantoned for the winter at Morristown, West Point, Albany, etc.[106]

The Commander-in-Chief's Guard.

On January 1, 1781, Major Gibbs, who had been in command of the Guard since its organization, was transferred to the Second Massachusetts Regiment; Surgeon Ebenezer Crosby resigned; and Second Lieutenant Levi Holden, of the Fourth Massachusetts Regiment, was detached and assigned to the Guard June 23, 1781; leaving Lieutenant Colfax the senior officer in command.

After Major Gibbs was transferred to the Second Massachusetts Regiment the Commander-in-Chief was pleased to compliment his valuable and distinguished services in orders*, which read:

"Head-quarters, New Windsor, April 23, 1781.
"Major Gibbs having been in the late arrangement of the army appointed to and having joined the Second Massachusetts Regiment, the Commander-in-Chief takes occasion to express his approbation of his conduct while in the command of his Corps of Guards and to return him thanks for his very particular attention to the several duties incident to that station."

In reply thereto Major Gibbs addressed General Washington the following letter:[107]

"Near the Garrison of West Point April 26, 1781
"Accept the warmest acknowledgements, My Dear General, of a heart filled with gratitude for your kind care and fatherly attention to me, while I had the honor to make part of your Excellency's family.

"I want words to express the many obligations I am under to you, and can only wish I may ever be so happy, as to have it in my power to make compensation.

"The General order of the 23rd inst. is a fresh mark of your

Excellency's friendship, for which, My dear Sir, accept my sincerest thanks.

"Forgive me for being so much unnerved when I took my leave of you and Mrs Washington, but be assured, sir, it was the fullness of a heart conscious of the many benefits I had rec'd from you during the five years I had the happiness to be nigh your Excellency's person.

"I shall ever make it my study to conduct myself in such a manner, as to gain the confidence of mankind, and particularly endeavor to merit the approbation of your Excellency.

"It is natural for all young military men to wish to have it in their power to show such credentials of their service, as to make them appear respectable in any part of the world where fortune may call them. This is my wish, and at a leisure hour when Your Excellency's mind is relaxed from the hurries and perplexities of a busy day, (which you are constantly engaged in) You will be so kind as to give me such a certificate as your own superior judgement may think proper.

"With great respect,
"Yr. Excellency's Most obdt.

"GENL WASHINGTON   C. GIBBS."

On the twenty-second of the following May, General Washington and the Count de Rochambeau, General-in-Chief of the French forces, met at Wethersfield, Connecticut, when a combined attack on Sir Henry Clinton and the British army in New York was determined upon. Various movements of the American and French troops then began towards the Hudson River above and around New York. At three o'clock in the morning on the second of July, Washington, whose head-quarters had been at the Van Cortlandt Mansion—two miles east of Peekskill—since June 25, moved the army towards Valentine's Hill in order to cover the detached troops, where he arrived at sunrise the following day and spent most of the morning in reconnoitering the enemy's works at the upper end of New York, near King's Bridge. As Washington moved leisurely along with the Guard and a detachment of New England troops making observations, he was discovered by a foraging party of the enemy, 1,500 strong, who had sallied out at daybreak to scour the country, when an irregular skirmish ensued, which resulted very disastrously to the Guard, as will appear from the following return:[108]

"HEAD-QUARTERS, 11th July, 1781.
"To CAPTAIN PEMBERTON:

"Return of killed, wounded and missing of His Excellency's Guard in the late skirmish at King's Bridge—one lieutenant and one sergeant wounded; fourteen rank and file wounded—one missing, and three of the wounded since dead.

"Your H'ble Servt,
"L. HOLDEN, *Lt Comd't*
"*Com'dr in Chief's Guard.*"

In the afternoon the Guard and the detachment retired to Valentine's Hill, four miles from King's Bridge, with the main army. On the following morning, at three o'clock, the army moved up twelve miles and encamped at Phillipsburg, near Dobbs Ferry, when Washington made his headquarters at the house of Joseph Appleby, on the cross road from Dobbs Ferry to White Plains, about three and a half miles from the ferry.[109]

On Friday, August 14, Washington, in consequence of the receipt of the well known dispatches from Admiral the

REVOLUTIONARY WAR.

Count de Grasse, which necessitated an entire change of the campaign against the enemy at New York, notified the admiral of his plans and movements for the environment, the assaulting, and the capture of Cornwallis on York River in Virginia. Still keeping up his successful feint against New York, he left Phillipsburg about noon on the nineteenth of August, and arrived at King's Ferry at ten o'clock the next day. While the allied armies were crossing the ferry he made his head-quarters at the house of Joshua Hett Smith, about two and a half miles below Stony Point, the western landing of the ferry. On the 23d, Washington, with the Guard, left for Philadelphia, via Haverstraw, Ramapo, Chatham, New Brunswick and Trenton, where he arrived at one o'clock in the afternoon of the thirtieth, and established head-quarters at the residence of Robert Morris, on South Front Street, waiting for the rear of the French army to come up.[110]

On Wednesday, September 5, Washington departed from Philadelphia with the Guard for the south; arriving at Baltimore Saturday afternoon, and reaching his home at Mount Vernon late Sunday night. The following Wednesday he proceeded to Williamsburg, Virginia, arriving there Friday afternoon at four o'clock, and established headquarters at the colonial mansion of George Wythe, one of the signers of the Declaration of Independence.[111]

The twenty-eighth of September, Washington left Williamsburg and arrived before Yorktown the next morning, where the Guard encamped in the rear of the allied armies,[112] adjacent to head-quarters, when the siege commenced. The assault was opened by the French at three o'clock in the afternoon of October 8, and continued daily with fierce cannonade of shot and shell until ten o'clock in the morning of the seventeenth, when a drummer beat a parley from the British works and the firing ceased. The articles of capitulation were signed October 19, at 11 A. M., and in the afternoon at two o'clock the sullen and despondent British troops were paraded, with their standards furled, to the music of an old English march "The World Turned Upside Down.[113]"

Washintgon, on November 5, 1781, accompanied by the Guard, left Yorktown and returned to Mount Vernon, via Eltham and Fredericksburg, where he arrived on the thirteenth, and there remained until the following Tuesday. He then passed north through Alexandria and Annapolis, and reached Baltimore Friday evening. The next morning he continued on towards Philadelphia, where he arrived Monday afternoon, November 26, and established head-quarters at the residence of Benjamin Chew, situated on South Third Street between Walnut and Spruce.[114] While the main army encamped at Morristown and in the Highlands near the Hudson, the Guard remained near head-quarters at Philadelphia during the winter,[115] where Washington was in conference with Congress and participating in the festivities over the Virginia campaign, so brilliantly conceived and rapidly executed.

On Friday morning, March 22, 1782, Washington pro-

ceeded with the Guard to Newburgh, New York,[116] via Burlington, Morristown, Pompton and Ringwood, where he arrived Sunday, March 31,[117] and established headquarters at the Hasbrouck House, situated on the brow of a hill in the southern part of the city, while the Guard occupied tents close by on the site now known as the corner of Ann and Liberty Streets.[118]

On May 17, 1782, Second Lieutenant Holden was commissioned First Lieutenant in the Sixth Massachusetts Regiment to rank from December 22, 1777, although retained as the junior officer in the Commander-in-Chief's Guard.[119]

While the army was encamped around and about Newburgh the Commander-in-Chief issued his first proclamation, in general orders, for the establishment of a Badge or order of military Merit to the non-commissioned officers and enlisted men of the army for long, honorable and faithful service, as well as for any special acts of heroism, which honors were likewise applicable to the members of the Guard. Washington was always ready to foster and encourage every species of military merit, and, as early as July 2, 1776, in general orders, announced his intention to notice and reward any officer or soldier for any special distinguished service. The proclamation* reads thus:

"HEAD-QUARTERS, NEWBURGH, August 7, 1782.

"Honorary badges of distinction are to be conferred on the veteran non-commissioned officers and soldiers of the army who have served more than three years with bravery, fidelity and good conduct; for this purpose a narrow piece of white cloth of an angular form is to be fixed to the left arm on the uniform coat. Non-commissioned officers and soldiers who have served with equal reputation more than six years are to be distinguished by two pieces of cloth set on parallel to each other in a similar form. Should any who are not entitled to these honors have the insolence to assume the badges of them they shall be severely punished. On the other hand it is expected (that) those gallant men who are thus designated will, on all occasions, be treated with particular confidence and consideration.

"The General, ever desirous to cherish a virtuous ambition in his soldiers, as well as to foster and encourage every species of military merit, directs that whenever any singularly meritorious action is performed, the author of it shall be permitted to wear on his facings over the left breast the figure of a heart in purple cloth, or silk, edged with narrow lace or binding. Not only instances of unusual gallantry, but also extraordinary fidelity and essential service in any way shall meet with a due reward. Before this favor can be conferred on any man the particular fact, or facts, on which it is to be grounded must be set forth to the Commander-in-Chief accompanied with certificates from the commanding officers of the regiment and brigade to which the candidate for reward belonged, or other incontestable proofs; and upon granting it, the name and regiment of the person with the action so certified are to be enrolled in the book of merit, which will be kept at the orderly office. Men who have merited this last distinction to be suffered to pass all guards and sentinels which officers are permitted to do.

"The road to glory in a patriot army and a free country is thus open to all. This order is also to have retrospect to the earliest stages of the war, and to be considered as a permanent one."

By reason of a misapprehension of the above proclamation, or order, so much as was inconsistent with the following supplemental order* was abrogated:

"HEAD-QUARTERS, NEWBURGH, August 11, 1782.
"In order to prevent misapplication of the honorary badges of

REVOLUTIONARY WAR.

distinction to be conferred on the non-commissioned officers and soldiers in consequence of long and faithful service, through any mistake or misapprehension of the order of the 7th instant, the General thinks proper to inform the army that they are only attainable by an uninterrupted series of faithful and honorable services. A soldier who has once retired from the field of glory forfeits all pretensions to precedence from former services; and a man who has deservedly met an ignominious punishment or degradation cannot be admitted a candidate for any honorary distinction, unless he shall have wiped away the stain his reputation has suffered by some very brilliant achievement, or by serving with reputation after his disgrace the number of years which entitle other men to that indulgence. The badges which non-commissioned officers and soldiers are permitted to wear on the left arm as a mark of long and faithful service are to be of the same color with the facings of the corps they belong to and not white in every instance as directed in the orders of the 7th instant."

On the morning of August 31 Washington relinquished head-quarters at Newburgh and moved the army to Verplanck's Point, arriving there in the evening of the same day. Shortly after the following order* was issued for a review of the Guard, in connection with other troops, by the Commander-in-Chief:

"HEAD-QUARTERS, VERPLANCK'S POINT, September 5, 1782.
"Captain Von Heer's Corps of Cavalry, the Commander-in-Chief's Guard, the Corps of Light Infantry (except a small guard for the security of their camp) and the several regiments now in camp, will be reviewed by the Commander-in-Chief on Saturday next. The whole to be drawn up as shall hereafter be directed and ready to receive the General precisely at seven o'clock in the morning."

The following compliment was given by General Washington in orders* upon the appearance of the troops reviewed:

"HEAD-QUARTERS, VERPLANCK'S POINT, September 7, 1782.
"The appearance of the army today afforded the Commander-in-Chief the most sensible pleasure. He cannot too often repeat his thanks to the officers of all ranks for their unremitted care and attention to their respective duties."

Afterwards the following order* was given for creating a board to examine and report upon the applications of the candidates for the Badge of Merit:

"HEAD-QUARTERS, VERPLANCK'S POINT, September 9, 1782.
"The Inspector-General, or in his absence the Inspector of the Northern Army, the Adjutant-General, Brigadier-General Huntington, Lieutenant-Colonel Barber, or any three of them are appointed a board, to examine the pretensions of the non-commissioned officers and soldiers who are candidates for the Badge of Merit. The board will report their opinions to the Commander-in-Chief. All certificates and recommendations will be lodged with the Adjutant-General who will occasionally summon the board to assemble."

The principal reason for moving the army from Newburgh over to Verplanck's Point was in consequence of an agreement with Count de Rochambeau to form a junction of the American and French armies at that place,[120] out of respect to Washington's desire to pay homage to France as a slight recognition of her invaluable services.[121] Accordingly the first division of the French troops arrived from the south at King's Ferry, opposite Verplanck's Point, early on the morning of the fourteenth of September, when

REVOLUTIONARY WAR.

General Rochambeau forwarded his compliments, with the announcement of his arrival, to General Washington, who in turn invited the Count over to breakfast. He also hastily wrote the following order[122] to Lieutenant Holden to have the Guard in readiness to receive the distinguished guest at head-quarters:

"MR. HOLDEN: Have the Guard clean and ready to receive Count de Rochambeau, who is to be here to breakfast this morning.

"Yours, &c.,
"Saturday. G. WASHINGTON.
"The barge is to go over for the count. One of the gentlemen of the family will go over with it. You will therefore know when he is coming."

The whole army was also immediately paraded under arms, and formed into two lines extending up from the ferry. Upon the arrival of the Count, he and his staff were met and escorted by a troop of cavalry through the lines to head-quarters, where he was received with much pomp and ceremony. Sitting on his horse by the side of Washington the entire troops passed before him in review, when he expressed much gratification and astonishment upon their improved appearance and their rapid progress in military skill and discipline since he last reviewed them. Turning to Washington he said: "You must have formed an alliance with the King of Prussia. These troops are Prussians!"[123]

The following Saturday was another gala day to the Guard, who again had the honor of receiving General Rochambeau and his suite at head-quarters amid the roar of cannon becoming his rank. The whole army was drawn up and maneuvered before the distinguished guests in a manner much to the delight and satisfaction of the Commander-in-Chief.[124] A French officer writes: "It was a military festival given by the Americans in honor of their allies. Their camp was covered with garlands and pyramids, as so many trophies gratefully raised by the hands of liberty. The day terminated with an entertainment of more than ninety covers, served with true military magnificence; and the band of American music, which played during the dinner, added much to the gaiety of the company."[125]

On Saturday morning, October 26, 1782, Washington conducted the army to winter-quarters at New Windsor, the last cantonment of the main army, via West Point, which they reached the following Monday. He resumed head-quarters at Newburgh, two miles above, in the Hasbrouck House; to the westward of which the Guard again encamped.

It was while at these head-quarters that tradition points to a bold move that was made by the enemy to kidnap the Commander-in-Chief, which was more successfully resisted by the forethought of Washington than the ingenuity of the scheme, which seemed so easy of execution, through the interposition of a young lady and the fidelity of a detachment of the Commander-in-Chief's Guard.[126] At this time there was no road along the river to the south for some distance, for in front of head-quarters the bank was a hundred feet high, and went sheer down to the water.

This, with little variation, continued for a mile, or almost down to Lafayette's head-quarters. Half way down the Quassaick Creek, now Chambers Creek, bursts from a gorge into the Hudson. This chasm ran back into the interior nearly a mile before it sunk away so that it could be spanned by a bridge. As it approached the river the south bank swept off in a side semi-circle, but again crowded against the creek, just before it plunged into the Hudson. This semi-circle enclosed a beautiful little valley, known afterward as the Vale of Avoca. In passing the mouth of the creek in a boat, the lofty banks of the chasm, heavily wooded, presented a gloomy pass, only wide enough for the stream of water. In this little secluded valley lived a man named Ettrick. His house lay almost in a straight line south of Washington's head-quarters and within cannon range, though the shot sent from there would pass nearly a hundred feet over its top. This lay on the opposite side of the gorge, and could be reached only by a detour of nearly two miles back into the country. The tide set up close to the dwelling, and a boat could be sent from it on to the Hudson in five minutes, and in an hour more be carried to the fastness of the Highlands. This Ettrick professed to be a warm patriot, but those who knew him best looked on him with suspicion. This man and this spot were selected to effect Washington's capture. The plan proposed was to have a boat ready, and a party of Tories secreted in the wood near by when Washington should be invited to dinner. His daughter overheard a conversation that exposed this plot, and informed Washington of her suspicions, and begged him not to accept the invitation of her father to dinner. The dinner hour was to be late, so that it would be dark before the meal was over. Then the seizure was to be effected, and the captive borne off to the bosom of the Hudson. The boat, manned by strong rowers, would easily have reached the English vessels below West Point before Washington would be missed. He was accustomed, occasionally, to dine with Greene and Knox, three or four miles further south, and not be back till near midnight, and on these occasions was usually accompanied only by his black servant.

Instead of declining the invitation, he accepted it, but in the meantime ordered a detachment of his Guard to march to the place just at evening, and present themselves at the door. While Ettrick was engaged in conversation with his distinguished guest, he heard their footsteps and the low command of their leader, and laying his hand on Washington's shoulder, said: "I believe, General, you are my prisoner." "I believe not, sir, but you are mine," was the reply, as the Guard closed around and placed him under arrest. The story then goes along to relate the paroxysms of grief that befell the daughter over her father's arrest. She had not anticipated such a result, and besought Washington to repay her fidelity to him by the release of her father, which he finally did, after a brief confinement, upon his promise to leave the country, and he afterwards moved to Nova Scotia.

Roll and Muster of the [illegible] in Chief [illegible] [illegible] of [illegible]

Ranks	Names	Term of Inlistment	Casualties	Mustered.	Time since last Muster, or Inlistment.	Attestations since last Muster.
	[illegible] [illegible]			[illegible] [illegible] [illegible] [illegible]	[illegible] 30 [illegible] 20	
Serjt	William [illegible]			[illegible] [illegible]	[illegible] 30	
	James [illegible]			[illegible] [illegible]	[illegible]	
	Edward [illegible]				[illegible]	
Corporal	[illegible] [illegible]			[illegible] [illegible]	[illegible]	
	[illegible] [illegible]			[illegible] [illegible]	[illegible]	
	[illegible] [illegible]			[illegible] [illegible]	[illegible]	
Privates	1 [illegible] [illegible]			[illegible] [illegible]	[illegible]	
	2 [illegible] [illegible]			[illegible] [illegible]	[illegible]	
	3 [illegible] [illegible]			[illegible] [illegible]	[illegible]	
	4 [illegible] [illegible]			[illegible] [illegible]	[illegible]	
	5 [illegible] [illegible]			[illegible] [illegible]	[illegible]	
	6 [illegible] [illegible]			[illegible] [illegible]	[illegible]	
	7 [illegible] [illegible]			[illegible] [illegible]	[illegible]	
	8 [illegible] [illegible]			[illegible] [illegible]	[illegible]	
	9 [illegible] [illegible]			[illegible] [illegible]	[illegible]	
	10 [illegible] [illegible]			[illegible] [illegible]	[illegible]	
	11 [illegible] [illegible]			[illegible] [illegible]	[illegible]	
	12 [illegible] [illegible]			[illegible] [illegible]	[illegible]	

REVOLUTIONARY WAR.

While also at these head-quarters an anecdote[127] of Washington is related in which Sergeant Phillips, of the Guard, was an actor. A part of Sergeant Phillips's duties was to provide for the General's table. If there was one eatable that he preferred to all others it was eggs, and the army consumed all found and produced in the neighborhood of the village. The eggs ran out, and Phillips informed the General of the desperate state of affairs in that department of the provisions. As salt was very valuable and scarce among the inhabitants, Washington immediately made an order on the quartermaster's department for a butt of salt. The quartermaster could not imagine the purpose for which the General wanted so much salt; however, the draft was honored and the salt conveyed to its proper destination by two pairs of oxen, when Phillips was instructed to give out notice to the country people that salt would be exchanged for eggs at the camp. This had the desired effect in a few days, and eggs were as plenty as blackberries.

The sedentary life of the men in the Commander-in-Chief's Guard, followed by their long march from Philadelphia to Newburgh in March, 1782, must have been a welcome respite from the arduous duties exacted of them in the last seven campaigns of alternate victory and defeat, attended with hardships and sufferings. As time passed along the monotony of camp doubtless became less burdensome by reason of their manifold duties. Among them were their assignment, by detail, to guard head-quarters both by day and night; they were also the purveyors to headquarters; and from time to time performed domestic and other duties in Washington's official family. The muster roll[129] dated March 2, 1783, shows how the men were then employed, and besides those on regular duty it reports Ebenezer Carleton the purveyor; Daniel Hymer the baker; George Fischer and Adam Foutz cooks; and James Dady the hostler. Other miscellaneous papers[129] show that Privates McIntire and Sanderson were the steward and hostler, respectively, for a year ending September 19, 1779; Private Dyer assistant cook for the fifteen months previous to January 1, 1780; and Sergeant Edwards, steward for the six months terminating March 14, 1780. For this special service they received the following extra monthly allowance in addition to the pay of their rank in the Guard: Steward, ten dollars; Assistant Cook, eight dollars; and Hostler, three dollars. Besides these assignments they were obliged to drill twice a day, weather permitting; and while they were at Newburgh, Baron Steuben received much relaxation in the regular drills that he gave the Guard.[130] However irksome these duties must have been, much relief and joy was experienced when Washington informed the army in orders, March 19, 1783, of the receipt of a letter from Congress announcing their receipt of unofficial advices of the signing of a definite treaty of peace with Great Britain on January 21, which was forwarded by a sloop-of-war, called the "Triumph," dispatched by Count D'Estaing and General Lafayette from Cadiz on the fourteenth of the previous month.

Revolutionary War.

Early in March, 1783, an arrangement was effected with the firm of Melancthon, Smith & Co., wherein they advanced to the enlisted men of the Guard the sum of four hundred and thirty-five dollars, being the amount of their pay for the previous month, who agreed to wait for reimbursement until the corps was paid by Congress. They were secured by the individual receipts of the men, which Lieutenant Colfax indorsed "Accepted to pay when recovered from the paymaster-general." These receipts have considerable interest by reason of the signatures of the men attached thereto, which are in possession of the Colfax family.[181] In referring to the pay roll of the command for the month of April, 1778, we find that the officers and men were allowed the following pay: Captain, forty dollars; Lieutenants, twenty-seven dollars; Surgeon, sixty dollars; Sergeants, eight dollars; Corporals, Drummers and Fifers, each seven and one-third dollars; and Privates, six and two-thirds dollars. The pay for similar ranks in February, 1783, were the same, except the Sergeants were advanced to ten dollars per month, while the Drum-major, a rank created in the Guard the previous July, was allowed nine dollars per month.

On April 1, 1783, Lieutenant Colfax, who had been carried "on command" on the rolls of the Connecticut Line, was promoted to a captaincy in the Second Connecticut Regiment, notwithstanding he had, and continued to retain, the command of the Commander-in-Chief's Guard, Continental Troops, as its lieutenant-commandant.

The Commander-in-Chief's Guard.

In arranging the principles for the settlement of the officers and men in the Guard, as well as those in the entire army, who had not been paid for some time, the following order* appears in relation thereto:

"HEAD-QUARTERS, NEWBURGH, April 2, 1783.

"The following principles being adopted in the settlement now commencing with the army, it is desired that they be attended to by the officers concerned, viz:

*　　*　　*　　*　　*　　*　　*

"5th: The officers and men of the Commander-in-Chief's Guard to be settled with in their respective lines and regiments."

The rumors of peace that had from time to time reached the army from unofficial sources were at length confirmed by Washington in general orders,* which read:

"HEAD-QUARTERS, NEWBURGH, April 18, 1783.

"The Commander-in-Chief orders the cessation of hostilities between the United States of America and the King of Great Britain to be publicly proclaimed tomorrow at twelve o'clock, at the New Building, and that the Proclamation, which will be communicated herewith, be read tomorrow evening at the head of every regiment and corps of the army. After which the chaplain with the several brigades will render thanks to Almighty God for all His mercies, particularly for His over-ruling the wrath of man to His own glory, and causing the rage of war to cease among nations.

"Although the proclamation before alluded to extends only to the prohibition of hostilities, and not to the annunciation of a general peace, yet it must afford the most rational and sincere satisfaction to every benevolent mind, as it puts a period to a long and doubtful contest, stops the effusion of human blood, opens the prospect to a more splendid scene, and, like another morning star, promises the approach of a brighter day than hath hitherto illuminated the western hemisphere. On such a happy day, a day which is the

Revolutionary War.

harbinger of peace, a day which completes the eighth year of the war, it would be ingratitude not to rejoice; it would be insensibility not to participate in the general felicity.

"The Commander-in-Chief, far from endeavoring to stifle the feelings of joy in his bosom, offers his most cordial congratulations on the occasion to all the officers of every denomination; to all the troops of the United States in general, and, in particular, to those gallant and persevering men who had resolved to defend the rights of their invaded country so long as the war should continue. For these are the men who ought to be considered as the pride and boast of the American army; and who, crowned with well earned laurels, may soon withdraw from the field of glory to the more tranquil walks of civil life.

"While the General recollects the almost infinite variety of scenes through which we have passed, with a mixture of pleasure, astonishment and gratitude; while he contemplates the prospects before us with rapture, he cannot help wishing that all the brave men, of whatever condition they may be, who have shared in the toils and dangers of effecting this glorious revolution, of rescuing millions from the hand of oppression, and of laying the foundation of a great empire, might be impressed with a proper idea of the dignified part they have been called to act, under the smiles of Providence, on the stage of human affairs; for happy, thrice happy, shall they be pronounced hereafter, who have contributed anything, who have performed the meanest office in erecting this stupendous fabric of freedom and empire on the broad basis of independency; who have assisted in protecting the rights of human nature and establishing an asylum for the poor and oppressed of all nations and religions.

"The glorious task for which we first flew to arms being thus accomplished, the liberties of our country being fully acknowledged and firmly secured by the smiles of heaven on the purity of our cause and the honest exertions of a feeble people determined to be free, against a powerful nation disposed to oppress them, and the character of those who have persevered through every extremity of hardship, suffering and danger being immortalized by the illustrious appellation of the patriot army. Nothing now remains but for the actors of this mighty scene to preserve a perfect unvarying consistency of character through the very last act; to close the drama with applause; and to retire from the military theatre with the same approbation of angels and men which have crowned all their former virtuous actions."

On the following morning "the day of jubilee" was ushered in by the excited and joyful soldiers with the firing of guns and shouts and song till hill and valley rang again. Precisely at twelve o'clock, noon, the troops of the cantonment having been drawn up, the Proclamation of Congress, for the cessation of hostilities, was published at the door of the New Building, followed by three huzzas; after which a prayer was offered by the Rev. John Gano, when the army, with one voice and accompanied by the band, thundered forth the anthem "Independence," by Billings:[122]

> "The States, O Lord, with song of praise
> Shall in Thy strength rejoice;
> And, blest with Thy salvation, raise
> To heaven their cheerful voice."

When night came the piles of combustible materials that had been heaped on the summits of Berean Mountains and Storm King to signal the advance of the enemy were lighted up, not to herald the approach of the foe, but blazed from their lofty tops like great altar fires to the God of Peace.

As the great drama of the War for Independence was now drawing to a close, Congress immediately began formulating plans for reducing the strength of the army.

Revolutionary War.

On the second day of June Washington proclaimed to the army, in general orders, the Resolve of Congress of May 26, 1783, instructing him to grant furloughs to all non-commissioned officers and enlisted men, engaged to serve during the war, until the ratification of the definite treaty of peace, together with a proportionate number of commissioned officers. In consequence of this resolution the Commander-in-Chief directed the commanding officers of all the various organizations, including the Guard, to make immediate returns to head-quarters of all the men who would and would not be entitled to the provisions of the resolution. In obedience to the order* the following return[133] was made of the Guard:

"Return of the non-commissioned officers and privates in the Commander-in-Chief's Guard, who are engaged to serve during the war.

No.	Name.	Rank.	State they belong to.
1	Ebenezer Carleton	Private	New Hampshire
2	Samuel Smith	do	do
3	John Phillips	Sergeant	Massachusetts
4	John Herrick	Corporal	do
5	Isaac Manning	Fifer	do
6	Joseph Vinal	Private	do
7	John Barton	do	do
8	Joel Crosby	do	do
9	Davis Brown	Sergeant	Rhode Island
10	Randolph Smith	Private	do
11	Reuben Thompson	do	do
12	William Tanner	do	do
13	Solomon Dailey	do	do

The Commander-in-Chief's Guard.

No.	Name.	Rank.	State they belong to.
14	Elihu Hancock	Corporal	Connecticut
15	Diah Manning	Drum-major	do
16	Jared Goodrich	Fifer	do
17	Frederick Parks	do	do
18	Peter Holt	Private	do
19	Jedediah Brown	do	do
20	Levi Dean	do	do
21	James Dady	do	do
22	Henry Wakelee	do	do
23	Elijah Lawrence	do	do
24	John Robinson	do	New York
25	Jacob Schriver	do	do
26	Edward Wiley	do	do
27	John Cole	do	do
28	Jonathan Moore	do	New Jersey
29	Benjamin Eaton	do	do
30	Stephen Hetfield	do	do
31	Lewis Campbell	do	do
32	Samuel Bailey	do	do
33	William Martin	do	do
34	Laban Landon	do	do
35	Robert Blair	do	do
36	Benjamin Bonnel	do	do
37	John Fenton	Drummer	do
38	Charles Dougherty	Private	do
39	William Hunter	Sergeant	Pennsylvania
40	John Arnold	do	do
41	Enoch Wells	Corporal	do
42	Cornelius Wilson	Drummer	do
43	William Karnahan	Private	do
44	Robert Finley	do	do
45	John Dother	do	do
46	John Patton	do	do

REVOLUTIONARY WAR.

No.	Name.	Rank.	State they belong to.
47	Hugh Cull	do	do
48	James Hughes	do	do
49	John Finch	do	do
50	Dennis Moriarity	do	do
51	John Montgomery	do	do
52	Daniel Hymer	do	do
53	Thomas Forrest	do	do
54	William Hennusey	do	do
55	Adam Foutz	do	do
56	George Fischer	do	do
57	Edward Weed	do	Maryland
58	Jeremiah Driskel	do	do
59	Thomas Gillen	do	do
60	Reaps Mitchell	Sergeant	Virginia
61	Lewis Flemister	do	do
62	William Coram	do	do
63	William Pace	do	do
64	Joseph Timberlake	do	do

"The above list includes the whole of the Guard, 4th June, '83.
"W. COLFAX, *Lieut. Comd't.*"

On Friday, June 6, 1783, Lieutenant Holden and all the non-commissioned officers and men of the Guard were granted furloughs, with the exception of Sergeant Phillips, who chose to remain.[134] On the same morning the following order* appeared for the formation of the new Guard:

"HEAD-QUARTERS, NEWBURGH, June 6, 1783.
"One subaltern, three sergeants, three corporals, two drums and fifes, and thirty privates to relieve the Commander-in-Chief's Guard, and to parade at the new building tomorrow morning at twelve

The Commander-in-Chief's Guard.

o'clock. They will be taken from the three years men in the Massachusetts Line, in the following proportion:

	Sub.	Serg't.	Corp.	D. F.	Pri.
"1st Brigade	1	1	1		10
2d Brigade		1	1	1	10
3d Brigade		1	1	1	10"

The next morning the preceding order was revoked by the following*:

"HEAD-QUARTERS, NEWBURGH, June 7, 1783.
"The Commander-in-Chief's Guard will be furnished daily from the regiments which gives other guards, and not as directed in the order of yesterday."

In compliance with the above order it is shown in orders that the temporary Guard was furnished daily from the various Massachusetts regiments until the sixteenth of June*, and on that day the permanent and final reorganization was formed by detail from the New Hampshire Line —after the war's men had been completely furloughed in accordance with the general order of June 2, when the three year's men were formed the same day into what was designated in orders as the "new or reformed regiments." The rank and file of the new Guard consisted of thirty-eight men, twelve of whom were mounted,[185] whose uniforms consisted of a blue coat with white facings, white waistcoat and breeches, black half-gaiters, and a cocked hat with a blue and white feather,[186] agreeable to that prescribed in general orders on the third of the preceding March, and in harmony with that neatly painted on a white silk flag[187]—

REVOLUTIONARY WAR.

the first of the organization—upon which is shown a member of the Guard holding a horse, and in the act of receiving a flag from the Genius of Liberty, who is personified as a woman leaning upon the Union Shield, near which is the American Eagle; and the motto of the corps, "Conquer or Die," is upon a ribbon.

On the first day of July Lieutenant Colfax was granted an indefinite leave, and on September 4 was detached[188] and assumed the captaincy of the Eighth Company of Colonel Heman Swift's Connecticut Regiment.

While waiting for the arrival of the definite treaty of peace, Washington, in company with Governor Clinton, of New York, left Newburgh, Friday, July 18, on a tour of inspection to the northward, going as far as Ticonderoga and Crown Point, and as far west as Fort Stanwix, up the Mohawk Valley, and returning to Newburgh on the fifth day of August.[189] In his absence the Guard remained at head-quarters under the command of the orderly sergeant. On September 5, 1783, Lieutenant Bezaleel Howe was detached from the New Hampshire Battalion and assigned to the command of the Commander-in-Chief's Guard.

In pursuance of an invitation to visit and confer with the Continental Congress at Princeton, Washington, on Monday morning, August 18, relinquished the command of the army during his absence to Major-General Knox;* and, accompanied by the Guard, proceeded from Newburgh, via West Point, to Rocky Hill, four miles distant from Princeton, where he arrived on the twenty-fourth of the same month[140] and took up quarters at the two story frame house of Judge John Berrien, situated upon an eminence a short distance from the Millstone River, near the rustic mansion of John Van Horne,[141] which had been provided by Congress. The Guard, which consisted of New England yeomen's sons, none older than twenty, encamped in tents upon the lawn about fifty rods from the house,[142] near the entrance to which Lieutenant Howe occupied his marquee.[143]

While at Rocky Hill the following permit[144] was issued for the care of the sick in the Guard:

"ROCKY HILL, Sep. 18, 1783.
"To MR. JOHN VANTILBURGH:
"Permit Mr. Howe to take possession of one of your rooms for the sick of General Washington's Guard.
"ICHABOD LEIGH, *Justice.*"

On October 10, 1783, Lieutenant Howe was commissioned a captain, by brevet, by the Continental Congress.[145] On the ninth of the following month Washington issued the following letter of instructions[146] to Captain Howe with respect to the delivery of his papers and baggage to his home at Mount Vernon, Virginia:

"INSTRUCTIONS FOR CAPT. HOWE.
"Sir
"You will take charge of the Waggons which contain my baggage, and with the escort proceed with them to Virginia, and deliver the baggage at my house—ten Miles below Alexandria

"As you know they contain all my Papers which are of immense value to me, I am sure it is unnecessary to request your particular attention to them—but as you will have several ferries to pass and

Gentleman

You will make such arrange
ments for the Peace, with Col. Morgan
at his Place and Illinois, & in at his
discretion and deliberaington as may be
necessary under the circumstances.

I am with Respect, the above —

J.P. Green

REVOLUTIONARY WAR.

some of them wide particularly the Susquehannah & Potomack I must caution you against crossing them if the Wind should be high or if there is in your own Judgement or the opinion of others the least danger

"The Waggons should never be without a Sentinel over them always locked and the keys in your possession

"You will make such arrangements for the March with Col. Morgan at this place and Mr. Hodgsden at Philadelphia as may be necessary under all circumstances especially with respect to the expence—failure of Horses and breaking of Waggons

"Your Road will be through Philadelphia and Wilmington, thence by the Head of Elk to the lower ferry on the Susquehannah & thence by Baltimore, Bladensburgh, Georgetown and Alexandria to Mount Vernon

"You will enquire of Mr. Hodgsden and Colonel Biddle if Mrs. Washington left any thing in their care to be forwarded by the Waggons to Virginia, if she did and you can find room for it let it be carried if there is not—desire them to send it by some other good opportunity

"the Waggons and Teams, after the Baggage is delivered is to be surrendered to the order of Colonel Pickering which has I believe been handed to Mr. Roberts and is to deliver them to Col. Fitzgerald to be sold

"the Bundle which contains my accounts you will be carefull of and deliver them at the financiers Office with the Letter addressed to him—that is to Mr. Morris

"the other small bundle you will deliver to Mr. Cotringer in Chestnut Street

"Doctor McHenrys Trunk & parcels you will (as I suppose he has already directed) leave at his House in Baltimore

"You will have the Tents which are occupied by the Guard delivered to Coll. Morgan, whose receipt for them will be a Voucher for you to the Quarter Master General

"the remainder of the Guard under the care of a good Serjeant with very strict orders to prevent every kind of abuse to the

THE COMMANDER-IN-CHIEF'S GUARD.

Inhabitants on the March is to be conducted to their Corps at West point

"Given at Rockyhill this 9th day of Nov 1783
"Go. WASHINGTON"

Upon the receipt of this order Corporal Holt was assigned wagonmaster to His Excellency's baggage,[147] and the remaining portion of the infantry Guard was detached and ordered to rejoin their corps—afterwards resolved into the American Regiment—stationed in the garrison at West Point. The twelve mounted infantrymen (so far as can be ascertained), consisting of Sergeant Stratton, Corporal Redington and Privates Ames, Batchelder, Blair, Coston, Currier, Ferguson, Morrison, Luther Smith and Pierce, under the command of Captain Howe, immediately started southward, via Trenton, escorting the six baggage wagons of the Commander-in-Chief. On the following Tuesday evening they arrived in Philadelphia, whence they departed the next morning for Mount Vernon.[148] By reference to Captain Howe's expense account[149] of the journey, which amounted to one hundred and three pounds, four shillings and seven pence, we find that they proceeded from Philadelphia, via "Chester, Wilmington, New Point, Christian Bridge, Head of Elk, Susquehanna, Swan Creek, Harford, Leggets, Baltimore, Elk Ridge Landing, Snowden's Ferries, Bladensburg, Georgetown and Alexandria." Upon their return north they passed through "Alexandria, Georgetown, Marlboro, Annapolis, Head of Severn, Baltimore, Leggets, Bakertown, Susquehanna, Charlestown and Wilmington," whence

REVOLUTIONARY WAR.

they proceeded to West Point, New York, where the company was mustered out and discharged on Constitution Island,[150] December 20, 1783,[151] after being presented with their horses, accoutrements, etc., in conformity with the Resolution of Congress of October 6, 1783.

The definite treaty of peace having been concluded and signed at Paris, September 3, 1783, Lieutenant Holden and the men of the Guard, who were furloughed on the sixth of the previous June, were finally discharged November 3, 1783, by virtue of the following proclamation:

BY THE UNITED STATES IN CONGRESS ASSEMBLED,
A Proclamation!

"Whereas, in the progress of an arduous and difficult war, the armies of the United States of America have eminently displayed every military and patriotic virtue, and are not less to be applauded for their fortitude and magnanimity in the most trying scenes of distress than for a series of heroic and illustrious achievements, which exalt them to a high rank among the most zealous and successful defenders of the rights and liberties of mankind: And, whereas, by the blessing of Divine Providence on our cause and our arms, the glorious period is arrived when our national independence and sovereignty are established, and we enjoy the prospect of a permanent and honorable peace; we, therefore, the United States, in Congress assembled, thus impressed with a lively sense of the distinguished merit and good conduct of the said armies, do give them the thanks of their country for their long, eminent and faithful services. And it is our will and pleasure that such part of the federal armies as stands engaged to serve during the war, and as by our acts of the 26th day of May, the 11th day of June, the 9th day of August and the 26th day of September last were furloughed, shall, from and after the 3d day of November next, be absolutely discharged, by virtue of this our proclamation from the said service, and we do declare that the further services in the field of the officers who are deranged and on furlough in consequence of our aforesaid acts can now be dispensed with, and they have our full permission to retire from service, without being longer liable from their present engagements to be called into command. And of such discharge and permission to retire from service respectively all our officers, civil and military, and all others whom it may concern, are required to take notice and to govern themselves accordingly.

"Given under the seal of the United States, in Congress assembled, witness His Excellency, Elias Boudinot, our President in Congress, this 18th day of October, in the year of our Lord 1783, and of the sovereignty and independence of the United States of America the eighth."

Fac Simile Signatures of the Officers and Men.

John Arnold

Samuel Baily

John Barlow X mark

Nathaniel Berry

Robert Blain

John Blundin

John Bodine

Benjamin Bonnel

James Brooks

Davis Brown

Jedidiah Brown

Lewis Campbell

Ebenr Carleton

Timothy Carleton

Nathan'l Chapman

Rawleigh E Christian

Benjamin Church

Lemuel Coffin

John + Cole

Martin Cole

Willm Colfax

Daniel Cook

William Coram

Eben^r Crosby

Joel Crosby

Hughey + Cull

Nathl Cunningham

James Dady

Solomon Daley

Levi Dean

John Lio × Dowthar
      Mark

Jeramiah Driskell

Levi Dunton

Benjamin Eaton

John Edge

David Emery

John Sinten
John Finch
Robert + Findby
George Fischer
Elijah Fisher
Lewis + his Flemister
     mark
Thomas Forrest
Adam Foutz
Carswell Gardner

Caleb Gibbs

Thomas Gillen

Jared Goodrich

Benjr Grymes

Elihu Hancock

William Harris

Wm Hennessey

John Herrick

Stephen Hetfield

Levi Holden

Peter X Holls

Bez.l Howe

Isaac Howel

James Hughes

Daniel X Hiner

John Ives

William Kernham

Ch. King

John King

James Knox

Laban Landon

Joseph Lard

Elijah Lawrence

Geo „ Lewis

Henry Ph: Livingston

Zenas Macomber

Diah Manning

Isaac Manning

William + Martin
his
mark

78 M⁵ In line

Reaps Mitchel

John Montgomery

Jonathan Moore

Dennis Moriarty

John Nicholas

Wm x Pace

Frederick Park

John Patten

John Phillips

Abner Pitcher

Elijah Hallock

Thomas Prentiss

Randolph

Samuel Raymond

Saml Reeves

Samuel Reid

Zebulon Richmond

John W Roberson

Elnathan Sanderson
Jacob Schriver
Samuel Sherman
Jesse Smith
Randall Smith
Samuel Smith
Timothy Smith
Henry Sparks
Nehemiah Stratton
Seth Sturtevant

William Tanner

Daniel Thompson

Reuben Thompson

Joseph McTimberlake

Michael Titcomb

Simon Tubbs

Abraham Vansickle

Jesse Vebart

Joseph Vinall

Henry Wakelee

Wm Pearrington

Edwd Wade

Sam Whitmarsh

Edward Wileys X Marsh

Enoch Wills

Cornelious Wilson

John Wilson

Saml Workman

REVOLUTIONARY WAR.

Roster of the Infantry Guard.

Major-Commandant.
Caleb Gibbs.

Captains.
Bezaleel Howe,
Henry Philip Livingston.

Lieutenants.
William Colfax,   Levi Holden,
Benjamin Grymes,   George Lewis,
John Nicholas.

Ensign.
George Augustine Washington.

Surgeons.
Ebenezer Crosby,   Samuel Hanson,

Drum-Major.
Diah Manning.

Sergeants.
John Arnold,   Nathaniel Cunningham,
Samuel Bliss,   Cornelius Drake,
Davis Brown,   Bildad Edwards,
——— Clements,   Lewis Flemister,
Martin Cole,   James Frazier,
William Coram,   Carswell Gardner,

The Commander-in-Chief's Guard.

Thomas Harris,
Daniel Holt,
William Hunter,
John Jones,
John Justice,
William McIntire,
Reaps Mitchell,
John Morris,
William Pace,
John Phillips,
Thomas Prentiss,
David Rice,
Peter Richards,
William Roach,
Nehemiah Stratton,
John Sturm,
Joseph Timberlake,
John Wilson,
Francis Wood,
Frederick Young.

Corporals.

Moses Cutter,
John Dent,
Ephraim Eddy,
Joshua Forbes,
Elihu Hancock,
John Herrick,
Thomas Holland,
Joel Holt,
Joseph Law,
Henry Randolph,
Asa Redington,
Henry Sparks,
Seth Sturtevant,
Levi Talbot,
Enoch Wells,
Samuel Wortman.

Drummers.

John Fenton,
Theophilus Frink,
William Green,
Roger Manning,
William Simpson,
Cornelius Wilson.

Fifers.

Elias Brown,
Jared Goodrich,
James Johnson,
Isaac Manning,
Samuel Odiorne,
Frederick Parks.

Privates.

Asa Adams,
George Albin,
Thomas Allen,
Richard Alling,
Stephen Ames,
David Ashby,

REVOLUTIONARY WAR.

Samuel Bailey,
Amos Baker,
Andrew Baker,
Benjamin Barham,
John Barnes,
John Barton,
William Batchelder,
John Bell,
Asa Benjamin,
John Berry,
Nathaniel Berry,
James Blair,
Robert Blair,
Thomas Blair,
John Blundin,
John Bodine,
Benjamin Bonnel,
Mills Bourn,
James Bradley,
James Brooks,
Ebenezer Brown,
Jedediah Brown,
Moses Brown,
Zachariah Brown,
———— Bullard,
John Bush,
Lewis Campbell,
Ebenezer Carleton,
Timothy Carleton,
Nathaniel Chapman,
Jonathan Chenoweth,
Raleigh Christian,
Benjamin Church,
John Coffin,
Lemuel Coffin,

John Cole,
William Condel,
———— Connor,
Daniel Cook,
Wilmer Cooper,
Ebenezer Coston,
James Craig,
Samuel Craig,
Joel Crosby,
Aaron Crumbie,
Hugh Cull,
Abraham Currier,
James Dady,
Solomon Daley,
William Darrah,
Joseph Davis,
John Daws,
William Day,
Levi Dean,
Joseph Delano,
Henry Desperate,
Antipas Dodge,
John Dother,
Charles Dougherty,
George Dougherty,
James Dougherty,
Jeremiah Driskel,
Levi Dunton,
Daniel Dyer,
Robert Eakin,
Henry Eastman,
———— Eaton,
Benjamin Eaton,
John Edge,
Clayborne Elder,

The Commander-in-Chief's Guard.

David Emery,
John English,
Jacob Erwin,
Eliphalet Everett,
Laban Fairbanks,
George Farmer,
William Ferguson,
John Finch,
Robert Finley,
George Fischer,
Elijah Fisher,
Thomas Forrest,
Adam Foutz,
William Gilbert,
William Gill,
Thomas Gillen,
James Gordon,
Edmund Griffin,
John Griffith,
Hugh Hagerty,
Silvanus Hall,
Thomas Harmon,
Thomas Harris,
William Harris,
William Harris,
Andrew Harrison,
Caleb Hendee,
William Henussey,
Stephen Hetfield,
Thomas Hickey,
Spencer Hill,
Joseph Hilton,
Peter Holt,
Philip Holt,
Isaac Howell,
Thomas Howell,
James Hughes,
John Hurring,
———— Hutchinson,
Daniel Hymer,
Pendleton Isbell,
John Ives,
Zachariah Jackson,
Solomon Janet,
Asa Johnson,
James Johnson,
Levi Johnson,
Ephraim Jones,
Joseph Jones,
William Jones,
John Kenney,
William Kernahan,
John Kidder,
Charles King,
John King,
James Knox,
Laban Landon,
Jasper Langley,
Elijah Lawrence,
John Leary,
Benjamin Lester,
Hezekiah Linton,
Jesse Linton,
William Logan,
Simeon Lothrop,
John Lovejoy,
Seth Lovell,
Ephraim Lucas,
Michael Lynch,
Zenas Macomber,

Revolutionary War.

Phineas Mapes,
Peter Martin,
William Martin,
William McCown,
James McDonald,
James Milsom,
John Montgomery,
Hezekiah Moor,
Jonathan Moore,
Dennis Moriarity,
———— Morrill,
David Morrison,
———— Norris,
Jesse Nott,
Reuben Odell,
William O'Neil
John Paddington,
William Palmer,
Joseph Parker,
John Patton,
John Pease,
Henry Perry,
Benjamin Pierce,
John Pillar,
Shadrack Pinkstone,
Thomas Piper,
Abner Pitcher,
Elijah Pollock,
———— Pope,
Robert Preston,
William Price,
Andrew Pritchett,
Henry Pullen,
John Putnam,
Samuel Raymond,

Daniel Reed,
Samuel Reeves,
Samuel Reid,
William Reiley,
Zebulon Richmond,
Timothy Ricker,
Dixon Robinson,
John Robinson,
Christopher Rodamer,
Jonathan Rundlett,
———— Sanborn,
Elnathan Sanderson,
Able Sargent,
John Savory,
Jacob Schriver,
Samuel Sherman,
Micajah Sherwood,
Joseph Shipman,
John Shorey,
William Simmons,
John Slocum,
Francis Smith,
Jesse Smith,
John Smith,
Luther Smith,
Randolph Smith,
Robinson Smith,
Samuel Smith,
Timothy Smith,
Henry Snow,
John Standard,
John Stockdell,
Joseph Stripe,
Michael Sutton,
William Tanner,

The Commander-in-Chief's Guard.

Daniel Thompson,
Reuben Thompson,
Ezekiel Thurston,
John Tipper,
Michael Titcomb,
Zebulon Titcomb,
Solomon Townsend,
John Trask,
Simon Tubbs,
Abraham Van Sickle,
Jesse Vibbart,
Joseph Vinal,
Robert Wadsworth,
Henry Wakelee,
Moses Walton,
Benjamin Ward,
Daniel Warner,
William Warrington,
Edward Weed,
Edward Whelan,
Samuel Whitmarsh,
Edward Wiley,
John Williams,
Joseph Winch,
William Wyman.

Roster of the Cavalry Guard.

Captain.
George Lewis.

Lieutenant.
Robert Randolph.

Quartermaster Sergeant.
Charles King.

Sergeants.
Isaac Davenport,   Francis Wood.

Corporals.
John Druce,   Carswell Gardner,
James Knox.

Revolutionary War.

Saddler.
Jeremiah Low.

Farrier.
Thomas McCarty.

Trumpeter.
Nathan Pushee.

Privates.

John Blundin,
William Boyd,
Nathaniel Brackett,
Jonathan Bryant,
Michael Caswell,
Oliver Chapin,
John Coffin,
Lemuel Coffin,
Philip Disclow,
William Dunn,
William Garret,
Charles Gavat,
Thomas Harris,
Caleb Hendee,
Daniel Hersey,
William Hincher,
Samuel Huston,
Isaac Kidder,
Abraham Lawell,
George Layard,
Samuel Leverich,
Zenas Macomber,
Alexander McCulloch,
Nathaniel Potter,
Samuel Raymond,
Samuel Reynolds,
Samuel Sherman,
Jesse Smith,
Simeon Stow,
Michael Titcomb,
Zebulon Titcomb.

REVOLUTIONARY WAR.

Records of the Officers and Men.

ADAMS, ASA: Enlisted, Norfolk, Conn., May 5, 1777, for three pears, a private, Captain Titus Watson's Company, Seventh Connecticut Regiment, commanded by Colonel Heman Swift; transferred, Valley Forge, Pa., March 19, 1778, to the Commander-in-Chief's Guard, commanded by Captain Caleb Gibbs; at battle of Monmouth, N. J., June 28, 1778; discharged, Morristown, N. J., May 5, 1780.

ALBIN, GEORGE:* Enlisted, Winchester, Va., February 28, 1776, for two years, a private, Captain Thomas Berry's Company, Eighth Virginia Regiment, commanded by Colonel Peter Muhlenberg; transferred, Morristown, N. J., May 1, 1777, to the Commander-in-Chief's Guard, commanded by Captain Caleb Gibbs; at battle of Brandywine, Del., September 11, 1777; battle of Germantown, Pa., October 4, 1777; discharged, Valley Forge, Pa., February 28, 1778; re-enlisted March 3, 1778, Captain Jeremiah Dunn's Company of Express Riders, Continental Troops; on rolls to November 24, 1778.

Born,[1] Winchester, Va., February 15, 1758; married Jane Green (born August 18, 1760; died, Steubenville, Ohio, August 8, 1839), Virginia, 1783; died, Steubenville, Ohio, January 29, 1840, with the following issue: Polly, born, Winchester, Va., October 11, 1784, and died, Melmore, Ohio, July, 1850 (married Thomas Edgington); William, born, Winchester, Va., March 22, 1786, and died, Canal Fulton, Ohio, July 1, 1845 (married, first, Elizabeth Shane, Jefferson County, Ohio, 1808; second, Jane Whitcraft, Stark County, Ohio, September, 1824; third, Isabella McCaughey,

Stark County, Ohio, June 9, 1840); John, born February
20, 1788, and died 1830 (married Susan Cox); Emerson,
born November 17, 1789, and died unmarried; Elizabeth,
born, Steubenville, Ohio, July 9, 1792, and died, Findlay,
Ohio, October, 1877 (married John Patterson, Jefferson
County, Ohio, August 17, 1809); Leah, born, Virginia,
April 4, 1794, and died, Wyandotte County, Ohio, July 1,
1855 (married Henry Crabbs); George, born March 6, 1796,
and died, Steubenville, Ohio, September 15, 1861 (married
Nancy Cox); Aaron, born, Steubenville, Ohio, March 24,
1798, and died, Nevada, Ohio, October 4, 1874 (married
Ann Patterson, Steubenville, Ohio, February 17, 1820);
Abram, born, Steubenville, Ohio, November 20, 1800, and
died, Washington County, Ohio, April 12, 1864 (married
Eliza Pyles in 1829); and Nancy, born November 10, 1804,
and died at Steubenville, Ohio, unmarried.

ALLEN, THOMAS: Enlisted January 6, 1777, for three
years, a private, Captain James Gray's Company, Fifteenth
Virginia Regiment, commanded by Lieutenant-Colonel
James Innes; transferred, Morristown, N. J., May 1, 1777,
to the Commander-in-Chief's Guard, commanded by Captain Caleb Gibbs; at battle of Brandywine, Del., September
11, 1777; battle of Germantown, Pa., October 4, 1777; battle
of Monmouth, N. J., June 28, 1778; discharged, Morristown,
N. J., January 6, 1780.

ALLING, RICHARD: "Appointed" May 25, 1779, a private,
Commander-in-Chief's Guard, commanded by Major Caleb
Gibbs; at battle of Connecticut Farms, N. J., June 7, 1780;
deserted, Tappan, N. Y., August 15, 1780.

AMES, STEPHEN:* Enlisted, Amherst, N. H., March 17,
1781, for three years, a private, Captain Moses Dustin's
Company, Second New Hampshire Regiment, commanded
by Lieutenant-Colonel George Reid; taken prisoner, Mohawk
River, N. Y., June 21, 1782, and confined in Canada; exchanged, Boston, Mass., November 28, 1782; rejoined Cap-

REVOLUTIONARY WAR.

tain Joseph Potter's Company, April 1, 1783; transferred, Newburgh, N. Y., June 16, 1783, to the Commander-in-Chief's Guard, commanded by Lieutenant-Commandant William Colfax; discharged, West Point, N. Y., December 20, 1783, and re-enlisted, as substitute, Captain Joseph Potter's Company, Colonel Henry Jackson's Regiment, Continental Infantry; discharged June 30, 1784.

Born October, 1762-63; occupation, blacksmith; moved from Groton, N. H., to Kirtland Township, Geauga County, Ohio, 1816, where he was residing, June 27, 1820, with wife Dorcas (born 1766) and son Ezra (born 1801); died November 2, 1825.

ARNOLD, JOHN: Enlisted April 19, 1777, for the war, a corporal, Fifth Pennsylvania Regiment, commanded by Colonel Francis Johnston; transferred, Valley Forge, Pa., March 19, 1778, to the Commander-in-Chief's Guard, commanded by Captain Caleb Gibbs, and assigned private; at battle of Monmouth, N. J., June 28, 1778; promoted 5th corporal, April 1, 1780; promoted 4th corporal, May 1, 1780; promoted 3d corporal, June 1, 1780; at battle of Connecticut Farms, N. J., June 7, 1780; promoted 1st corporal, July 1, 1781; at skirmish of King's Bridge, N. Y., July 3, 1781; battle of Yorktown, Va., October 19, 1781; promoted 5th sergeant, November 1, 1782; promoted 4th sergeant, February 1, 1783; furloughed, Newburgh, N. Y., June 6, 1783, until the ratification of the definite treaty of peace; discharged November 3, 1783.

ASHBY, DAVID: Private, Virginia Line; transferred, Morristown, N. J., May 1, 1777, to the Commander-in-Chief's Guard, commanded by Captain Caleb Gibbs; on rolls to August 11, 1777, without remark.

BAILEY, SAMUEL: Private, Captain Joseph Pancoast's (4th) Company, First Burlington Regiment, New Jersey Militia, commanded by Colonel William Shreve, May, 1778; re-enlisted June 3, 1778, for nine months, Captain Alexander

Mitchell's (3d) Company, Fourth New Jersey Regiment, commanded by Colonel Ephraim Martin, Brigadier-General William Maxwell's Brigade; born, U. S., 1759; height, five feet, nine inches; well built; complexion, fair; hair, light; residence, Springfield, Burlington County, N. J.; at battle of Monmouth, N. J., June 28, 1778; re-enlisted for the war and transferred to Major Richard Howell's Company, Second New Jersey Regiment, commanded by Colonel Israel Shreve, Brigadier-General Maxwell's Brigade, February 1, 1779; assigned with Regiment and Brigade to Major-General John Sullivan's Division, Continental Army, engaged in an expedition against the Six Nations of Indians in Western Pennsylvania and New York, May 26 to October 26, 1779; transferred, Morristown, N. J., March 20, 1780, to the Commander-in-Chief's Guard, commanded by Major Caleb Gibbs; at battle of Connecticut Farms, N. J., June 7, 1780; skirmish of King's Bridge, N. Y., July 3, 1781; battle of Yorktown, Va., October 19, 1781; furloughed, Newburgh, N. Y., June 6, 1783, until the ratification of the definite treaty of peace; discharged November 3, 1783.

BAKER, AMOS: Enlisted, Lincoln, Mass., March 4, 1776, a private, Captain John Hartwell's Company, Colonel Eleazer Brooks's Regiment; discharged March 9, 1776; re-enlisted December 20, 1776, Captain Moses Harrington's Company, Colonel Nicholas Dike's Regiment; discharged March 1, 1777; re-enlisted August 16, 1777, Captain George Minot's Company, Colonel Samuel Bullard's Regiment; discharged September 30, 1777; re-enlisted November 3, 1777, Captain Simon Hunt's Company, Colonel Eleazer Brooks's Regiment; discharged April 3, 1778; re-enlisted, New Ipswich, N. H., February 27, 1781, for three years, Eighth Company, First New Hampshire Regiment, commanded by Colonel Alexander Scammell; transferred, Newburgh, N. Y., June 16, 1783, to the Commander-in-Chief's Guard, commanded by Lieutenant-Commandant William Colfax; on return dated Rocky Hill, N. J., October 22, 1783, with remark "Present."

REVOLUTIONARY WAR.

Born,[2] Dunstable, Mass., January, 1764; married Betsey Walker; died, Buffalo, N. Y., October 7, 1814; issue: Henry Knox, born, Canaan, Me., December 2, 1806, and died, Hallowell, Me., June, 1902, married.

BAKER, ANDREW: Enlisted, Groton, Conn., April 2, 1777, for three years, a private, Captain Aaron Steven's Company, Seventh Connecticut Regiment, commanded by Colonel Heman Swift; transferred, Valley Forge, Pa., March 19, 1778, to the Commander-in-Chief's Guard, commanded by Captain Caleb Gibbs; at battle of Monmouth, N. J., June 28, 1778; discharged, Morristown, N. J., April 1, 1780; re-enlisted and stationed at Fort Griswold, Conn., under the command of Captain Oliver Coit, September, 1781; killed at battle of Groton Heights, Conn., September 6, 1781.

Born,[3] Groton, Conn., March 22, 1756; occupation, shoemaker; married Mary ———; issue: one child.

BARHAM, BENJAMIN:[*] Enlisted February 13, 1776, for two years, a private, Captain John Walker's Company, Fourth Virginia Regiment, commanded by Colonel Adam Stephens; at battle of Trenton, N. J., December 26, 1776; battle of Princeton, N. J., January 3, 1777; transferred, Morristown, N. J., May 1, 1777, to the Commander-in-Chief's Guard, commanded by Captain Caleb Gibbs; sick-hospital, June 1 to August 11, 1777; at battle of Germantown, Pa., October 4, 1777; discharged, Valley Forge, Pa., February 13, 1778.

Born 1754; residing in Southampton County, Va., September 1, 1818; married, with issue; will admitted to probate, Southampton County, Va., September 16, 1822.

BARNES, JOHN: Private, Commander-in-Chief's Guard, commanded by Captain Caleb Gibbs; in arrest, New York, June 22, 1776; committed to prison in city hall, New York, July 12, 1776.

The Commander-in-Chief's Guard.

BARTON, JOHN :* Enlisted, Duxbury, Mass., January 1, 1776, for one year, a private, Captain Samuel Bradford's Company, Twenty-third Regiment, Continental Infantry, commanded by Colonel John Bailey; re-enlisted May 15, 1777, for the war, Captain Joseph Wadsworth's Company, Fourteenth Massachusetts Regiment, commanded by Colonel Gamaliel Bradford; deserted December 15, 1778; rejoined February 1, 1779, and transferred to Captain Zebulon King's Company; transferred, West Point, N. Y., November 1, 1779, to the Commander-in-Chief's Guard, commanded by Major Caleb Gibbs; at battle of Connecticut Farms, N. J., June 7, 1780; skirmish of King's Bridge, N. Y., July 3, 1781; battle of Yorktown, Va., October 19, 1781; sick at New Windsor Hospital, N. Y., November, 1782; furloughed, Newburgh, N. Y., June 6, 1783, until the ratification of the definite treaty of peace; discharged November 3, 1783.

Born,[4] England, 1759; occupation, farmer; married Abigail Simmons (born, Duxbury, Mass., May 24, 1753; died, Duxbury, Mass., November 6, 1807), 1784; died, Duxbury, Mass., December 20, 1835, with the following issue: George Washington, born, Duxbury, Mass., July 23, 1785; John Douglas, born, Duxbury, Mass., February 9, 1788; Jedediah, born, Duxbury, Mass., December 31, 1789 (married Sally Weston); Anderson, born, Duxbury, Mass., February 17, 1793, and died October 6, 1796; and Matthew, born, Duxbury, Mass., September 2, 1795.

BATCHELDER, WILLIAM :* Enlisted, Chester, N. H., May 9, 1782, for three years, a private, Captain Samuel Cherry's Company, Second New Hampshire Regiment, commanded by Lieutenant-Colonel George Reid; transferred, Newburgh, N. Y., June 16, 1783, to the Commander-in-Chief's Guard, commanded by Lieutenant-Commandant William Colfax; discharged, West Point, N. Y., December 20, 1783.

Born 1765; occupation, shoemaker; married Joanna Blackwell (born 1772; residing at Pittston, Me., May 30, 1853), Vienna, Me., February 6, 1812, by James Chapman, J. P.; died, Pittston, Me., November 4, 1840.

REVOLUTIONARY WAR.

BELL, JOHN: Enlisted July 28, 1776, for three years, a private, Virginia Line; transferred, Morristown, N. J., May 1, 1777, to the Commander-in-Chief's Guard, commanded by Captain Caleb Gibbs; at battle of Brandywine, Del., September 11, 1777; battle of Germantown, Pa., October 4, 1777; battle of Monmouth, N. J., June 28, 1778; on furlough, January 8, 1779; discharged, West Point, N. Y., July 28, 1779.

BENJAMIN, ASA:* Enlisted, Worthington, Mass., May 4, 1775, for eight months, a private, Captain Ebenezer Webber's Company, Eighth Regiment, Continental Infantry, commanded by Colonel John Fellows; discharged December 23, 1775; re-enlisted, Dorchester, Mass., January 1, 1776, for one year, Captain Samuel Bartlett's Company, Twenty-first Regiment, Continental Infantry, commanded by Colonel Jonathan Ward; at battle of Long Island, N. Y., August 27, 1776; battle of Harlem Plains, N. Y., September 16, 1776; battle of White Plains, N. Y., October 28, 1776; discharged, Peekskill, N. Y., December 31, 1776; re-enlisted January 1, 1777, for three years, Captain Samuel Bartlett's Company, Ninth Massachusetts Regiment, commanded by Colonel James Wesson; at siege of Fort Stanwix, N. Y., August 22, 1777; battles of Stillwater, N. Y., September 19 and October 7, 1777; transferred, Valley Forge, Pa., March 19, 1778, to the Commander-in-Chief's Guard, commanded by Captain Caleb Gibbs; sick-absent, June, 1778; discharged, Morristown, N. J., December 26, 1779; re-enlisted July 12, 1780, for six months, Captain Samuel Bartlett's Company, Ninth Massachusetts Regiment, commanded by Colonel James Wesson; discharged January 12, 1781; re-enlisted August 10, 1781, for three months, a corporal, Captain Ebenezer Strong's Company, Colonel Sears's Hampshire County Regiment, Massachusetts Militia; discharged November 20, 1781; re-enlisted May 17, 1782; for three years, Captain Abbott's Company, Tenth Massachusetts Regiment, commanded by Colonel Benjamin Tupper (also given Captain Peter Claye's Company, Lieutenant-Colonel

THE COMMANDER-IN-CHIEF'S GUARD.

Calvin Smith's Regiment); discharged, West Point, N. Y., at close of war.

Born,⁵ Connecticut, October 27, 1753; married Polly Brumley (born January 16, 1763; died, Pierpont, Ohio, August 10, 1845), Worthington, Mass., January 5, 1787; died, Pierpont, Ohio, December 28, 1825, with the following issue: Polly, born, Worthington, Mass., August 22, 1789, and died, Kingsville, Ohio, 1870 (married Jacob Pratt at Pierpont, Ohio); Reuben, born, Worthington, Mass., December 29, 1792, and died, Pierpont, Ohio, January 30, 1864 (married, first, Lydia Pratt; second, Almira Prince at Pierpont, Ohio); Priscilla, born, Worthington, Mass., April 7, 1796, and died, Pierpont, Ohio, December 27, 1830 (married Asahel Cleveland at Pierpont, Ohio); Ansell, born, Worthington, Mass., December 19, 1798, and died, Pierpont, Ohio, September 2, 1831 (married Marriba Snow at Pierpont, Ohio); Philander, born, Worthington, Mass., May 3, 1805, and died November 15, 1804(?); and George Nelson, born Worthington, Mass., February 28, 1807, and died at Newark, Ohio (married Elizabeth Rawson).

BERRY, JOHN :* Enlisted, Philadelphia, Pa., January, 1776, for one year, a private, Captain Alexander Graydon's Company, Third Pennsylvania Battalion, commanded by Colonel John Shee; re-enlisted April, 1777, for three years, Captain James Long's Company, Tenth Pennsylvania Regiment, commanded by Lieutenant-Colonel Adam Hubley; transferred, Valley Forge, Pa., March 19, 1778, to the Commander-in-Chief's Guard, commanded by Captain Caleb Gibbs; at battle of Monmouth, N. J., June 28, 1778; deserted, Morristown, N. J., March 1, 1780; re-enlisted, Egg Harbor, N. J., May, 1781, for six months, on privateer "Rattlesnake," commanded by Captain William Treen.

Born, Gloucester County, N. J., 1757; occupation, farmer; residing in Hamilton Township, Gloucester County, N. J., June, 1823, with wife Phebe (born 1760), and the following children: Elisha, born 1800; and Priscilla, born 1803.

Revolutionary War.

BERRY, NATHANIEL:* Enlisted, Gardnerstown, Mass., January 1, 1777, for three years, a private, Captain Isaiah Stetson's Company, Fourteenth Massachusetts Regiment, commanded by Colonel Gamaliel Bradford; at battles of Stillwater, N. Y., September 19 and October 7, 1777; transferred, Valley Forge, Pa., March 19, 1778, to the Commander-in-Chief's Guard, commanded by Captain Caleb Gibbs; at battle of Monmouth, N. J., June 28, 1778; discharged, Morristown, N. J., January 1, 1780.

Born,⁶ Georgetown, Me., December 22, 1755; married Lydia Berry (born, Gardiner, Me., August 22, 1765, and residing at Gardiner, Me., May 22, 1820); died, Pittston, Me., August 20, 1850, with the following issue: Rhoda, born, Gardiner, Me., 1779, and died, Pittston, Me., September 7, 1848 (married Ichabod Wentworth, Gardiner, Me., April 29, 1798); John, born, Gardiner, Me., February 17, 1783, and died, Gardiner, Me., October 14, 1860 (married Elizabeth Robinson, Litchfield, Me., November 8, 1804); Josiah, died unmarried; Deborah, born, Gardiner, Me., 1786, and died, Pittston, Me., June 23, 1855 (married, first, Abram Lord, Pittston, Me., February 27, 1808; second, Pardon Grey, Pittston, Me., February 5, 1813); and Sally, born, Gardiner, Me., 1791, and died, Pittston, Me., December 25, 1879 (married Leonard Blanchard).

BLAIR, JAMES:* Enlisted, Londonderry, N. H., March 21, 1781, for three years, a private, Captain Joseph Potter's Company, Second New Hampshire Regiment, commanded by Lieutenant-Colonel George Reid; transferred, Newburgh, N. Y., June 16, 1783, to the Commander-in-Chief's Guard, commanded by Lieutenant-Commandant William Colfax; discharged, West Point, N. Y., December 20, 1783.

Born,⁷ Ireland, 1763; occupation, farmer; married Mollie Chaffee (born in Scotland; died, Mill Village, Pa., 1822); died, Mill Village, Pa., 1848, with the following issue: Robert, died Somerset County, Ky., 1847 (married Rachel Copley, Blairsville, Pa., March 24, 1828); Archibald, died, Mill Village, Pa., 1891 (married Elizabeth Cottrell); Elizabeth, died, Mill Village, Pa., 1860 (married Mr. Johnson); Mary Ann, died, Mill Village, Pa., 1893 (married Aaron Everly, Medina, Ohio, August 6, 1836); and Samuel, died unmarried.

BLAIR, ROBERT:* Enlisted, Burlington, N. J., May 1, 1777, for the war, a private, Captain John Hollinshead's (6th) Company, Second New Jersey Regiment, commanded by Colonel Israel Shreve, Brigadier-General William Maxwell's Brigade; at battle of Short Mills, N. J., June 26, 1777; battle of Brandywine, Del., September 11, 1777; battle of Germantown, Pa., October 4, 1777; transferred, Valley Forge, Pa., March 19, 1778, to the Commander-in-Chief's Guard, commanded by Captain Caleb Gibbs; at battle of Monmouth, N. J., June 28, 1778; battle of Connecticut Farms, N. J., June 7, 1780; skirmish of King's Bridge, N. Y., July 3, 1781; battle of Yorktown, Va., October 19, 1781; furloughed, Newburgh, N. Y., June 6, 1783, until the ratification of the definite treaty of peace; discharged November 3, 1783.

Born,[8] Ireland, 1762; died, Newburgh, N. Y., March 11, 1841, unmarried.

BLAIR, THOMAS:* Enlisted August 14, 1776, for three years, a private, Captain John Finley's Company, Eighth Pennsylvania Regiment, commanded by Colonel Daniel Broadhead; transferred, Valley Forge, Pa., March 19, 1778, to the Commander-in-Chief's Guard, commanded by Captain Caleb Gibbs; at battle of Monmouth, N. J., June 28, 1778; discharged, West Point, N. Y., August 25, 1779.

Born 1757; married; residing in Spencer County, Ind., February 3, 1826; died January 1, 1833.

BLISS, SAMUEL: Transferred, Morristown, N. J., March 20, 1780, to the Commander-in-Chief's Guard, commanded by Major Caleb Gibbs, and assigned third sergeant; at battle of Connecticut Farms, N. J., June 7, 1780; deserted September 15, 1780.

Revolutionary War.

BLUNDIN, JOHN :* Enlisted, Brookline, Mass., April 19, 1775, a private, Captain Thomas White's Company of Minute-men; re-enlisted April 26, 1775, for eight months, a corporal, Captain Timothy Corey's Company, Thirty-eighth Regiment, Continental Infantry, commanded by Colonel Samuel Gerrish; re-enlisted January 1, 1776, for one year, a private, Captain Thomas Mighill's Company, Twenty-sixth Regiment, Continental Infantry, commanded by Colonel Loammi Baldwin; transferred, Cambridge, Mass., March 12, 1776, to the Commander-in-Chief's Guard, commanded by Captain Caleb Gibbs; at battle of White Plains, N. Y., October 28, 1776; discharged, Newtown, Pa., December 14, 1776, and re-enlisted for three years, Captain George Lewis's Troop, Third Regiment, Continental Dragoons, commanded by Colonel George Baylor; assigned to the Cavalry of the Commander-in-Chief's Guard, commanded by Captain George Lewis, May 1, 1777; at battle of Brandywine, Del., September 11, 1777; battle of Germantown, Pa., October 4, 1777; battle of Monmouth, N. J., June 28, 1778; rejoined Regiment, September 26, 1778; at skirmish of Tappan, N. Y., September 28, 1778; discharged, Schuylkill Barracks, Philadelphia, Pa., December 13, 1779.

Born⁰ June 16, 1747; married Letitia (died, Hulmeville, Pa., September 26, 1831); died, Hulmeville, Pa., August 13, 1829, with the following issue: Samuel, born, Hulmeville, Pa., June 29, 1798, and died, Hulmeville, Pa., June 22, 1847 (married Rachel Dunlap); Rachel, born, Hulmeville, Pa., February 23, 1800; Joseph, born Hulmeville, Pa., November 21, 1801 (married Amy Lott); George, born, Hulmeville, Pa., December 19, 1803; Richard, born, Hulmeville, Pa., August 30, 1806, and died, Philadelphia, Pa., January 4, 1860 (married Martha Newlin, who died, Philadelphia, Pa., March 15, 1901); Ann, born, Hulmeville, Pa., January 21, 1808; John, born, Hulmeville, Pa., January 28, 1810; William, born, Hulmeville, Pa., June 5, 1812, and died, Philadelphia, Pa., May, 1872 (married Sarah Noble, Philadelphia, Pa., 1833); Susan, born, Hulmeville, Pa., August 9, 1814, and died, Hulmeville, Pa., 1856 (married Mr. Rue); and Maria, born, Hulmeville, Pa., May 19, 1817, and residing in Camden, N. J., February 2, 1902 (married Mr. Thompson).

BODINE, JOHN:* Enlisted, Martinsburg, Va., January 22, 1777, for three years, a private, Captain Joseph Mitchell's Company, Twelfth Virginia Regiment, commanded by Colonel James Wood; transferred, Morristown, N. J., May 6, 1777, to the Commander-in-Chief's Guard, commanded by Captain Caleb Gibbs; at battle of Brandywine, Del., September 11, 1777; battle of Germantown, Pa., October 4, 1777; battle of Monmouth, N. J., June 28, 1778; discharged, Morristown, N. J., January 22, 1780.

Born 1744; residing in Ross County, Ohio, April 1, 1821; died September 2, 1822.

BONNEL, BENJAMIN: Enlisted August 19, 1777, for the war, a private, Captain John Conway's (3d) Company, First New Jersey Regiment, commanded by Colonel Matthias Ogden, Brigadier-General William Maxwell's Brigade; deserted at battle of Brandywine, Del., September 11, 1777; rejoined April 1, 1778; at battle of Monmouth, N. J., June 28, 1778; assigned with Regiment and Brigade to Major-General John Sullivan's Division, Continental Army, engaged in an expedition against the Six Nations of Indians in Western Pennsylvania and New York, May 26 to October 26, 1779; promoted corporal, January 21, 1780; at battle of Connecticut Farms, N. J., June 7, 1780; battle of Springfield, N. J., June 23, 1780; deserted December 13, 1780; rejoined January 1, 1781, and reduced to the ranks; detached, Morristown, N. J., February 26, 1781, to Captain Jonathan Forman's (1st) Company, Third Battalion, Lieutenant-Colonel Francis Barber, First Brigade, Brigadier-General Peter Muhlenberg, First Division, Light Infantry, commanded by Major-General Lafayette; at battle of Green Springs, Va., July 6, 1781; battle of Yorktown, Va., October 19, 1781; rejoined Company and Regiment, October 26, 1781; transferred, Newburgh, N. Y.,

REVOLUTIONARY WAR.

April 30, 1782, to the Commander-in-Chief's Guard, commanded by Lieutenant-Commandant William Colfax; furloughed, Newburgh, N. Y., June 6, 1783, until the ratification of the definite treaty of peace; discharged November 3, 1783.

Born[10] and died near Chatham, N. J.; married Hannah Ward; issue: Enos (married Rachel Ball); Matthias (married Sally Ward); Sarah (married Enos B. Townley); Phebe (married Dr. Amos King); and Prussia (married Bonnel Brant).

BOURN, MILLS: Enlisted January 9, 1777, for three years, a private, Virginia Line; transferred, Morristown, N. J., May 1, 1777, to the Commander-in-Chief's Guard, commanded by Captain Caleb Gibbs; sick at Morristown, N. J., August 11, 1777; at battle of Monmouth, N. J., June 28, 1778; sick at Quaker Hill Hospital, November 26, 1778, to February 26, 1779; discharged, Morristown, N. J., January 9, 1780.

BOYD, WILLIAM :* Enlisted June 24, 1775, for one year, a private, Captain Michael Cresap's (1st) Company, Maryland Rifles; re-enlisted, Staten Island, N. Y., July 1, 1776, Captain Garret Graff's Company, Lieutenant-Colonel Peter Kachlein's Battalion, Pennsylvania Militia; at battle of Long Island, N. Y., August 27, 1776; re-enlisted January, 1778, Captain George Lewis's Troop, assigned as the Cavalry to the Commander-in-Chief's Guard; at battle of Monmouth, N. J., June 28, 1778; transferred with Troop to Third Regiment, Continental Dragoons, commanded by Colonel George Baylor, September 26, 1778; at skirmish of Tappan, N. Y., September 28, 1778; discharged, Schuylkill Barracks, Philadelphia, Pa., December 13, 1779.

Born 1754; ocupation, shoemaker; residing at Upper Bluelicks, Fleming County, Ky., September 6, 1821; died December 30, 1828.

BRACKETT, NATHANIEL: Enlisted January 1, 1777, for three years, a private, Captain George Lewis's Troop, Third

Regiment, Continental Dragoons, commanded by Colonel George Baylor; assigned to the Cavalry of the Commander-in-Chief's Guard, commanded by Captain George Lewis, May 1, 1777; on rolls to August 1, 1777, without remark.

BRADLEY, JAMES: Enlisted May 16, 1776, for three years, a private, Captain John Nelson's Company, Fourth North Carolina Regiment, commanded by Colonel Thomas Polk (also given Captain Griffith J. McRee's Company, First North Carolina Regiment, commanded by Colonel Thomas Clark); transferred, Valley Forge, Pa., March 19, 1778, to the Commander-in-Chief's Guard, commanded by Captain Caleb Gibbs; at battle of Monmouth, N. J., June 28, 1778; sick in quarters, March, 1779; discharged, Middlebrook, N. J., May 5, 1779.

BROOKS, JAMES:* Enlisted, Haddam, Conn., January 15, 1777, for three years, a private, Captain John Mills's Company, Second Connecticut Regiment, commanded by Colonel Charles Webb; transferred, Valley Forge, Pa., March 19, 1778, to the Commander-in-Chief's Guard, commanded by Captain Caleb Gibbs; at battle of Monmouth, N. J., June 28, 1778; discharged, Morristown, N. J., January 17, 1780.

Born,[11] Haddam, Conn., November, 1758; occupation, rigger and pilot; married Lydia King (born, Long Island, N. Y., December 2, 1763; died, Carlisle, Ohio, December 3, 1847), Haddam, Conn., April 15, 1782, by Joseph Brooks, Esquire; died, Carlisle, Ohio, December 30, 1832, with the following issue: Sally, born, Chester, Conn., 1784, and died, Meriden, Conn., September, 1863 (married ——— Loveland); Samuel, born, Haddam, Conn., February 27, 1786, and died, Carlisle, Ohio, December 20, 1874 (married Sophia Johnson, Connecticut, November 4, 1810); Hannah, born, Haddam, Conn., August, 1789, and died, Elyria, Ohio, February 2, 1870 (married Riley Smith); Hezekiah, born, Haddam, Conn., April 10, 1791, and died, Carlisle, Ohio, January 24, 1862 (married Hannah Johnson, Connecticut, March 11, 1812, who died, Cleveland, Ohio, July 22, 1880);

Revolutionary War.

Fanny, born, Haddam, Conn., March, 1793, and died, Oberlin, Ohio, August 16, 1856 (married Stephen Hull); Stephen, born, Haddam, Conn., January 13, 1796, and died, Philadelphia, Pa., unmarried; David S., born, Haddam, Conn., August 22, 1798, and died, Hartford, Conn., June 18, 1881 (married Rosanna Loveland January 12, 1823); James, born, Haddam, Conn., July 28, 1800, and died October, 1835, unmarried; Elisha, born, Haddam, Conn., November 13, 1801, and died, Cleveland, Ohio, April 13, 1874 (married Emily Noble, Lagrange, Ohio, November 26, 1834); Calvin, born, Haddam, Conn., February 17, 1806, and died, Carlisle, Ohio, August 20, 1852 (married Amanda Webster at Carlisle, Ohio); and Heman, born, Haddam, Conn., July 28, 1809, and died, Illinois, September 30, 1866 (maried Jane Van Derbury, Carlisle, Ohio, January, 1835).

Brown, Davis: Enlisted March 24, 1777, for three years, a private, Captain David Dexter's Company, Second Rhode Island Regiment, commanded by Colonel Israel Angell; transferred, Valley Forge, Pa., March 19, 1778, to the Commander-in-Chief's Guard, commanded by Captain Caleb Gibbs; at battle of Monmouth, N. J., June 28, 1778; furloughed fifty days, May 15, 1779; promoted 4th corporal, April 1, 1780; promoted 3d corporal, May 1, 1780; promoted 2d corporal, June 1, 1780; at battle of Connecticut Farms, N. J., June 7, 1780; promoted 4th sergeant, July 1, 1781; at skirmish of King's Bridge, N. Y., July 3, 1781; battle of Yorktown, Va., October 4, 1781; promoted 3d sergeant, February 1, 1783; furloughed, Newburgh, N. Y., June 6, 1783, until the ratification of the definite treaty of peace; discharged November 3, 1783.

Born, Cumberland, R. I., July 10, 1756.

Brown, Ebenezer: Enlisted, Tolland, Conn., April 24, 1777, for three years, a corporal, Captain Josiah Child's Company, Fifth Connecticut Regiment, commanded by Colonel Philip B. Bradley; at battle of Germantown, Pa.,

October 4, 1777; reduced to the ranks, February 1, 1778; transferred, Valley Forge, Pa., March 19, 1778, to the Commander-in-Chief's Guard, commanded by Captain Caleb Gibbs; at battle of Monmouth, N. J., June 28, 1778; discharged, Morristown, N. J., May 1, 1780.

Married,[12] first, —————— ——————; no issue; second, Sarah Gee (died at South Lansing, N. Y.) in Orange County, N. Y.; issue: Martha, born at South Lansing, N. Y., and died in Wisconsin (maried Gilbert Gibbs); Eunice, born at South Lansing, N. Y., and died in Missouri (married Bruce Packard); Polly, died, South Lansing, N. Y., 1817 (married Manly Packard); Sarah, born at South Lansing, N. Y., and died at West Groton, N. Y. (married, first, Joseph Head; second, James Stevenson); William, died at Fort Erie, War 1812-15, unmarried; Benoni, born, South Lansing, N. Y., 1799, and died, West Groton, N. Y., 1894 (married Hannah Townley, Ludlowville, N. Y., 1826); and James, born, South Lansing, N. Y., 1804, and died, Ithaca, N. Y., 1882 (married Katharine Hays at South Lansing, N. Y.); third, Mrs. Abigail Baldwin (died at South Lansing, N. Y.) at South Lansing, N. Y.; died at South Lansing, N. Y., with the following issue: Electa, died, Peruville, N. Y., 1874 (married Alvin Allen); and Julia, born, South Lansing, N. Y., 1817, and died, Peruville, N. Y., January 17, 1901 (married John S. Lanterman).

BROWN, ELIAS:* Enlisted, Windsor, Conn., April 1, 1777, for the war, a fifer, Captain Abner Prior's Company, Fifth Connecticut Regiment, commanded by Colonel Philip B. Bradley; transferred, White Plains, N. Y., August 1, 1778, to the Commander-in-Chief's Guard, commanded by Major Caleb Gibbs; in arrest, Fredericksburg, N. Y., October 18, 1778; court-martialed October 22, 1778, and found guilty of a breach of article 21, section 13, of the articles of war, and sentenced to death; sentence approved by the Commander-in-Chief, October 23, 1778, who directed that he be hanged immediately in Major-General McDougall's Division; escaped; pardoned, and rejoined regiment; promoted fife-major, September 7, 1781; furloughed, New Windsor, N. Y., June 5, 1783, until the ratification of the definite treaty of peace; discharged November 3, 1783.

Born, Windsor, Conn., March 18, 1758; occupation, farmer; married, first, Prudence Fitch (born, Windsor, Conn., March 15, 1761); issue: Eurastus Fitch, born, Windsor, Conn., March 20, 1779, and died, Hamilton, Bermuda, 1807 (maried Mrs. Susanna Ingham Steele, Hamilton, Bermuda, 1803); Joseph, born, Windsor, Conn., July 30, 1792; Harriet Prudence, born, Windsor, Conn., January 30, 1796; and Julia Maria, born, Windsor, Conn., December 7, 1798, and residing in Berlin District, Conn., January 24, 1851 (married ———— Humphrey); second, Mrs. Nancy Hart (born 1765; died, New Britain, Conn., June 8, 1850); died Farmington, Conn., January 18, 1843.

BROWN, JEDEDIAH :* Enlisted February 10, 1777, for the war, a private, Captain John McGregor's Company, Fourth Connecticut Regiment, commanded by Colonel John Durkee; transferred, Morristown, N. J., March 20, 1780, to the Commander-in-Chief's Guard, commanded by Major Caleb Gibbs; at battle of Connecticut Farms, N. J., June 7, 1780; skirmish of King's Bridge, N. Y., July 3, 1781—wounded in both arms; battle of Yorktown, Va., October 19, 1781; furloughed, Newburgh, N. Y., June 6, 1783, until the ratification of the definite treaty of peace; discharged November 3, 1783.

Born 1754; occupation, farmer; married Lydia, widow of Ebenezer Johnson; residing at Canterbury, Conn., 1820; died November 2, 1827.

BROWN, MOSES: Rank, private; transferred, Valley Forge, Pa., March 19, 1778, to the Commander-in-Chief's Guard, commanded by Captain Caleb Gibbs; at battle of Monmouth, N. J., June 28, 1778; discharged, White Plains, N. Y., August 27, 1778.

BROWN, ZACHARIAH : Rank, private; transferred, Valley Forge, Pa., March 19, 1778, to the Commander-in-Chief's

The Commander-in-Chief's Guard.

Guard, commanded by Captain Caleb Gibbs; on rolls to May 1, 1778, without remark.

BRYANT, JONATHAN :* Enlisted, Lynn, Mass., April 19, 1775, a private, Captain Ezra Newhall's Company of Minutemen; re-enlisted May 2, 1775, for eight months, Captain Ezra Newhall's Company, Nineteenth Regiment, Continental Infantry, commanded by Colonel John Mansfield; re-enlisted January 1, 1776, for one year, Captain Ezra Newhall's Company, Twenty-seventh Regiment, Continental Infantry, commanded by Colonel Israel Hutchinson; at battle of Trenton, N. J., December 26, 1776; discharged, Newtown, Pa., December 30, 1776, and re-enlisted for three years, Captain George Lewis's Troop, Third Regiment, Continental Dragoons, commanded by Colonel George Baylor; assigned to the Cavalry of the Commander-in-Chief's Guard, commanded by Captain George Lewis, May 1, 1777; at battle of Brandywine, Del., September 11, 1777; battle of Germantown, Pa., October 4, 1777; battle of Monmouth, N. J., June 28, 1778; rejoined regiment, September 26, 1778; at skirmish of Tappan, N. Y., September 28, 1778; discharged, Schuylkill Barracks, Philadelphia, Pa., December 13, 1779.

Born October, 1755; occupation, shoemaker and sexton of St. Michael's Church, Trenton, N. J.; residing at Trenton, N. J., August 2, 1820, with wife Jane (born June, 1755), and grand-daughter Jane Ann Davenport (born 1808); died September 21, 1831.

BULLARD, ———: Private, New Hampshire Line; transferred, Newburgh, N. Y., June 16, 1783, to the Commander-in-Chief's Guard, commanded by Lieutenant-Commandant William Colfax; on return dated Rocky Hill, N. J., October 22, 1783, with remark "Present."

BUSH, JOHN: Private, Massachusetts Line; transferred, West Point, N. Y., September 11, 1779, to the Commander-in-Chief's Guard, commanded by Major Caleb Gibbs; deserted, Morristown, N. J., February 28, 1780; age, 23;

height, five feet, ten and a half inches; complexion, dark; occupation, carpenter; residence, Northampton, Mass.

CAMPBELL, LEWIS: Enlisted, Woodbridge, N. J., July 1, 1776, for five months, a private, Colonel David Forman's Regiment, Brigadier-General Nathaniel Heard's Brigade, New Jersey State Troops, assigned to Major-General Nathaniel Greene's Division, Continental Troops, on Long Island, N. Y., August 12, 1776; at battle of Long Island, N. Y., August 27, 1776; battle of White Plains, N. Y., October 28, 1776; discharged December 1, 1776; re-enlisted, Woodbridge, N. J., December 5, 1776, for the war, Captain John Anderson's (2d) Company, Fourth New Jersey Regiment, commanded by Colonel Ephraim Martin, Brigadier-General William Maxwell's Brigade; transferred to Captain Jonathan Forman's (6th) Company, April 1, 1777; at battle of Short Hills, N. J., June 26, 1777; battle of Brandywine, Del., September 11, 1777; battle of Germantown, Pa., October 4, 1777; transferred, Valley Forge, Pa., March 19, 1778, to the Commander-in-Chief's Guard, commanded by Captain Caleb Gibbs; at battle of Monmouth, N. J., June 28, 1778; battle of Connecticut Farms, N. J., June 7, 1780; skirmish of King's Bridge, N. Y., July 3, 1781—wounded; battle of Yorktown, Va., October 19, 1781; furloughed, Newburgh, N. Y., June 6, 1783, until the ratificaton of the definite treaty of peace; discharged November 3, 1783.

CARLETON, EBENEZER:*‡ Enlisted, Wilton, N. H., May 2, 1775, for eight months, a private, Captain Benjamin Mann's Company, Third Regiment, Continental Infantry, commanded by Colonel James Reed; re-enlisted January 1, 1776, for one year, Captain James Keith's Company, Sixteenth Regiment, Continental Infantry, commanded by Colonel Paul D. Sargent; re-enlisted March 21, 1777, for the war, Captain Isaac Frye's Company, Third New Hampshire Regiment, commanded by Colonel Alexander Scammell; transferred, Valley Forge, Pa., March 19, 1778, to the Commander-in-Chief's Guard, commanded by Captain

The Commander-in-Chief's Guard.

Caleb Gibbs; at battle of Monmouth, N. J., June 28, 1778; furloughed fifty-five days, May 15, 1779; deserted July 9, 1779; rejoined August 1, 1780; at skirmish of King's Bridge, N. Y., July 3, 1781; battle of Yorktown, Va., October 19, 1781; furloughed, Newburgh, N. Y., June 6, 1783, until the ratification of the definite treaty of peace; discharged November 3, 1783.

Born,[13] Litchfield, N. H., April 2, 1754; married Rebecca Farrar (born May 29, 1754; died, Hill, N. H., September 7, 1832), January 3, 1784; died, Hill, N. H., December 8, 1836, with the following issue: Timothy, born, Hill, N. H., April 9, 1785, and died, Hill, N. H., February 7, 1866, unmarried; Ebenezer, born, Hill, N. H., March 9, 1787, and died in Vermont, September 7, 1832 (married Betsey Moony); Rebecca, born, Hill, N. H., April 25, 1789, and died, Waterford, Pa., August 9, 1885 (married Samuel Wells, Hill, N. H., February 4, 1810); Jeremiah, born, Hill, N. H., February 7, 1792, and died, Hill, N. H., October 19, 1878 (married Betsey Tenney, Hill, N. H., January 20, 1820); and John M., born, Hill, N. H., October 12, 1795, and died, Hill, N. H., January 31, 1829 (married Lavinia Wells).

CARLETON, TIMOTHY:* Enlisted, Lunenburg, Mass., June 2, 1777, for three years, a private, Captain Sylvanus Smith's Company, Fifteenth Massachusetts Regiment, commanded by Colonel Timothy Bigelow; transferred, Valley Forge, Pa., March 19, 1778, to the Commander-in-Chief's Guard, commanded by Captain Caleb Gibbs; at battle of Monmouth, N. J., June 28, 1778; discharged, Morristown, N. J., June 1, 1780.

Born,[14] England, 1753; occupation, carpenter; married Mary White (born, Charlestown, N. H., 1764; died at Charlestown, N. H.); died, Charlestown, N. H., 1825, with the following issue: Alpheus, born and died at Charlestown, N. H., unmarried; Guy, born and died at Charlestown, N. H., unmarried; Lewis, born, Charlestown, N. H., 1802, and died, Charlestown, N. H., 1836 (married Roxanna

REVOLUTIONARY WAR.

Chalis, Charlestown, N. H., January 10, 1830); Shedia, born at Charlestown, N. H., and died at Ballston Spa, N. Y., unmarried; Sallie, born at Charlestown, N. H., and died at Ballston Spa, N. Y. (married Thomas Radford at Charlestown, N. H.); Polly, born at Charlestown, N. H., and died at Ballston Spa, N. Y. (married John Radford at Charlestown, N. H.); Esther, born at Charlestown, N. H., and died at Springfield, Vt., unmarried; and Lucy, born at Charlestown, N. H., and died at Cannonsville, N. Y. (married John Call at Charlestown, N. H.).

CASWELL, MICHAEL: Enlisted, Newburyport, Mass., May 2, 1775, for eight months, a private, Captain Ezra Lunt's Company, Seventeenth Regiment, Continental Infantry, commanded by Colonel Moses Little; re-enlisted, Newtown, Pa., December 14, 1776, for three years, Captain George Lewis's Troop, Third Regiment, Continental Dragoons, commanded by Colonel George Baylor; assigned to the Cavalry of the Commander-in-Chief's Guard, commanded by Captain George Lewis, May 1, 1777; at battle of Brandywine, Del., September 11, 1777; battle of Germantown, Pa., October 4, 1777; battle of Monmouth, N. J., June 28, 1778; rejoined regiment, September 26, 1778; at skirmish of Tappan, N. Y., September 28, 1778; discharged, Schuylkill Barracks, Philadelphia, Pa., December 13, 1779.

CHAPIN, OLIVER:* Enlisted, Mendon, Mass., September 30, 1775, a private, Captain Abishai Brown's Company, Fifth Regiment, Continental Infantry, commanded by Colonel John Nixon; discharged December 31, 1775; re-enlisted, Newtown, Pa., December 14, 1776, for three years, Captain George Lewis's Troop, Third Regiment, Continental Dragoons, commanded by Colonel George Baylor; assigned to the Cavalry of the Commander-in-Chief's Guard, commanded by Captain George Lewis, May 1, 1777; at battle of Brandywine, Del., September 11, 1777; battle of Germantown, Pa., October 4, 1777; battle of Monmouth, N. J., June 28, 1778; rejoined regiment,

September 26, 1778; at skirmish of Tappan, N. Y., September 28, 1778; discharged, Schuylkill Barracks, Philadelphia, Pa., December 13, 1779.

Born,[15] Milford, Mass., October 1, 1759; married Mary Jones (born, Milford, Mass., 1765; died, Brattleboro, Vt., August 27, 1849), Milford, Mass., April 29, 1784; died, Brattleboro, Vt., June 26, 1811, with the following issue: Cyrus, born, Milford, Mass., June 10, 1785, and died, Brattleboro, Vt., April 27, 1811, unmarried; Jonathan, born, Milford, Mass., May 6, 1787, and died, Orange, Mass., July 14, 1793; Abigail, born, Orange, Mass., July 2, 1789, and died, Jaffrey, N. H., August 3, 1870 (married Thomas Harris of Charlestown, Mass.); Mary, born, Orange, Mass., February 10, 1793, and died in infancy; Oliver, born, Orange, Mass., May 10, 1801, and died in infancy; and Charles, born, Orange, Mass., July 10, 1803, and died, Brattleboro, Vt., January 6, 1878 (married, first, Elizabeth B. Bridge of Charlestown, Mass., May 8, 1827, who died March 28, 1828; second, Sophia D. Orne of Springfield, Mass., January 6, 1830).

CHAPMAN, NATHANIEL:* Enlisted, Lunenburgh, Mass., April 25, 1775, for eight months, a private, Captain John Fuller's Company, Twenty-third Regiment, Continental Infantry, commanded by Colonel Asa Whitcomb; at battle of Bunker Hill, Mass., June 17, 1775; re-enlisted, Prospect Hill, Mass., January 1, 1776, for one year, Captain Gideon Parker's Company, Twelfth Regiment, Continental Infantry, commanded by Colonel Moses Little; at battle of Harlem Heights, N. Y., October 16, 1776; re-enlisted, Peekskill, N. Y., January 1, 1777, for three years, Captain Joseph Pettingill's Company, Ninth Massachusetts Regiment, commanded by Colonel James Wesson; at siege of Fort Stanwix, N. Y., August 4-22, 1777; battles of Stillwater, N. Y., September 19 and October 7, 1777; transferred, Valley Forge, Pa., March 19, 1778, to the Commander-in-Chief's Guard, commanded by Captain Caleb Gibbs; at battle of Monmouth, N. J., June 28, 1778; sick in camp,

REVOLUTIONARY WAR.

August, 1778; sick in quarters, March, 1779; sick in hospital, May and June, 1779; discharged, Morristown, N. J., January 1, 1780.

Born, Lunenburgh, Mass., 1759; married Mrs. Sarah Gott (died, Stark, Me., August 10, 1848), Norridgewock, Me., June 16, 1788, by Oliver Wood, Esquire; died, Kingfield, Me., January 2, 1819, with the following issue: Nathaniel, born and died at Stark, Me. (married Eleanor Brainard); Moses, died at Kingfield, Me., unmarried; John, died at Newburgh, Me. (married Deborah Simpson); James, born, 1796, and died, Stark, Me., March, 1875 (married Sarah Jewell); Betsey, died at New Portland, Me. (married Joseph Knowlton, Sr.); William, died, Newburgh, Me., October 30, 1869 (married Eliza Morrill, Newburgh, Me., May 24, 1823); Laodicea, died at Hampden, Me. (married Esther Lowell); Mary, born, Mt. Vernon, Me., April 25, 1799, and died, New Portland, Me., December 3, 1871 (married William Knowlton); Aaron, died, Newport, Me., April 9, 1883 (married, first, Annise Phillips; second, Mrs. Sarah E. Burgess); Stephen, born, Mercer, Me., October 3, 1805, and died, Newburgh, Me., March 14, 1874 (married Almira Smith, New Vinyard, Me., January 21, 1830); George (married Celia Spencer of New Vinyard, Me.); Moses (married Abigail Snow of Newburgh, Me.); and Harrison (married Almira Pease of Newburgh, Me.).

CHENOWETH, JONATHAN: Private, Virginia Line; transferred, Morristown, N. J., May 1, 1777, to the Commander-in-Chief's Guard, commanded by Captain Caleb Gibbs; on rolls to August 11, 1777, with remark "Tends on the sick."

CHRISTAIN, RALEIGH CHINN:* Enlisted April 10, 1776, for three years, a private, Captain Thomas Gaskin's Company, Fifth Virginia Regiment, commanded by Colonel Charles Scott; at battle of Trenton, N. J., December 26, 1776; battle of Princeton, N. J., January 3, 1777; transferred, Morristown, N. J., May 1, 1777, to the Commander-in-Chief's Guard, commanded by Captain Caleb Gibbs; sick-hospital, June, 1777; at battle of Brandywine, Del.,

September 11, 1777; battle of Germantown, Pa., October 4, 1777; battle of Monmouth, N. J., June 28, 1778; re-enlisted and furloughed ninety days, January 18, 1779; deserted April 28, 1779 (soldier claims while home ordered by Colonel Gaskin to join Fourth Virginia Regiment, and shot in left hand and right thigh at battle of Guilford, N. C., March 15, 1781); rejoined July 1, 1781; at skirmish of King's Bridge, N. Y., July 3, 1781; battle of Yorktown, Va., October 19, 1781; deserted, Philadelphia, Pa., February 1, 1782 (soldier claims discharge).

Born,[17] Northumberland County, Va., 1754; occupation, farmer; married Elizabeth Pope (born 1753; died, Lancaster County, Va., January 28, 1840), Northumberland County, Va., July 4, 1782; died, Northumberland County, Va., July 4, 1828, with the following issue: Ann Richardson, born, Northumberland County, Va., October 10, 1789, and died, Clear View, Lancaster County, Va., April 13, 1862 (married Thomas Armstrong July 18, 1810); William, died, Williamsburg, Va., April 30, 1853 (married Caroline Robinson); and Elizabeth, died, Northumberland County, Va., May 8, 1865 (married Rodham Booth).

CHURCH, BENJAMIN:* Enlisted, Cambridge, Mass., January 1, 1776, for one year, a private, Twelfth Regiment, Continental Infantry, commanded by Colonel Moses Little, and transferred to Major-General Charles Lee's Guard, commanded by Ensign Benjamin Gould; transferred to Major-General Artemas Ward's Guard, March 17, 1776; transferred, Fort Washington, N. Y., August, 1776, to Captain Edward Burbeck's Company, Colonel Henry Knox's Regiment, Continental Artillery; at battle of White Plains, N. Y., October 28, 1776; transferred, White Plains, N. Y., October 30, 1776, to the Commander-in-Chief's Guard, commanded by Captain Caleb Gibbs; at battle of Trenton, N. J., December 26, 1776; battle of Princeton, N. J., January 3, 1777; discharged, Morristown, N. J., February 10, 1777.

Born, Fall River, Mass., November 27, 1756; residing at Holland, Mass., October 4, 1832.

REVOLUTIONARY WAR.

CLEMENTS, ———: Sergeant, Commander-in-Chief's Guard, commanded by Captain Caleb Gibbs; court-martialed, New York, September 13, 1776, and found guilty of neglect of duty, when reduced to the ranks and ordered to rejoin his regiment.

COFFIN, JOHN: Enlisted, Newburyport, Mass., August 3, 1775, a private, Captain Benjamin Perkins's Company, Seventeenth Regiment, Continental Infantry, commanded by Colonel Moses Little; re-enlisted January 1, 1776, for one year, Captain Benjamin Perkins's Company, Twelfth Regiment, Continental Infantry, commanded by Colonel Moses Little; transferred, Cambridge, Mass., March 12, 1776, to the Commander-in-Chief's Guard, commanded by Captain Caleb Gibbs; at battle of White Plains, N. Y., October 28, 1776; discharged, Newtown, Pa., December 14, 1776, and re-enlisted for three years, Captain George Lewis's Troop, Third Regiment, Continental Dragoons, commanded by Colonel George Baylor; assigned to the Cavalry of the Commander-in-Chief's Guard, commanded by Captain George Lewis, May 1, 1777; at battle of Brandywine, Del., September 11, 1777; battle of Germantown, Pa., October 4, 1777; battle of Monmouth, N. J., June 28, 1778; rejoined regiment, September 26, 1778; at skirmish of Tappan, N. Y., September 28, 1778; discharged, Schuylkill Barracks, Philadelphia, Pa., December 13, 1779.

Born,[18] Newburyport, Mass., August 12, 1757; married Mary Palmer, November 20, 1785; issue: Henry, born February 23, 1783; John, born November 20, 1785; and Jeremiah, born August 21, 1787 (married Rebecca Stone October 23, 1811).

COFFIN, LEMUEL:* Enlisted, Newburyport, Mass., May 9, 1775, for eight months, a private, Captain Benjamin Perkins's Company, Seventeenth Regiment, Continental Infantry, commanded by Colonel Moses Little; at battle of Bunker Hill, Mass., June 17, 1775; re-enlisted January 1, 1776, for one year, Captain Benjamin Perkins's Company, Twelfth Regiment, Continental Infantry, commanded by Colonel

Moses Little; transferred, Cambridge, Mass., March 12, 1776, to the Commander-in-Chief's Guard, commanded by Captain Caleb Gibbs; at battle of White Plains, N. Y., October 28, 1776; discharged, Newtown, Pa., December 14, 1776, and re-enlisted for three years, Captain George Lewis's Troop, Third Regiment, Continental Dragoons, commanded by Colonel George Baylor; assigned to the Cavalry of the Commander-in-Chief's Guard, commanded by Captain George Lewis, May 1, 1777; at battle of Brandywine, Del., September 11, 1777; battle of Germantown, Pa., October 4, 1777; battle of Monmouth, N. J., June 28, 1778; rejoined regiment, September 26, 1778; at skirmish of Tappan, N. Y., September 28, 1778; discharged, Schuylkill Barracks, Philadelphia, Pa., December 13, 1779.

Born,[18] Newburyport, Mass., November 20, 1755; occupation, shoemaker; married Catherine Cressal (born 1760; died, Newburyport, Mass., January 22, 1844), Frederick, Md., April 2, 1780, by Rev. Mr. Haneker; removed to Newburyport, Mass., November 16, 1785; died, Newburyport, Mass., June 29, 1837, with the following issue: Eliza, born, Frederick, Md., August 18, 1781; John, born, Frederick, Md., July 9, 1783, and died September 16, 1784; Olive, born, Frederick, Md., July 14, 1785 (married Jonathan Pearson); Joseph, born, Newburyport, Mass., March 25, 1788, and died, Gaudaloupe, October 28, 1816; Rachel, born, Newburyport, Mass., August 9, 1790; Abel, born, Newburyport, Mass., October 21, 1792; Catherine, born, Newburyport, Mass., January 19, 1795, and died in 1875; Sarah, born, Newburyport, Mass., July 29, 1797, and died in infancy; Michael, born, Newburyport, Mass., March 17, 1800, and died October 11, 1801; and Sarah, born, Newburyport, Mass., November 16, 1802 (married ——— Loud).

COLE, JOHN:* Enlisted, Blooming Grove, N. Y., March, 1776, a private, Captain Seth Marvin's Company, Colonel Samuel Drake's Regiment, New York Troops; at battle of Long Island, N. Y., August 27, 1776; battle of White Plains, N. Y., October 28, 1776; re-enlisted, Greenwich,

Revolutionary War.

Sussex County, N. J., May 12, 1777, for the war, Captain David Lyon's Company, Colonel Oliver Spencer's Regiment, Continental Infantry, Brigadier-General Thomas Conway's Brigade; at battle of Brandywine, Del., September 11, 1777; battle of Germantown, Pa., October 4, 1777; transferred, Valley Forge, Pa., March 19, 1778, to the Commander-in-Chief's Guard, commanded by Captain Caleb Gibbs; at battle of Monmouth, N. J., June 28, 1778; battle of Connecticut Farms, N. J., June 7, 1780; skirmish of King's Bridge, N. Y., July 3, 1781; battle of Yorktown, Va., October 19, 1781; furloughed, Newburgh, N. Y., June 6, 1783, until the ratification of the definite treaty of peace; discharged November 3, 1783.

Born 1752 (also given 1759); residing at Newburgh, N. Y., May, 1820.

COLE, MARTIN :* Enlisted September 23, 1775, for six months, a private, Captain Alfred Moore's Company, First North Carolina Regiment, commanded by Lieutenant-Colonel Francis Nash; re-enlisted November 18, 1776, for the war, a corporal, Captain John Walker's Company, First North Carolina Regiment, commanded by Colonel Francis Nash; at battle of Brandywine, Del., September 11, 1777; battle of Germantown, Pa., October 4, 1777; transferred, Valley Forge, Pa., March 19, 1778, to the Commander-in-Chief's Guard, commanded by Captain Caleb Gibbs, and assigned 1st corporal; at battle of Monmouth, N. J., June 28, 1778; promoted 5th sergeant, August 2, 1778; promoted 4th sergeant, December 11, 1778; promoted 3rd sergeant, August 25, 1779; rejoined regiment, November 1, 1779; at battle of Fort Moultrie, S. C., May 7, 1780; taken prisoner, Charleston, S. C., May 12, 1780, and confined at Williamsburg, Va.; exchanged and rejoined regiment at Ashley Ferry, S. C.; discharged, James Island, S. C., August, 1783.

Born 1758; occupation, blacksmith; residing in Spartanburg District, S. C., April, 1825.

COLFAX, WILLIAM :* Enlisted, New London, Conn., May 1, 1775, a private, Captain William Coit's Company, Thirteenth Regiment, Continental Infantry, commanded by Colonel Samuel H. Parsons; at battle of Bunker Hill, Mass., June 17, 1775; discharged December 10, 1775; re-enlisted January 1, 1776, for one year, sergeant-major, Captain James Eldridge's Company, Tenth Regiment, Continental Infantry, commanded by Colonel Samuel H. Parsons; at battle of Long Island, N. Y., August 27, 1776; battle of White Plains, N. Y., October 28, 1776—wounded; discharged December 31, 1776; ensign, Captain Christopher Ely's Company, First Connecticut Regiment, commanded by Colonel Jedediah Huntington, January 1, 1777; at battle of Germantown, Pa., October 4, 1777; promoted 2d lieutenant, January 1, 1778; detached, Valley Forge, Pa., March 18, 1778, and assigned to the Commander-in-Chief's Guard, commanded by Captain Caleb Gibbs; at battle of Monmouth, N. J., June 28, 1778; promoted 1st lieutenant, March 16, 1779, to rank from March 18, 1778; on furlough, September, 1779; furloughed five weeks, November 6, 1779; at battle of Connecticut Farms, N. J., June 7, 1780; lieutenant-commandant, Commander-in-Chief's Guard, January 1, 1781 (transferred, January 1, 1781, to Captain Selah Benton's (7th) Company, Fifth Connecticut Regiment—"On command with His Excellency's Guard."); at skirmish of King's Bridge, N. Y., July 3, 1781—wounded; battle of Yorktown, Va., October 19, 1781; furloughed thirty days, April 4, 1782 (transferred, November 17, 1782, to Captain Ephraim Chamberlain's (2d) Company, Second Connecticut Regiment—"On command with His Excellency's Guard."); furloughed eighty days, November 26, 1782 (promoted captain, April 1, 1783, Second Connecticut Regiment—"On command with His Excellency's Guard."); furloughed July, 1783; detached, September 5, 1783, and assumed the captaincy of the Eighth Company, Colonel Heman Swift's Connecticut Regiment; discharged November 3, 1783; brevetted captain, by Congress, February 23, 1784; major, Third Regiment, Bergen County New Jersey Militia, June 5, 1793; lieutenant-colonel, November 25, 1806; brigadier-general commanding Brigade of New Jersey detailed Militia

REVOLUTIONARY WAR.

in Third Military District, war with Great Britain, August 12, 1814, to December 8, 1814; commanding a Brigade of Consolidated Militia and Sea Fencibles in Third Military District, at New York, January 11, 1815.

Born,[19] New London, Conn., July 3, 1756; occupation, farmer; married Esther Schuyler (born, Pompton, N. J., 1763; died, Pompton, N. J., October 27, 1839), Pompton, N. J., August 27, 1793, by Rev. Benjamin Vanderlinder; died, Pompton, N. J., September 6, 1838, with the following issue: George Washington, born, Pompton, N. J., November 3, 1784, and died at Pompton, N. J. (married Eliza Colfax, Pompton, N. J., December 11, 1811); Lucy, born, Pompton, N. J., November 18, 1789, and died, Pompton, N. J., March 24, 1861 (married Henry Berry, Pompton, N. J., August 3, 1815); Schuyler, born, Pompton, N. J., August 3, 1792, and died, Pompton, N. J., October 30, 1822 (married Hannah D. Stryker, New York City, April 25, 1820); Elizabeth, born, Pompton, N. J., August 8, 1794, and died, Pompton, N. J., May 15, 1836 (married James L. Baldwin, Pompton, N. J., July 30, 1810); William W., born, Pompton, N. J., April 26, 1797, and died, Pompton, N. J., February 28, 1876 (married Hester Mandeville, Pompton, Plains, N. J., May 21, 1826); and Mary, born, Pompton, N. J., July 3, 1800, and died, Pompton, N. J., July 26, 1823 (married Abraham Williams, Pompton, N. J., January 14, 1822).

CONDEL, WILLIAM: Enlisted, Boston, Mass., January 12, 1777, for three years, a private, Captain Samuel King's Company, Tenth Massachusetts Regiment, commanded by Colonel Thomas Marshall; transferred, Valley Forge, Pa., March 19, 1778, to the Commander-in-Chief's Guard, commanded by Captain Caleb Gibbs; at battle of Monmouth, N. J., June 28, 1778; discharged, Morristown, N. J., January 12, 1780.

CONNOR, ——————: Private, New Hampshire Line; transferred, Newburgh, N. Y., June 16, 1783, to the Commander-

THE COMMANDER-IN-CHIEF'S GUARD.

in-Chief's Guard, commanded by Lieutenant-Commandant William Colfax; on return dated Rocky Hill, N. J., October 22, 1783, with remark "Present."

COOK, DANIEL: Enlisted, Rochester, N. H., May 22, 1777, for three years, a private, Captain Frederick M. Bell's Company, Second New Hampshire Regiment, commanded by Colonel Nathan Hale; transferred, Valley Forge, Pa., March 19, 1778, to the Commander-in-Chief's Guard, commanded by Captain Caleb Gibbs; at battle of Monmouth, N. J., June 28, 1778; furloughed sixty days, May 15, 1779; deserted July 14, 1779.

Born,[20] Acton, Me., April 23, 1757; married Mehitable Gilman (born, Wakefield, N. H., November 14, 1760; died, Wakefield, N. H., September 26, 1849); died, Wakefield, N. H., January 11, 1832, with the following issue: Mary, born, Acton, Me., October 8, 1784, and died, Wakefield, N. H., February 25, 1877 (married John Fellows at Wakefield, N. H.); Mehitable, born, Acton, Me., July 21, 1786, and died, Acton, Me., September 26, 1853 (married ——— Remick at Acton, Me.); Benjamin G., born, Acton, Me., September 28, 1788, and died, Middletown, N. H., October 30, 1816, unmarried; and Annie, born, Acton, Me., January 1, 1791, and died, Wakefield, N. H., August 9, 1866, unmarried.

COOPER, WILMER: Enlisted November, 1776, for three years, a private, Captain John Gregory's Company, Fifteenth Virginia Regiment, commanded by Lieutenant-Colonel James Innes; transferred, Morristown, N. J., May 1, 1777, to the Commander-in-Chief's Guard, commanded by Captain Caleb Gibbs; at battle of Brandywine, Del., September 11, 1777; battle of Germantown, Pa., October 4, 1777; battle of Monmouth, N. J., June 28, 1778; discharged, Morristown, N. J., December 16, 1779.

CORAM, WILLIAM: Private, Virginia Line; transferred, Morristown, N. J., May 1, 1777, to the Commander-in-

REVOLUTIONARY WAR.

Chief's Guard, commanded by Captain Caleb Gibbs; at battle of Brandywine, Del., September 11, 1777; battle of Germantown, Pa., October 4, 1777; sick-absent, Valley Forge, Pa., June to October, 1778; re-enlisted and furloughed ninety days, January 18, 1779; sick in quarters, April and May, 1779; at battle of Connecticut Farms, N. J., June 7, 1780; skirmish of King's Bridge, N. Y., July 3, 1781; battle of Yorktown, Va., October 19, 1781; sick at New Windsor, N. Y., June 30 to September 1, 1782; promoted sergeant, June 4, 1783; furloughed, Newburgh, N. Y., June 6, 1783, until the ratification of the definite treaty of peace; discharged November 3, 1783.

COSTON, EBENEZER:* Enlisted, Francestown, N. H., May 7, 1782, for three years, a private, Captain Isaac Frye's Company, First New Hampshire Regiment, commanded by Lieutenant-Colonel Henry Dearborn; transferred, Newburgh, N. Y., June 16, 1783, to the Commander-in-Chief's Guard, commanded by Lieutenant-Commandant William Colfax; discharged, West Point, N. Y., December 20, 1783.

Born,[21] Francestown, N. H., 1765; married Sarah J. Hale (born, Beverly, N. H., June 1, 1763; married Hezekiah Eastman, who died June, 1832; died, Sherburne, N. Y., March 26, 1857), Francestown, N. H., January 14, 1783; died, Lysander, N. Y., February 17, 1814, with the following issue: Elizabeth, born, Greenfield, N. H., June 26, 1786, and died, Oshkosh, Wis., October 17, 1876 (married Alfred Skinner, Sherburne, N. Y., December 12, 1802); Ebenezer; Jane, died, Sherburne, N. Y., August 14, 1853 (married Joshua Williams Leonard); Jemima, died, Jersey City, N. J., 1890 (married Samuel C. Love); Alfred; Zara, died, Lawrence, Kan., May, 1874 (married Jane Wallace of Pittsburgh, Pa.); and Tinette, died, Fredonia, N. Y., 1893 (married Solomon Cushman).

CRAIG, JAMES: Enlisted, York County, Pa., January 4, 1777, for the war, a private, Captain Thomas Church's Company, Fifth Pennsylvania Regiment, commanded by Colonel

THE COMMANDER-IN-CHIEF'S GUARD.

Francis Johnston; transferred, Morristown, N. J., March 20, 1780, to the Commander-in-Chief's Guard, commanded by Major Caleb Gibbs; at battle of Connecticut Farms, N. J., June 7, 1780; skirmish of King's Bridge, N. Y., July 3, 1781; battle of Yorktown, Va., October 19, 1781; deserted, Philadelphia, Pa., March 22, 1782.

CRAIG, SAMUEL: Enlisted, York County, Pa., December 1, 1776, for the war, a private, Captain Thomas Church's Company, Fifth Pennsylvania Regiment, commanded by Colonel Francis Johnston; transferred, Morristown, N. J., March 20, 1780, to the Commander-in-Chief's Guard, commanded by Major Caleb Gibbs; at battle of Connecticut Farms, N. J., June 7, 1780; skirmish of King's Bridge, N. Y., July 3, 1781; battle of Yorktown, Va., October 19, 1781; deserted, Philadelphia, Pa., March 22, 1782.

CROSBY, EBENEZER:‡ Surgeon's Mate, Cambridge Hospital, Mass., January 1, 1777; 2d surgeon, Flying Hospital, Middle Department, April 11, 1777; surgeon, Commander-in-Chief's Guard, commanded by Major Caleb Gibbs, June 22, 1779; at battle of Connecticut Farms, N. J., June 7, 1780; resigned January 1, 1781.

Born,[22] Braintree, Mass., September 30, 1753; married Catherine Bedlow (born, New York, May 19, 1757; died, New York, February 19, 1789), New Windsor, N. Y., October 11, 1781, by Rev. John Moffat; died, New York, July 16, 1788, with the following issue: John Player, born, New York, January 15, 1785, and died, Island of Jamaica, about 1807, unmarried; William Bedlow, born, New York, February 7, 1786, and died, New York, March 18, 1865 (married Harriet A. Clarkson February 7, 1807, who died, New York, December 13, 1859); and Henry Rutger, born, New York, June 11, 1787, and died, New York, May 22, 1788.

CROSBY, JOEL:* Enlisted, Billerica, Mass., April 7, 1777, for the war, a private, Captain Benjamin Heywood's Com-

REVOLUTIONARY WAR.

pany, Sixth Massachusetts Regiment, commanded by Colonel Thomas Nixon; transferred, New Windsor, N. Y., June 23, 1781, to the Commander-in-Chief's Guard, commanded by Lieutenant-Commandant William Colfax; at skirmish of King's Bridge, N. Y., July 3, 1781; battle of Yorktown, Va., October 19, 1781; furloughed sixty days, December 5, 1781; rejoined March 5, 1782; furloughed, Newburgh, N. Y., June 6, 1783, until the ratification of the definite treaty of peace; discharged November 3, 1783.

Born,[23] Lexington, Mass., February 9, 1763; occupation, farmer; married Hannah Blanchard (died, Leominster, Mass., 1846), May 7, 1794; died, Leominster, Mass., October 20, 1833, without issue.

CRUMBIE, AARON :* Enlisted, Rowley, Mass., May 15, 1776, for eight months, a private, Captain Nathaniel Wade's Company, Seventeenth Regiment, Continental Infantry, commanded by Colonel Moses Little, and immediately transferred to Captain Samuel Gridley's Company, Colonel Richard Gridley's Regiment of Artillery; at battle of Bunker Hill, Mass., June 17, 1775; re-enlisted for one year, January 1, 1776; transferred, Cambridge, Mass., March 12, 1776, to the Commander-in-Chief's Guard, commanded by Captain Caleb Gibbs; at battle of White Plains, N. Y., October 28, 1776; battle of Trenton, N. J., December 26, 1776; battle of Princeton, N. J., January 3, 1777; discharged, Morristown, N. J., February 10, 1777; re-enlisted April 28, 1777, for the war, Captain Thomas Wooster's Company, Colonel Samuel B. Webb's Regiment, Continental Infantry; promoted sergeant, November 19, 1777; reduced to the ranks, November 4, 1778; promoted corporal, November 28, 1778; transferred to Captain Elisha Hopkins's Company, Third Connecticut Regiment, commanded by Colonel Samuel B. Webb, January 1, 1781; reduced to the ranks, July 1, 1781; furloughed, New Windsor, N. Y., June 6, 1783, until the ratification of the definite treaty of peace; discharged November 3, 1783.

Born[24] June 11, 1753; married Mary (born October 30, 1767); residing at Rowley, Mass., April 20, 1818, and died

THE COMMANDER-IN-CHIEF'S GUARD.

at Danbury, N. H., with the following issue: John, born November 5, 1787; Mary, born January 24, 1789; Aaron, born February 15, 1790, and died May 23, 1869 (married Dolly Dorman October 31, 1812); Benjamin, born January 25, 1792, and died, Georgetown, Mass., December 18, 1863; William, born May 21, 1794; Charlotte, born November 15, 1795, and died, Georgetown, Mass., October 8, 1862; Nathaniel, born November, 1799, and died at Georgetown, Mass.; and Thomas N., born, Georgetown, Mass., November 11, 1802, and died, Groveland, Mass., August 15, 1884 (married Ruth M. Noyes).

CULL, HUGH: Enlisted January 13, 1777, for the war, a private, Captain Alexander Parker's Company, Seventh Pennsylvania Regiment, commanded by Colonel William Irvine; transferred, August 1, 1780, to the Commander-in-Chief's Guard, commanded by Major Caleb Gibbs; at skirmish of King's Bridge, N. Y., July 3, 1781; battle of Yorktown, Va., October 19, 1781; furloughed, Newburgh, N. Y., June 6, 1783, until the ratification of the definite treaty of peace; discharged November 3, 1783.

CUNNINGHAM, NATHANIEL:* Enlisted, Prince Edward County, Va., September 1, 1775, for one year, a private, Captain Robert Ballard's Company, First Virginia Regiment, commanded by Colonel Edward Read; re-enlisted August 4, 1776, for three years, Captain John Morton's Company, Fourth Virginia Regiment, Commanded by Colonel Thomas Elliott; at battle of Trenton, N. J., December 26, 1776; battle of Princeton, N. J., January 3, 1777; promoted corporal, May 1, 1777; transferred, Morristown, N. J., May 6, 1777, to the Commander-in-Chief's Guard, commanded by Captain Caleb Gibbs; promoted 3d sergeant, June 4, 1777; at battle of Brandywine, Del., September 11, 1777; battle of Germantown, Pa., October 4, 1777; promoted 2d sergeant, March 1, 1778; reduced to the ranks, April 1, 1778; transferred, Valley Forge, Pa., May 1, 1778, to Captain William Cunningham's Company, First Virginia Regiment, commanded by Colonel Richard Parker; promoted sergeant,

June 1, 1778; at battle of Monmouth, N. J., June 28, 1778; on rolls to May 7, 1779, with remark "On Georgia Command."

Born,[25] Petersburg, Va., 1754; occupation, schoolmaster; married Elizabeth Sneed (born 1772; residing in Putnam County, Ind., April 10, 1843), Caswell County, N. C., September 25, 1790; died, Putnam County, Ind., August 16, 1832, with the following issue: Alexander, died unmarried; Amelia, born October, 1794, and residing in Putnam County, Ind., November 19, 1838, unmarried; Susanna, born July 2, 1801, and died, Savannah, Mo., about 1869 (married Jeremiah Stiles of Stilesville, Ind., September 27, 1827, who died at Savannah, Mo., June 23, 1855); Elizabeth, born 1798, and died, Fillmore, Ind., March, 1866 (married Absalom Brown); John W., born 1800, and died, Oskaloosa, Iowa, 1887 (married Elizabeth Johnson); Benjamin Sneed, born, Randolph County, N. C., 1805, and died, Keithsburg, Ill., March 27, 1893 (married Margaret Humphreys, Putnam County, Ind., 1834); and Lucinda, born, Randolph County, N. C., March 15, 1812, and died, Doniphan County, Kan., January 17, 1881 (married William Bailey about 1834, who died at Troy, Kan., 1863).

CURRIER, ABRAHAM:* Enlisted, Hopkinton, N. H., April 5, 1781, for three years, a private, Captain Daniel Livermore's Company, First New Hampshire Regiment, commanded by Colonel Alexander Scammell; transferred. Newburgh, N. Y., June 16, 1783, to the Commander-in-Chief's Guard, commanded by Lieutenant-Commandant William Colfax; discharged, West Point, N. Y., December 20, 1783.

Born[26] 1764; married Polly Cressy (born, Hopkinton, N. H., April 1, 1770; died, Bradford, N. H., January 29, 1852), Hopkinton, N. H., November 26, 1789, by Rev. Jacob Cram; died, Bradford, N. H., September 22, 1825, without issue.

CUTTER, MOSES: Enlisted, Jaffrey, N. H., March 16, 1781, for three years, a private, Eighth Company, First New Hampshire Regiment, commanded by Colonel Alexander

Scammell; transferred, Newburgh, N. Y., June 16, 1783, to the Commander-in-Chief's Guard, commanded by Lieutenant-Commandant William Colfax, and assigned 2d corporal; on return dated Rocky Hill, N. J., October 22, 1783, with remark "Present"; afterwards captain, Twelfth Regiment, New Hampshire Militia.

Born,[27] Shrewsbury, Mass., March 26, 1760; married Rachel Turner (born, Jaffrey, N. H., September 30, 1769; died, Jaffrey, N. H., August 21, 1849) at Jaffrey, N. H.; died, Bradford, N. H., April 10, 1816, with the following issue: Jane, born, Jaffrey, N. H., August 4, 1787, and died, Jaffrey, N. H., October 14, 1838 (married Samuel Bates, Jaffrey, N. H., June 21, 1810); Susan, born, Jaffrey, N. H., May 19, 1789, and died, Bradford, N. H., July 7, 1818, unmarried; Rachel, born, Jaffrey, N. H., October 31, 1792, and died October 14, 1848 (married Abel Nutting of Groton, Mass., January 1, 1815, who died, Marlboro, N. H., June 10, 1863); Mary, born, Jaffrey, N. H., March 22, 1794, and died, Albany, N. Y., 1832 (married Richard Hoyt of Bradford, N.H.); Moses, born, Jaffrey, N.H., November 11, 1795, and died, Princeton, Mass., February 21, 1854 (married Abigail Davidson of Peterborough, N. H., December 28, 1826); William Turner, born, Jaffrey, N. H., March 5, 1798, and died, East Jaffrey, N. H., June 4, 1866 (married Lydia Jennings of Waltham, Mass., March 7, 1832); Sarah, born, Jaffrey, N. H., November 13, 1801 (married Artemas Law of Jaffrey, N. H., who died November 12, 1836); Pamelia, born, Jaffrey, N. H., August 8, 1803, and died, Jaffrey, N. H., October 10, 1867 (married, first, Charles G. Gilmore of Jaffrey, N. H., December 25, 1829, who died May 12, 1838; second, John Sanderson, September, 1852); Willard, born, Jaffrey, N. H., July 14, 1806, and died, Meadville, Pa., February 8, 1860, (married Eliza Shirley of Waltham, Mass., July 30 1830); Caroline, born, Bradford, N. H., October 26, 1809, and died December 26, 1861 (married Luther Cutter of Jaffrey, N. H., September 15, 1830); and John, born, Bradford, N. H., July 11, 1812, and died, Jaffrey, N. H., March 12, 1842.

Revolutionary War.

DADY, JAMES: Enlisted, Suffield, Conn., March 31, 1777, for the war, a sergeant, Captain John Harmon's Company, Fourth Connecticut Regiment, commanded by Colonel John Durkee; reduced to the ranks, September 1, 1777; transferred, Valley Forge, Pa., March 19, 1778, to the Commander-in-Chief's Guard, commanded by Captain Caleb Gibbs; at battle of Monmouth, N. J., June 28, 1778; battle of Connecticut Farms, N. J., June 7, 1780; skirmish of King's Bridge, N. Y., July 3, 1781; battle of Yorktown, Va., October 19, 1781; furloughed, Newburgh, N. Y., June 6, 1783, until the ratification of the definite treaty of peace; discharged November 3, 1783.

DALEY, SOLOMON:‡ Enlisted June 17, 1777, for the war, a corporal, Captain Thomas Hughes's Company, Second Rhode Island Regiment, commanded by Colonel Israel Angell; transferred, Valley Forge, Pa., March 19, 1778, to the Commander-in-Chief's Guard, commanded by Captain Caleb Gibbs, and assigned private; at battle of Monmouth, N. J., June 28, 1778; battle of Connecticut Farms, N. J., June 7, 1780—wounded; skirmish of King's Bridge, N. Y., July 3, 1781; battle of Yorktown, Va., October 19, 1781; furloughed, Newburgh, N. Y., June 6, 1783, until the ratification of the definite treaty of peace; discharged November 3, 1783.

Born,[28] Smithfield, R. I., April 13, 1754; married Miss Butler; issue: Warren, born 1787, and killed at New Orleans, La., war of 1812-15, unmarried; Owen, born 1799, and died unmarried; Martha, born, Elizabethtown, Ky., 1803, and died in infancy; Frances, born, Elizabethtown, Ky., July 4, 1806, and died, St. Louis, Mo., March 2, 1846 (married William W. Graham, Elizabethtown, Ky., 1826).

DARRAH, WILLIAM: Enlisted, Litchfield, N. H., July 9, 1775, a drummer, Captain John Parker's Company, Colonel Timothy Bedel's Regiment of Rangers; age, 18; discharged December 17, 1775; re-enlisted January 1, 1776, for one year, a private, Fifth Regiment, Continental Infantry, com-

THE COMMANDER-IN-CHIEF'S GUARD.

manded by Colonel John Stark; transferred, Cambridge, Mass., March 12, 1776, to the Commander-in-Chief's Guard, commanded by Captain Caleb Gibbs; at battle of White Plains, N. Y., October 28, 1776; battle of Trenton, N. J., December 26, 1776; discharged December 30, 1776; re-enlisted January, 1777, for the war, Captain William Scott's Company, First New Hampshire Regiment, commanded by Colonel John Stark; on rolls to February 14, 1781, with remark "Present."

DAVENPORT, ISAAC HOWE: Enlisted, Dorchester, Mass., April 29, 1775, for eight months, a private, Captain Elijah Vose's Company, Thirty-sixth Regiment, Continental Infantry, commanded by Colonel John Greaton; re-enlisted, Newtown, Pa., December 30, 1776, for three years, a sergeant, Captain George Lewis's Troop, Third Regiment, Continental Dragoons, commanded by Colonel George Baylor; assigned to the Cavalry of the Commander-in-Chief's Guard, commanded by Captain George Lewis, May 1, 1777; at battle of Brandywine, Del., September 11, 1777; battle of Germantown, Pa., October 4, 1777; battle of Monmouth, N. J., June 28, 1778; rejoined regiment, September 26, 1778; killed at skirmish of Tappan, N. Y., September 28, 1778.

Born,[29] Dorchester, Mass., August 14, 1756, and died unmarried.

DAVIS, JOSEPH:[*] Enlisted, Chester, N. H., April 5, 1781, for three years, a private, Captain Enoch Chase's Company, Second New Hampshire Regiment, commanded by Lieutenant-Colonel George Reid; transferred, Newburgh, N. Y., June 16, 1783, to the Commander-in-Chief's Guard, commanded by Lieutenant-Commandant William Colfax; on return dated Rocky Hill, N. J., October 22, 1783, with remark "Deserted October 14, 1783."

Born 1763; occupation, farmer; residing at Chester, N. H., July 18, 1820.

Revolutionary War.

DAWS, JOHN: Enlisted March 8, 1777, for three years, a private, Captain Edward Garland's Company, Fourteenth Virginia Regiment, commanded by Colonel Charles Lewis; transferred, Morristown, N. J., May 1, 1777, to the Commander-in-Chief's Guard, commanded by Captain Caleb Gibbs; at battle of Brandywine, Del., September 11, 1777, battle of Germantown, Pa., October 4, 1777; battle of Monmouth, N. J., June 28, 1778; discharged, West Point, N. Y., November 16, 1779.

DAY, WILLIAM: Private, Virginia Line; transferred, Morristown, N. J., May 1, 1777, to the Commander-in-Chief's Guard, commanded by Captain Caleb Gibbs; on rolls to August 11, 1777, without remark.

DEAN, LEVI: Enlisted, Norwich, Conn., January 8, 1777, for three years, a private, Captain Benjamin Throop's Company, First Connecticut Regiment, commanded by Colonel Jedediah Huntington; transferred, Valley Forge, Pa., March 19, 1778, to the Commander-in-Chief's Guard, commanded by Captain Caleb Gibbs; at battle of Monmouth, N. J., June 28, 1778; deserted, West Point, N. Y., August 7, 1779; rejoined August 11, 1780; at skirmish of King's Bridge, N. Y., July 3, 1781; battle of Yorktown, Va., October 19, 1781; furloughed thirty days, January 31, 1783; furloughed, Newburgh, N. Y., June 6, 1783, until the ratification of the definite treaty of peace; discharged November 3, 1783.

DELANO, JOSEPH: Enlisted, Plymouth, Mass., March 5, 1777, for three years, a private, Captain George Dunham's Company, Second Massachusetts Regiment, commanded by Colonel John Bailey; transferred, Valley Forge, Pa., March 19, 1778, to the Commander-in-Chief's Guard, commanded by Captain Caleb Gibbs; at battle of Monmouth, N. J., June 28, 1778; discharged, Morristown, N. J., March 5, 1780.

DENT, JOHN:* Enlisted, Buck Tavern, Anne Arundel County, Md., May 1, 1777, for the war, a private, Third

The Commander-in-Chief's Guard.

Maryland Regiment, commanded by Colonel Mordecai Gist; transferred, Morristown, N. J., December 31, 1779, to the Commander-in-Chief's Guard, commanded by Major Caleb Gibbs; at battle of Connecticut Farms, N. J., June 7, 1780; promoted 4th corporal, July 1, 1781; at skirmish of King's Bridge, N. Y., July 3, 1781—lost an eye; battle of Yorktown, Va., October 19, 1781; promoted 3d corporal, April 1, 1782; promoted 2d corporal, October 23, 1782; promoted 1st corporal, March 1, 1783; invalided May 1, 1783.

Born 1757; married Ellenor Cissell (born 1760; residing in Anne Arundel County, Md., March 1, 1842), St. James Parish, Anne Arundel County, Md., January 19, 1777, by Rev. Walter Magowan; died, Prince George County, Md., March, 1808; issue: Arasmus; John; Richard; James; and Elizabeth.

DESPERATE, HENRY: Enlisted January 5, 1776, a private, Captain Samuel Benezet's Company, Fifth Pennsylvania Battalion, commanded by Colonel Robert Magaw; taken prisoner, Fort Washington, N. Y., November 16, 1776; exchanged; re-enlisted February 5, 1777, for the war, Sixth Pennsylvania Regiment, commanded by Colonel Robert Magaw; transferred, Valley Forge, Pa., March 19, 1778, to the Commander-in-Chief's Guard, commanded by Captain Caleb Gibbs; at battle of Monmouth, N. J., June 28, 1778; battle of Connecticut Farms, N. J., June 7, 1780; skirmish of King's Bridge, N. Y., July 3, 1781; battle of Yorktown, Va., October 19, 1781; deserted, Philadelphia, Pa., March 22, 1782.

DISCLOW, PHILIP: Private, Third Regiment, Continental Dragoons, commanded by Colonel George Baylor; assigned to the Cavalry of the Commander-in-Chief's Guard, commanded by Captain George Lewis, May 1, 1777; on rolls without remark.

DODGE, ANTIPAS: Enlisted, Brookfield, Mass., October 1, 1776, a private, Captain Thomas Wellington's Company,

REVOLUTIONARY WAR.

Sixth Regiment, Continental Infantry, commanded by Colonel Asa Whitcomb; re-enlisted January 1, 1777, for the war, Captain Elisha Brewer's Company, Twelfth Massachusetts Regiment, commanded by Colonel Samuel Brewer; born, 1760; height, five feet, six inches; complexion, dark; occupation, hatter; transferred, Valley Forge, Pa., March 19, 1778, to the Commander-in-Chief's Guard, commanded by Captain Caleb Gibbs; at battle of Monmouth, N. J., June 28, 1778; furloughed thirty days, Morristown, N. J., January 8, 1780; deserted February 8, 1780.

Born,[20] Brookfield, Mass., 1760; married Lucy Woodward (born May 10, 1755), Westminster, Mass., March 8, 1782; issue: Nancy, born September 22, 1782; and Polly, born October 5, 1784.

DOTHER, JOHN: Enlisted, Marsh Creek, Pa., January 1, 1777, for the war, a private, First Pennsylvania Regiment, commanded by Colonel Edward Hand; transferred, Valley Forge, Pa., March 19, 1778, to the Commander-in-Chief's Guard, commanded by Captain Caleb Gibbs; at battle of Monmouth, N. J., June 28, 1778; battle of Connecticut Farms, N. J., June 7, 1780; skirmish of King's Bridge, N. Y., July 3, 1781; battle of Yorktown, Va., October 19, 1781; furloughed, Newburgh, N. Y., June 6, 1783, until the ratification of the definite treaty of peace; discharged November 3, 1783.

DOUGHERTY, CHARLES: Enlisted, Hackensack, N. J., June 1, 1781, for the war, a private, Captain William Piatt's Company, First New Jersey Regiment, commanded by Colonel Matthias Ogden, Colonel Elias Dayton's Brigade—assigned to the Second Brigade, Second Division, Major-General Benjamin Lincoln, September 24, 1781; at battle of Yorktown, Va., October 19, 1781; transferred, Newburgh, N. Y., March 1, 1783, to the Commander-in-Chief's Guard, commanded by Lieutenant-Commandant William Colfax; furloughed, Newburgh, N. Y., June 6, 1783, until the ratification of the definite treaty of peace; discharged November 3, 1783.

THE COMMANDER-IN-CHIEF'S GUARD.

DOUGHERTY, GEORGE: Enlisted, Chester County, Pa., May 1, 1777, for the war, a private, Captain John Davis's Company, Ninth Pennsylvania Regiment, commanded by Lieutenant-Colonel George Nagel; transferred, Valley Forge, Pa., March 19, 1778, to the Commander-in-Chief's Guard, commanded by Captain Caleb Gibbs; at battle of Monmouth, N. J., June 28, 1778; battle of Connecticut Farms, N. J., June 7, 1780; on return dated April 8, 1781, with remark "Present."

DOUGHERTY, JAMES :* Enlisted, Lancaster County, Pa., June 25, 1775, a private, Captain Arthur Smith's Company, Second Regiment, Continental Infantry, commanded by Colonel William Thompson; taken prisoner, Quebec, January 1, 1776; released on parole August 3, 1776; re-enlisted, Philadelphia, Pa., December 15, 1776, for the war, Captain John Brady's Company, Twelfth Pennsylvania Regiment, commanded by Colonel William Cook; at battle of Short Hills, N. J., June 26, 1777; transferred, Middlebrook, N. J., to Captain Clark's Artillery Company; transferred to Captain Carnes's Artillery Company; at battle of Brandywine, Del., September 11, 1777; battle of Germantown, Pa., October 4, 1777; transferred, Valley Forge, Pa., March 19, 1778, to the Commander-in-Chief's Guard, commanded by Captain Caleb Gibbs; at battle of Monmouth, N. J., June 28, 1778; battle of Connecticut Farms, N. J., June 7, 1780; skirmish of King's Bridge, N. Y., July 3, 1781; battle of Yorktown, Va., October 19, 1781; furloughed eight days, November 6, 1782; furloughed eight days, December 6, 1782; deserted February 1, 1783.

Born December 25, 1759; married; residing in Center County, Pa., August 28, 1820; died, Franklin, Pa., 1849.

DRAKE, CORNELIUS: Enlisted 1777, for two and a half years, a sergeant, Captain James Gee's Company, Second North Carolina Regiment, commanded by Colonel Alexander Martin; transferred, Valley Forge, Pa., March 19, 1778,

Revolutionary War.

to the Commander-in-Chief's Guard, commanded by Captain Caleb Gibbs, and assigned 1st sergeant; at battle of Monmouth, N. J., June 28, 1778; discharged, White Plains, N. Y., August 2, 1778.

DRISKEL, JEREMIAH: Private, Fourth Maryland Regiment; transferred, Morristown, N. J., December 31, 1779, to the Commander-in-Chief's Guard, commanded by Major Caleb Gibbs; at battle of Connecticut Farms, N. J., June 7, 1780; skirmish of King's Bridge, N. Y., July 3, 1781; battle of Yorktown, Va., October 19, 1781; furloughed, Newburgh, N. Y., June 6, 1783, until the ratification of the definite treaty of peace; discharged November 3, 1783.

DRUCE, JOHN: Enlisted, Wrentham, Mass., April 27, 1775, for eight months, a private, Captain Oliver Pond's Company, Twentieth Regiment, Continental Infantry, commanded by Colonel Joseph Read; re-enlisted, Newtown, Pa., December 30, 1776, for three years, a corporal, Captain George Lewis's Troop, Third Regiment, Continental Dragoons, commanded by Colonel George Baylor; assigned to the Cavalry of the Commander-in-Chief's Guard, commanded by Captain George Lewis, May 1, 1777; on rolls to August 1, 1777, without remark.

DUNN, WILLIAM: Enlisted, Sudbury, Mass., April 19, 1775, a private, Captain John Nixon's Company of Minutemen, commanded by Colonel Abijah Pierce; re-enlisted May 13, 1775, for eight months, Captain Isaac Gray's Company, Sixth Regiment, Continental Infantry, commanded by Colonel Jonathan Brewer; re-enlisted, Newtown, Pa., December 14, 1776, for three years, Captain George Lewis's Troop, Third Regiment, Continental Dragoons, commanded by Colonel George Baylor; assigned to the Cavalry of the Commander-in-Chief's Guard, commanded by Captain George Lewis, May 1, 1777; at battle of Brandywine, Del., September 11, 1777; battle of Germantown, Pa., October 4, 1777; battle of Monmouth, N. J., June 28, 1778; rejoined regiment, September 26, 1778; at skirmish of Tappan, N. Y., September 28, 1778; discharged, Schuylkill Barracks, Philadelphia, Pa., December 13, 1779.

DUNTON, LEVI:* Enlisted, Southborough, Mass., March 24, 1777, for three years, a private, Captain Daniel Barnes's Company, Fifteenth Massachusetts Regiment, commanded by Colonel Timothy Bigelow; born, 1756; height, five feet, seven inches; complexion, dark; occupation, laborer; transferred, Valley Forge, Pa., March 19, 1778, to the Commander-in-Chief's Guard, commanded by Captain Caleb Gibbs; at battle of Monmouth, N. J., June 28, 1778; furloughed fifty days, Middlebrook, N. J., May 15, 1779; deserted July 4, 1779.

Residing at Harvard, Mass., July 10, 1820; married, with issue; died July 26, 1827.

DYER, DANIEL: Enlisted, Cape Elizabeth (also given Salisbury), Mass., May 23, 1775, for eight months, a private, Captain Samuel Dunn's Company, Thirty-first Regiment, Continental Infantry, commanded by Colonel Edmund Phinney; re-enlisted January 1, 1776, for one year, Captain Hart Williams's Company, Eighteenth Regiment, Continental Infantry, commanded by Colonel Edmund Phinney; re-enlisted January 1, 1777, for three years, Captain George Smith's Company, First Massachusetts Regiment, commanded by Colonel Joseph Vose; transferred, Valley Forge, Pa., March 19, 1778, to the Commander-in-Chief's Guard, commanded by Captain Caleb Gibbs; at battle of Monmouth, N. J., June 28, 1778; discharged, Morristown, N. J., January 1, 1780.

EAKIN, ROBERT: Enlisted February 28, 1777, for the war, a private, Captain Robert Wilkins's Company, Sixth Pennsylvania Regiment, commanded by Colonel Josiah Harmer; transferred, Morristown, N. J., March 20, 1780, to the Commander-in-Chief's Guard, commanded by Major Caleb Gibbs; at battle of Connecticut Farms, N. J., June

REVOLUTIONARY WAR.

7, 1780; skirmish of King's Bridge, N. Y., July 3, 1781; battle of Yorktown, Va., October 19, 1781; deserted, Philadelphia, Pa., February 10, 1782.

EASTMAN, HENRY: Enlisted, Henniker, N. H., July 13, 1781, for three years, a private, Third Company, First New Hampshire Regiment, commanded by Colonel Alexander Scammell; transferred, Newburgh, N. Y., June 16, 1783, to the Commander-in-Chief's Guard, commanded by Lieutenant-Commandant William Colfax; on return dated Rocky Hill, N. J., October 22, 1783, with remark "Present."

EATON, ———: Private, New Hampshire Line; transferred, Newburgh, N. Y., June 16, 1783, to the Commander-in-Chief's Guard, commanded by Lieutenant-Commandant William Colfax; on return dated Rocky Hill, N. J., October 22, 1783, with remark "Present."

EATON, BENJAMIN:* Enlisted, Pomfret, Conn., April 20, 1775, a private, Captain Israel Putnam's Company of Minutemen; re-enlisted, Cambridge, Mass., May 1, 1775, for eight months, Captain Jedediah Waterman's Company, Thirty-fourth Regiment, Continental Infantry, commanded by Lieutenant-Colonel Experience Storrs; detached, Cambridge, Mass., September 7, 1775, to Captain Ezekiel Scott's Company, Provisional Regiment, Continental Infantry, commanded by Colonel Benedict Arnold; upon Canadian expedition, and retreated from Dead River under the command of Lieutenant-Colonel Roger Enos, October 26, 1775; rejoined Company and Regiment at Cambridge, Mass., November 25, 1775; re-enlisted January 1, 1776, for one year, Captain John Keyes's Company, Twentieth Regiment, Continental Infantry, commanded by Lieutenant-Colonel John Durkee; discharged, Newtown, Pa., December 18, 1776; re-enlisted December 21, 1776, for the war, Captain Noadiah Wade's (3d) Company, Fourth New Jersey Regiment, commanded by Colonel Ephraim Martin, Brigadier-General William Maxwell's Brigade; at battle of Short Hills, N. J.,

THE COMMANDER-IN-CHIEF'S GUARD.

June 26, 1777; battle of Brandywine, Del., September 11, 1777; battle of Germantown, Pa., October 4, 1777; battle of Monmouth, N. J., June 28, 1778; transferred, February 1, 1779, to Captain Alexander Mitchell's Company, First New Jersey Regiment, commanded by Colonel Matthias Ogden; assigned with Regiment and Brigade to Major-General John Sullivan's Division, Continental Army, engaged in an expedition against the Six Nations of Indians in Western Pennsylvania and New York, May 26 to October 26, 1779; transferred, Morristown, N. J., March 20, 1780, to the Commander-in-Chief's Guard, commanded by Major Caleb Gibbs; at battle of Connecticut Farms, N. J., June 7, 1780; skirmish of King's Bridge, N. Y., July 3, 1781; battle of Yorktown, Va., October 19, 1781; furloughed, Newburgh, N. Y., June 6, 1783, until the ratification of the definite treaty of peace; discharged November 3, 1783; served in the War of 1812-15 from New York State.

Born[81] 1758; married; died, Cuddebackville, N. Y., October 16, 1843, with the following known issue: Samuel; Abigail (married ———— Kelly); and Benjamin W., born December 30, 1791, and died, Cuddebackville, N. Y., January 13, 1857 (married Margaret Duvall; born August 8, 1795, and died April 4, 1870).

EDDY, EPHRAIM:[*] Enlisted, Middleborough, Mass., March 1, 1777, for three years, a corporal, Captain Joshua Eddy's Company, Fourteenth Massachusetts Regiment, commanded by Colonel Gamaliel Bradford; transferred, Valley Forge, Pa., March 19, 1778, to the Commander-in-Chief's Guard, commanded by Captain Caleb Gibbs, and assigned private; at battle of Monmouth, N. J., June 28, 1778; promoted 4th corporal, August 2, 1778; promoted 2d corporal, September 1, 1778; discharged, Morristown, N. J., March 1, 1780; assistant commissary of issues, Eastern Department, Vermont, June 10, 1781; resigned April 1, 1782.

Born,[82] Middleborough, Mass., December 21, 1759; married Mary Safford (born April 4, 1763; married Frye Bayley, Chelsea, Vt., April 13, 1812; died, Chelsea, Vt.,

REVOLUTIONARY WAR.

February 12, 1841), Woodstock, Vt., October 10, 1782; died, Woodstock, Vt., September 3, 1799, with the following issue: Safford, born, Woodstock, Vt., October 20, 1783, and died, Chelsea, Vt., February 25, 1810 (married Clara Meachan, Woodstock, Vt., February 1, 1810); Lucinda, born, Woodstock, Vt., May 28, 1785, and died, Chelsea, Vt., August 1, 1871 (married Harry Hale, Chelsea, Vt., November 14, 1815); Polly, born, Woodstock, Vt., June 22, 1787, and died at Woodstock, Vt. (married Henry C. Dennison at Woodstock, Vt.); Claunda, born, Woodstock, Vt., May 8, 1789; Henry Highton, born, Woodstock, Vt., October 6, 1791; and Laura C., born, Woodstock, Vt., January 14, 1794, and died, Chelsea, Vt., August 9, 1840 (married John W. Smith at Chelsea, Vt.).

EDGE, JOHN:* Enlisted, Frederick County, Va., February 10, 1777, for three years, a private, Captain Thomas Blackwell's Company, Tenth Virginia Regiment, commanded by Colonel Edward Stevens; transferred, Morristown, N. J., May 1, 1777, to the Commander-in-Chief's Guard, commanded by Captain Caleb Gibbs; at battle of Brandywine, Del., September 11, 1777; battle of Germantown, Pa., October 4, 1777; battle of Monmouth, N. J., June 28, 1778; discharged, Morristown, N. J., February 16, 1780.

Born 1753; occupation, farmer; married Nancy Cummins (born 1760; died, Belmont County, Ohio, February 5, 1856), Fauquier County, Va., January 6, 1781; died, Belmont County, Ohio, July 4, 1830, with the following issue: Molly, born November 7, 1781; Rosanch, born September 1, 1783 (married ——— Dunfee); Israel, born April 30, 1785; John, born August 20, 1786; Levincy, born September 5, 1787; and Letice, born November 11, 1791.

EDWARDS, BILDAD: Enlisted, Groton, Conn., March 6, 1777, for three years, a sergeant, Captain Christopher Darrow's Company, First Connecticut Regiment, commanded by Colonel Jedediah Huntington; transferred, Valley Forge, Pa., March 19, 1778, to the Commander-in-Chief's Guard, commanded by Captain Caleb Gibbs, and assigned 2d sergeant; at battle of Monmouth, N. J., June 28, 1778; promoted 1st sergeant, August 2, 1778; discharged, Morristown, N. J., March 14, 1780.

ELDER, CLAYBORNE: Enlisted April 1, 1777, for two years, a private, Captain Alexander Rose's Company, Sixth Virginia Regiment, commanded by Lieutenant-Colonel James Hendricks; transferred, Morristown, N. J., May 6, 1777, to the Commander-in-Chief's Guard, commanded by Captain Caleb Gibbs; on rolls to August 11, 1777, without remark.

EMERY, DAVID:* Enlisted, Canaan, Mass., January 1, 1776, for one year, a private, Captain William Scott's Company, Sixteenth Regiment, Continental Infantry, commanded by Colonel Paul D. Sargent; re-enlisted, Winslow, Mass., March 12, 1777, for three years, Captain Josiah Jenkins's Company, Twelfth Massachusetts Regiment, commanded by Colonel Samuel Brewer; transferred, Valley Forge, Pa., March 19, 1778, to the Commander-in-Chief's Guard, commanded by Captain Caleb Gibbs; sick-absent, June, 1778; discharged, Morristown, N. J., March 12, 1780.

Born,[33] Dracut, Mass., September 24, 1754; occupation, farmer; married Abigail Goodwin (born 1763; died, Fairfield, Me., August 28, 1840), Lincoln County, Me., April 5, 1782; died, Fairfield, Me., November 18, 1830, with the following issue: John, born at Fairfield, Me., and died, Waterville, Me., November 24, 1860 (married Abigail Brown, Clinton, Me., October 18, 1805—died, Waterville, Me., January 26, 1851); Benjamin, born, Fairfield, Me., June 13, 1784, and died, Upper Stillwater, Me., April 28, 1871 (married Mary Whilden, Canaan, Me., 1808—died, Upper Stillwater, Me., May 2, 1873); Jonathan, born, Fairfield, Me., January 3, 1786, and died, Harmony, Me., December 17, 1863 (married Hannah Cheney, Fairfield, Me., 1810—died October, 1848); Cynthia, born, Fairfield, Me., 1793, and died 1865, unmarried; Caleb, born, Fairfield,

REVOLUTIONARY WAR.

Me., January 1, 1794 (married Emily Chase October 24, 1819); Jerusha, born, Fairfield, Me., and died, Fairfield, Me., 1866 (married Moses Wyman at Fairfield, Me.); Miles, born, Fairfield, Me., November 29, 1799, and died, Fort Kent, Me., October 18, 1884 (married Mary D. Nedean, Tobique, Victoria, N. B., March 17, 1832); Rachel, born, Fairfield, Me., 1800, and died March 15, 1887 (married Isaac Chase, Fairfield, Me., December 1, 1825); Nehemiah, born at Fairfield, Me. (married, first, Nancy Carpenter at Lincoln, Me.; second, ——— Adams at Lincoln, Me.); and Susannah, born, Fairfield, Me., 1809, and died 1869, unmarried.

ENGLISH, JOHN: Private, Virginia Line; transferred, Morristown, N. J., May 1, 1777, to the Commander-in-Chief's Guard, commanded by Captain Caleb Gibbs; on rolls to August 11, 1777, without remark.

ERWIN, JACOB: Enlisted, Philadelphia, Pa., January 22, 1777, for the war, a private, Captain Joseph Erwin's Company, Ninth Pennsylvania Regiment, commanded by Colonel James Irvine; transferred, Valley Forge, Pa., March 19, 1778, to the Commander-in-Chief's Guard, commanded by Captain Caleb Gibbs; at battle of Monmouth, N. J., June 28, 1778; battle of Connecticut Farms, N. J., June 7, 1780; on return dated April 8, 1781, with remark "Present."

EVERETT, ELIPHALET:[*] Enlisted, Sharon, Conn., March 3, 1777, for three years, a private, Captain Theodore Woodbridge's Company, Seventh Connecticut Regiment, commanded by Colonel Heman Swift; height, five feet, eight inches; hair, dark; at battle of Germantown, Pa., October 4, 1777; battle of Whitemarsh, Pa., December 8, 1777; transferred, Valley Forge, Pa., March 19, 1778, to the Commander-in-Chief's Guard, commanded by Captain Caleb Gibbs; at battle of Monmouth, N. J., June 28, 1778; discharged, Morristown, N. J., March 3, 1780.

Born,[34] Sharon, Conn., December 3, 1757; married Rhoda Peck (born 1763; died, Watertown, N. Y., June 2, 1851),

Cornwall, Conn., November 19, 1786, by Rev. Hezekiah
Gold; died, Watertown, N. Y., March 27, 1815, with the
following issue: Lorania, born September 18, 1787, and
died, Brownville, N. Y., February 4, 1882 (married Henry
Hatch October 18, 1806); Elias, born 1792, and drowned,
Lake Ontario, November, 1835 (married Emma Brown,
Watertown, N. Y., 1825); Mary, born 1797, and died,
Decatur, Mich., September, 1867 (married Oliver Bartholomew, Watertown, N. Y., 1819); Austin, born, Sharon,
Conn., December 11, 1797, and died, Watertown, N. Y.,
1860 (married Minerva Crandall at Johnstown, N. Y.); and
Hampton, born October, 1802, and died, Watertown, N. Y.,
1862, unmarried.

FAIRBANKS, LABAN: Enlisted, Mendon, Mass., May 18,
1777, for three years, a private, Captain Isaac Warren's
Company, Second Massachusetts Regiment, commanded by
Colonel John Bailey; transferred, Valley Forge, Pa., March
19, 1778, to the Commander-in-Chief's Guard, commanded
by Captain Caleb Gibbs; at battle of Monmouth, N. J., June
28, 1778; discharged, Morristown, N. J., May 19, 1780.
Born,[35] Dedham, Mass., October 1, 1755; married Mary
Wheelock, March 9, 1785; died, Mendon, Mass., March
27, 1799, with the following issue: Clarissa, born, Mendon,
Mass., January 26, 1786 (married Daniel Rawson of Oakham, Mass., January 20, 1814); Lewis, born, Mendon, Mass.,
July 21, 1788, and died, Georgia, Vt., March 22, 1826 (married, first, Susan, Bowker, Georgia, Vt., December 25, 1815
—died April 27, 1824; second, Emily Bowker, Georgia, Vt.,
July 3, 1825—died December 8, 1863); Samuel, born, Mendon, Mass., May 29, 1791, and died, Georgia, Vt., October
11, 1857 (married Maria Ballard, Georgia, Vt., June 27,
1817—died April 19, 1848); Almira, born, Mendon, Mass.,
March 20, 1794, and died January 6, 1833, unmarried;
Nancy, born, Mendon, Mass., February 14, 1796, and died,
Mendon, Mass., February, 1834 (married Thomas Gardner
of Hingham, Mass., October 16, 1814—died March 30,
1872); and Laban, born, Mendon, Mass., November 14,

Revolutionary War.

1798, and died, Georgia, Vt., 1827 (married Lucy Burrell —no issue).

FARMER, GEORGE: Enlisted, Springfield, N. J., January 7, 1777, for the war, a private, Captain Jonathan Kinsey's (5th) Company, Fourth New Jersey Regiment, commanded by Colonel Ephraim Martin, Brigadier-General William Maxwell's Brigade; at battle of Short Hills, N. J., June 26, 1777; battle of Brandywine, Del., September 11, 1777; battle of Germantown, Pa., October 4, 1777; transferred, Valley Forge, Pa., March 19, 1778, to the Commander-in-Chief's Guard, commanded by Captain Caleb Gibbs; at battle of Monmouth, N. J., June 28, 1778; battle of Connecticut Farms, N. J., June 7, 1780; on rolls to January 15, 1781, without remark.

Born,[86] New York, March 17, 1761; married, first, Gertrude Coejemans (born, Raritan, N. J., December 4, 1770; died, New Brunswick, N. J., February 17, 1810), Princeton, N. J., October 9, 1793; issue: Samuel Staats, born, New Brunswick, N. J., July 21, 1794, and died September 18, 1794; Mary Leacraft, born, New Brunswick, N. J., January 29, 1796, and died, New Brunswick, N. J., March 11, 1870 (married, first, William Raborg February 28, 1819; second, Benito T. Caro, Claiborne, Ala., March 29, 1823); Arietta Schuyler, born, New Brunswick, N. J., March 15, 1798, and died, Apalachicola Bay, Fla., November 25, 1832 (married John Jenkins, New Brunswick, N. J., October 10, 1825); Catherine Neilson, born, New Brunswick, N. J., January 31, 1800, and died, New Brunswick, N. J., April 2, 1890 (married Theophilus M. Holcombe, New Brunswick, N. J., November 20, 1821); Sarah Ann, born, New Brunswick, N. J., April 24, 1802, and died, Mobile, Ala., August 8, 1878 (married Hugh Munroe, New Brunswick, N. J., October 2, 1823); Gertrude Lott, born, New Brunswick, N. J., July 18, 1804, and died, New Brunswick, N. J., January 21, 1870 (married Alfred Bill, New Brunswick, N. J., September 9, 1834); second, Mrs. Jane Van Doren Coejemans (born, Millstone, N. J., and died at Auburn,

N. Y.), New Brunswick, N. J., September, 1811; died, New Brunswick, N. J., October 7, 1818, with the following issue: Jane, born, New Brunswick, N. J., July, 1813, and died, Long Branch, N. J., 1886 (married Jardman P. DeWees, New Brunswick, N. J., November 25, 1837); Gitty, born, New Brunswick, N. J., June 7, 1815, and died, New Brunswick, N. J., October 19, 1828; and Ellen, born, New Brunswick, N. J., May 4, 1817, and died, Apalachicola, Fla., July, 1841 (married Colonel Hawkins, Apalachicola, Fla., 1840).

FENTON, JOHN:[*][‡] Enlisted, 1776, for two months, a private, Captain William Blain's Company, New Jersey Militia; re-enlisted, 1776, for one month, a corporal, Lieutenant John Martin's Company, Colonel Ephraim Martin's Regiment, New Jersey Militia; re-enlisted, 1777, for nine months, a sergeant, Captain Thomas Wolverton's Company of Minute-men, New Jersey Militia; re-enlisted, 1778, for two years, a blacksmith, Corps of Artificers; transferred to Second New Jersey Regiment, commanded by Lieutenant-Colonel John N. Cumming, and assigned private; transferred, Philadelphia, Pa., September 1, 1781, to the Commander-in-Chief's Guard, commanded by Lieutenant-Commandant William Colfax, and assigned drummer; at battle of Yorktown, Va., October 19, 1781; deserted, Philadelphia, Pa., March 17, 1782; rejoined, Newburgh, N. Y., May 8, 1782; furloughed, Newburgh, N. Y., June 6, 1783, until the ratification of the definite treaty of peace; discharged November 3, 1783.

Born,[87] Deer Park, N. Y., May 8, 1752; married, first, Phebe Wells; second, Elizabeth; died, Romulus, N. Y., February 14, 1839, with the following issue: Amy (married, first, James Wickoff; second, Jonathan Swartout); Esther (married John Wickoff); James D., born, New Jersey, October 5, 1799, and died, Romulus, N. Y., December 28, 1871 (married Zerviah Seely, Romulus, N. Y., January 31, 1822); Asa S., died at Romulus, N. Y. [Michigan?] (married Harriet Watrus); Alva R., born January 22, 1806, and

Revolutionary War.

died, Romulus, N. Y., March 2, 1867 (married Mary Jane Winnie); Elijah S.; Josiah, born, Romulus, N. Y., June 21, 1810, and died, San Francisco, Cal., November 9, 1853 (married Frances A. Conklin, Geneva, N. Y., 1836); and William (married ——— Coan).

FERGUSON, WILLIAM :* Enlisted, Sandwich, N. H., March 7, 1781, for three years, a private, Captain John Dennett's Company, Second New Hampshire Regiment, commanded by Lieutenant-Colonel George Reid; transferred to Captain Isaac Frye's Company; transferred, Newburgh, N. Y., June 16, 1783, to the Commander-in-Chief's Guard, commanded by Lieutenant-Commandant William Colfax; discharged, West Point, N. Y., December 20, 1783.

Born 1762; married Betty Glines (born 1766; died, Sandwich, N. H., October 19, 1856), Moultonboro, N. H., November, 1784, by Rev. Jeremiah Shaw; died, Sandwich, N. H., July 17, 1826, with the following issue: John, residing at Moultonboro, N. H., September 10, 1838; Abigail, born 1803; and Bradbury, born 1809.

FINCH, JOHN: Private, Pennsylvania Line; transferred, Philadelphia, Pa., January 28, 1782, to the Commander-in-Chief's Guard, commanded by Lieutenant-Commandant William Colfax; furloughed, Newburgh, N. Y., June 6, 1783, until the ratification of the definite treaty of peace; discharged November 3, 1783.

FINLEY, ROBERT: Enlisted May 1, 1777, for the war, a private, Captain Christian Staddel's Company, Second Pennsylvania Regiment, commanded by Colonel James Irvine; transferred, Morristown, N. J., March 20, 1780, to the Commander-in-Chief's Guard, commanded by Major Caleb Gibbs; at battle of Connecticut Farms, N. J., June 7, 1780; skirmish at King's Bridge, N. Y., July 3, 1781; battle of Yorktown, Va., October 19, 1781; furloughed thirty days, January 8, 1783; furloughed, Newburgh, N. Y., June 6, 1783, until the ratification of the definite treaty of peace; discharged November 3, 1783.

THE COMMANDER-IN-CHIEF'S GUARD.

FISCHER, GEORGE: Enlisted February 18, 1777, for the war, a private, Captain Thomas Craig's Company, Third Pennsylvania Regiment, commanded by Colonel Joseph Wood; transferred, Philadelphia, Pa., January 1, 1782, to the Commander-in-Chief's Guard, commanded by Lieutenant-Commandant William Colfax; furloughed, Newburgh, N. Y., June 6, 1783, until the ratification of the definite treaty of peace; discharged November 3, 1783.

FISHER, ELIJAH :* Enlisted, Attleborough, Mass., May 5, 1775, for eight months, a private, Captain Moses Knapp's Company, Twentieth Regiment, Continental Infantry, commanded by Colonel Joseph Reed; re-enlisted January 1, 1776, for one year, Captain Moses Knapp's Company, Thirteenth Regiment, Continental Infantry, commanded by Colonel Joseph Reed; discharged, White Plains, N. Y., for inability, November 27, 1776; re-enlisted January 7, 1777, for three years, Captain Moses Knapp's Company, Fourth Massachusetts Regiment, commanded by Colonel William Shepard; at battles of Stillwater, N. Y., September 19 and October 7, 1777; transferred, Valley Forge, Pa., March 30, 1778, to the Commander-in-Chief's Guard, commanded by Captain Caleb Gibbs; at battle of Monmouth, N. J., June 28, 1778; discharged, Morristown, N. J., January 6, 1780; re-enlisted October 10, 1780, for six months, Eighth Company, Eleventh Massachusetts Regiment, commanded by Colonel Benjamin Tupper; promoted 1st sergeant, December 15, 1780; discharged, West Point, N. Y., April 10, 1781.

Born,[86] Norton, Mass., June 18, 1758; occupation, farmer; married Jerusha Keen (born, Taunton, Mass., July 1, 1764; died, Livermore, Me., August 20, 1840), Turner, Me., December 10, 1784; died, Livermore, Me., January 28, 1842, with the following issue: John, born August 27, 1786, and died, Parkman, Me., January 13, 1854 (married Jerusha Packard, Livermore, Me., December 1, 1814); Jerusha, born June 1, 1788, and died, Turner, Me., May 8, 1851 (married John Keen, Jr., Livermore, Me., March 27, 1814); Mary

B., born June 28, 1791, and died, Livermore, Me., June 28, 1841, unmarried; Elijah, born July 16, 1793, and died, Livermore, Me., June 18, 1855, unmarried; Grinfill, born June 28, 1795, and died, Livermore, Me., October 30, 1873 (married Mary A. Filoon, Livermore, Me., December 21, 1823); Sarah, born June 17, 1798, and died, Livermore, Me., October 27, 1878 (married Moses Berry, Livermore, Me., December 14, 1856); Priscilla, born January 9, 1801, and died, Winthrop, Me., September 12, 1893 (married Isaac Briggs, Livermore, Me., July 3, 1825); and Salome H., born March 22, 1806, and died, Livermore, Me., October 28, 1879 (married Jacob Woodsom, Livermore, Me., March 20, 1842).

FLEMISTER, LEWIS:*‡ Enlisted February 1, 1777, for three years, a private, Captain William Moseley's Company, Seventh Virginia Regiment, commanded by Colonel Alexander McClenachan; transferred, Morristown, N. J., May 6, 1777, to the Commander-in-Chief's Guard, commanded by Captain Caleb Gibbs; at battle of Brandywine, Del., September 11, 1777; battle of Germantown, Pa., October 4, 1777; battle of Monmouth, N. J., June 28, 1778; battle of Connecticut Farms, N. J., June 7, 1780; skirmish of King's Bridge, N. Y., July 3, 1781; battle of Yorktown, Va., October 19, 1781; promoted sergeant, June 4, 1783; furloughed, Newburgh, N. Y., June 6, 1783, until the ratification of the definite treaty of peace; discharged November 3, 1783.

Married[39] Ellender Chism (residing near Monticello, Ga., March 8, 1849), Halifax County, Va., February 27, 1790, by Rev. Hawkins Landrum; died, Jasper County, Ga., October 1, 1807-8, with the following issue: John; William (married ———— Wilson); Lewis (marreid ———— Wilson); Joseph; James C., (married ———— Wilson); Betsey (married ———— Parker); and Catherine (married ———— Lindsay).

FORBES, JOSHUA: Enlisted December 18, 1776, for three years, a sergeant, Captain Joseph Walker's Company,

The Commander-in-Chief's Guard.

Seventh North Carolina Regiment, commanded by Colonel James Hogan (also given private, Captain Howell Tatum's Company, First North Carolina Regiment, commanded by Colonel Thomas Clark); transferred, Valley Forge, Pa., March 19, 1778, to the Commander-in- Chief's Guard, commanded by Captain Caleb Gibbs, and assigned private; at battle of Monmouth, N. J., June 28, 1778; promoted 4th corporal, September 1, 1778; discharged, Morristown, N. J., December 18, 1779.

FORREST, THOMAS: Enlisted, Philadelphia, Pa., January 1, 1777, for the war, a sergeant, Captain Herculas Courtnay's Company, Fourth Regiment, Continental Artillery, commanded by Colonel Thomas Proctor; reduced to the ranks; transferred, Philadelphia, Pa., February 21, 1782, to the Commander-inChief's Guard, commanded by Lieutenant-Commandant William Colfax; furloughed, Newburgh, N. Y., June 6, 1783, until the ratification of the definite treaty of peace; discharged November 3, 1783.

FOUTZ, ADAM: Enlisted December 1, 1776, for the war, a private, Captain John Patterson's Company, Second Pennsylvania Regiment, commanded by Colonel James Irvine; transferred, Philadelphia, Pa., January 1, 1782, to the Commander-in-Chief's Guard, commanded by Lieutenant-Commandant William Colfax; furloughed, Newburgh, N. Y., June 6, 1783, until the ratification of the definite treaty of peace; discharged November 3, 1783.

FRAZIER, JAMES: Enlisted February 1, 1777, for the war, a sergeant, Third Pennsylvania Regiment, commanded by Colonel Joseph Wood; transferred, Valley Forge, Pa., March 19, 1778, to the Commander-in-Chief's Guard, commanded by Captain Caleb Gibbs, and assigned private; at battle of Monmouth, N. J., June 28, 1778, furloughed forty days, May 15, 1779; promoted 4th sergeant, November 1, 1779; promoted 3d sergeant, January 1, 1780; promoted 2d sergeant, March 14, 1780; at battle of Connecticut Farms, N. J.,

Revolutionary War.

June 7, 1780; skirmish of King's Bridge, N. Y., July 3, 1781; battle of Yorktown, Va., October 19, 1781; "on command" after deserters, June 30 to September 1, 1782; deserted, Newburgh, N. Y., February 1, 1783.

FRINK, THEOPHILUS: Enlisted, Preston, Conn., March 11, 1777, for the war, a drummer, Captain William Belcher's Company, First Connecticut Regiment, commanded by Colonel Jedediah Huntington; transferred, Teaneck, N. J., September 1, 1780, to the Commander-in-Chief's Guard, commanded by Major Caleb Gibbs; at skirmish of King's Bridge, N. Y., July 3, 1781; battle of Yorktown, Va., October 19, 1781; furloughed eight days, Newburgh, N. Y., May 11, 1782; deserted May 20, 1782.

GARDNER, CARSWELL:* Enlisted, Cambridge, Mass., January 1, 1776, for one year, a private, Captain Samuel Bartlett's Company, Twenty-first Regiment, Continental Infantry, commanded by Colonel Jonathan Ward; shortly after taken prisoner, Dorchester Neck, Mass., and confined on British transport "Empress of Russia" for six weeks, when he escaped and rejoined regiment; transferred, Cambridge, Mass., March 12, 1776, to the Commannder-in-Chief's Guard, commanded by Captain Caleb Gibbs, and assigned sergeant; at battle of White Plains, N. Y., October 28, 1776; discharged, Newtown, Pa., December 14, 1776, and re-enlisted, for three years, a corporal, Captain George Lewis's Troop, Third Regiment, Continental Dragoons, commanded by Colonel George Baylor; assigned to the Cavalry of the Commander-in-Chief's Guard, commanded by Captain George Lewis, May 1, 1777; at battle of Brandywine, Del., September 11, 1777; battle of Germantown, Pa., October 4, 1777; battle of Monmouth, N. J., June 28, 1778; rejoined regiment, Septembr 26, 1778; at skirmish of Tappan, N. Y., September 28, 1778; discharged, Schuylkill Barracks, Philadelphia, Pa., December 13, 1779.

Born November 19, 1755; married, first, Sarah McMarsters (born November 8, 1754), February 11, 1778; issue:

The Commander-in-Chief's Guard.

Benjamin, born September 27, 1790 (married Amy, issue: Sarah Jean, born July 25, 1812; and Eliza H., born November 16, 1815); second, Elizabeth Johnston (born 1778; residing in Chester County, Pa., August 17, 1853), April 13, 1825, by Rev. Robert Graham; died, New London, Chester County, Pa., October 20, 1840.

GARRET, WILLIAM: Enlisted, Newtown, Pa., January 1, 1777, for three years, a private, Captain George Lewis's Troop, Third Regiment, Continental Dragoons, commanded by Colonel George Baylor; residence, Massachusetts; assigned to the Cavalry of the Commander-in-Chief's Guard, commanded by Captain George Lewis, May 1, 1777; at battle of Brandywine, Del., September 11, 1777; battle of Germantown, Pa., October 4, 1777; battle of Monmouth, N. J., June 28, 1778; rejoined regiment, September 26, 1778; at skirmish of Tappan, N. Y., September 28, 1778; discharged, Schuylkill Barracks, Philadelphia, Pa., December 13, 1779.

GAVET, CHARLES: Enlisted July 12, 1777, for three years, a private, Captain George Lewis's Troop, assigned to the Cavalry of the Commander-in-Chief's Guard; residence, Massachusetts; at battle of Brandywine, Del., September 11, 1777; battle of Germantown, Pa., October 4, 1777; battle of Monmouth, N. J., June 28, 1778; transferred with troop to Third Regiment, Continental Dragoons, commanded by Colonel George Baylor, September 26, 1778; at skirmish of Tappan, N. Y., September 28, 1778; discharged, Schuylkill Barracks, Philadelphia, Pa., December 13, 1779.

GIBBS, CALEB :* Adjutant, Twenty-first Regiment, Continental Infantry, commanded by Colonel John Glover, April 21, 1775; adjutant, Fourteenth Regiment, Continental Infantry, commanded by Colonel John Glover, January 1, 1776; captain, commanding the Commander-in-Chief's Guard, Continental Troops, March 12, 1776; at battle of White Plains, N. Y., October 28, 1776; battle of Trenton,

N. J., December 26, 1776; battle of Princeton, N. J., January 3, 1777; battle of Brandywine, Del., September 11, 1777; battle of Germantown, Pa., October 4, 1777; battle of Monmouth, N. J., June 28, 1778; major, commanding the Commander-in-Chief's Guard, July 29, 1778; on furlough July, August and September, 1778; on furlough January and February, 1779; at battle of Connecticut Farms, N. J., June 7, 1780; transferred to Second Massachusetts Regiment, commanded by Lieutenant-Colonel Ebenezer Sprout, January 1, 1781; wounded in ankle before Yorktown, Va., October 14, 1781; transferred to Colonel Henry Jackson's Regiment, Continental Infantry, November 3, 1783; resigned June 20, 1784.

Born,[40] Newport, R. I., September 25, 1748; married Catherine Hall (born 1766; died, Boston, Mass., December 12, 1849), New South Church, Boston, Mass., January 14, 1787, by Rev. Oliver Everett; died, Charlestown Navy Yard, Mass., November 6, 1818, with the following issue: Margaret H., born 1789 (married Samuel Wells); Alexander H., born August 2, 1791, and died, Roxbury, Mass., March 5, 1827 (married Ellen Mary Hatch, Jamaica Plains, Mass., November 25, 1816); Sarah Blagge, born May, 1793, and died 1795; Caleb, born 1794, and died 1795; Hannah Hall, born 1786 (married James G. Wild, Boston, Mass., October 13, 1824); Catherine Hall, born 1798, and died 1798; Samuel Brown, born 1800; Catherine Susan Ward, born 1805; and Matilda Bartlett, born 1810, and died 1821.

GILBERT, WILLIAM: Enlisted, Hanover, Mass., May 27, 1777, for three years, a private, Captain Seth Drew's Company, Second Massachusetts Regiment, commanded by Colonel John Bailey; born 1757; height, five feet, eight inches; complexion, fresh; transferred, Valley Forge, Pa., March 19, 1778, to the Commander-in-Chief's Guard, commanded by Captain Caleb Gibbs; at battle of Monmouth, N. J., June 28, 1778; sick at Quaker Hill Hospital, November 26, 1778 to January 1, 1779; discharged, Morristown, N. J., May 30, 1780.

THE COMMANDER-IN-CHIEF'S GUARD.

GILL, WILLIAM:* Enlisted February 23, 1776, for two years, a private, Captain John Brent's Company, Fourth Virginia Regiment, commanded by Colonel Adam Stephen; transferred, Morristown, N. J., May 1, 1777, to the Commander-in-Chief's Guard, commanded by Captain Caleb Gibbs; at battle of Brandywine, Del., September 11, 1777; battle of Germantown, Pa., October 4, 1777; discharged, Valley Forge, Pa., February 23, 1778; re-enlisted, Prince Edward County, Va., for three months in 1781, Captain Ambrose Nelson's Company; at battle of Guilford, N. C., March 15, 1781; re-enlisted for three months in 1781, Captain Williamson Bird's Company, Major Charles Allen's Battalion of Virginia Militia; at battle of Yorktown, Va., October 19, 1781.

Born[41] July 12, 1761; occupation, carpenter; married Mary Wright (born, Cumberland County, Va., September 27, 1760; died, Buckingham County, Va., August 18, 1851), Littleton Parish, Cumberland County, Va., February 5, 1784, by Rev. Christopher Macrae; died, Buckingham County, Va., February 4, 1816, with the following issue: Thomas Wright, born, Cumberland County, Va., January 7, 1785, and died unmarried; Sarah Perkins, born, Cumberland County, Va., April 7, 1787, and died, Powhatan County, Va., June 9, 1878 (married Joseph McDearmon); George W., born, Cumberland County, Va., March 27, 1789, and died, Buckingham County, Va., January 4, 1817 (married Judith Lancaster of Cumberland County, Va.); William, born, Cumberland County, Va., October 10, 1792, and died, Buckingham County, Va., August 5, 1883 (married Elizabeth Hix, Buckingham County, Va., April 19, 1821); Polly, born December 25, 1794, and died, Prince Edward County, Va., March 14, 1852 (married Wesley Wilkerson, Buckingham County, Va., September 6, 1820); Archibald, born March 4, 1797, and died, Buckingham County, Va., December 10, 1869 (married Lucy Gill, Bedford County, Va., October 25, 1820); and James, born February 12, 1800, and died, Buckingham County, Va., August 18, 1842 (married Elizabeth Davis of Curdsville, Va.).

Revolutionary War.

GILLEN, THOMAS :*‡ Enlisted, Queen Anne County, Md., May 19, 1778, for the war, a private, Captain John Hawkins's Company, Fifth Maryland Regiment, commanded by Colonel William Richardson; at battle of Monmouth, N. J., June 28, 1778; transferred, Preakness, N. J., July 1, 1780, to the Commander-in-Chief's Guard, commanded by Major Caleb Gibbs; at skirmish of King's Bridge, N. Y., July 3, 1781; battle of Yorktown, Va., October 19, 1781; furloughed, Newburgh, N. Y., June 6, 1783, until the ratification of the definite treaty of peace; discharged November 3, 1783.

Born 1757; occupation, farmer; married Mary (born 1763); residing at Wallkill, N. Y., September 4, 1820; died September 12, 1831; issue: Nancy, born 1795 (married ———— Ross; issue: Mary, born 1817; and Eliza, born 1819); and grandson, Thomas Gillen, residing in Anne Arundel County, Md., April, 1833.

GOODRICH, JARED :* Enlisted, Wethersfield, Conn., January 1, 1776, for one year, a fifer, Captain Samuel Wright's Company, Twenty-second Regiment, Continental Infantry, commanded by Colonel Samuel Wyllys; re-enlisted January 1, 1777, for the war, Captain John Barnard's Company, Third Connecticut Regiment, commanded by Colonel Samuel Wyllys; transferred, Middlebrook, N. J., February 1, 1779, to the Commander-in-Chief's Guard, commanded by Major Caleb Gibbs; at battle of Connecticut Farms, N. J., June 7, 1780; skirmish of King's Bridge, N. Y., July 3, 1781; battle of Yorktown, Va., October 19, 1781; furloughed, Newburgh, N. Y., June 6, 1783, until the ratification of the definite treaty of peace; discharged November 3, 1783.

Born,[42] Rocky Hill, Conn., 1760; married Deborah Griswold (born, Rocky Hill, Conn., 1768; died, Rocky Hill, Conn., 1841), Rocky Hill, Conn., September 15, 1793; died, Rocky Hill, Conn., November 24, 1833, without issue.

GORDON, JAMES :* Enlisted, Bedford, N. H., July 1, 1782, for three years, a private, Captain Ebenezer Frye's Company, First New Hampshire Regiment, commanded by

The Commander-in-Chief's Guard.

Lieutenant-Colonel Henry Dearborn; transferred, Newburgh, N. Y., June 16, 1783, to the Commander-in-Chief's Guard, commanded by Lieutenant-Commandant William Colfax; transferred November 9, 1783, to Colonel Henry Jackson's Regiment, Continental Infantry; discharged, West Point, N. Y., June 30, 1784.

Born,[48] Leeds, Scotland, March, 1752; occupation, weaver; married, first, Jerusha Tarbell (born, Groton, Mass., September 25, 1753; died, Rushford, N. Y., March 8, 1834); issue: Thomas, born, Mason, N. H., August 23, 1780, and died, Reading, Vt., March 25, 1813 (married Olive Harris, Fitchburg, Mass., 1804); Kastorn, born, Mason, N. H., July 23, 1781; James, born, Mason, N. H., October 30, 1783, and died, Rushford, N. Y., October 24, 1868 (married Abigail Bowen); Tarbell, born, Mason, N. H., January 21, 1785, and died, Rushford, N. Y., February 21, 1845 (married Lucy Lawrence); William, born, Mason, N. H., October 7, 1787, and died, Rushford, N. Y., April 5, 1870 (married, first, Mira Gary; second, Martha Gary); John, born, Cavendish, Vt., August 4, 1790, and died, Rushford, N. Y., February 12, 1842 (married Harmony Woodworth January 24, 1810); Wilson, born, Cavendish, Vt., June 4, 1794, and died, Rushford, N. Y., February 29, 1879 (married, first, Lydia Pratt; second, Palina Walker); and Samuel, born, Cavendish, Vt., September 6, 1797, and died, Cavendish, Vt., March 16, 1809; second, Mrs. Abigail Chapman (residing at Rushford, N. Y., August 11, 1853); died, Rushford, N. Y., December 4, 1844.

GREEN, WILLIAM: Enlisted January 1, 1776, for one year, a drummer, Captain Thomas Migill's Company, Twenty-sixth Regiment, Continental Infantry, commanded by Colonel Loammi Baldwin; transferred, Cambridge, Mass., March 12, 1776, to the Commander-in-Chief's Guard, commanded by Captain Caleb Gibbs; in arrest, New York, June 22, 1776; committed to prison in City Hall, New York, July 12, 1776.

Revolutionary War.

GRIFFIN, EDMUND: Enlisted November 7, 1776, for three years, a private, Captain Benjamin Williams's Company, Second North Carolina Regiment, commanded by Colonel Alexander Martin; transferred, White Plains, N. Y., August 1, 1778, to the Commander-in-Chief's Guard, commanded by Major Caleb Gibbs; discharged, West Point, N. Y., November 1, 1779.

GRIFFITH, JOHN: Enlisted January 20, 1777, for the war, a private, Captain Tilman Dixon's Company, First North Carolina Regiment, commanded by Lieutenant-Colonel Thomas Clark; transferred, Valley Forge, Pa., March 19, 1778, to the Commander-in-Chief's Guard, commanded by Captain Caleb Gibbs; at battle of Monmouth, N. J., June 28, 1778; discharged, West Point, N. Y., November 1, 1779.

GRYMES, BENJAMIN: First Lieutenant, Captain Cleon Moore's Company, Colonel William Grayson's Regiment, Continental Infantry, January 18, 1777; detached, Valley Forge, Pa., March 19, 1778, to the Commander-in-Chief's Guard, commanded by Captain Caleb Gibbs; at battle of Monmouth, N. J., June 28, 1778; on furlough from October, 1778, until resigned, March 26, 1779.
Born,[44] "Eagle's Nest," King George County, Va., January 2, 1756; married Ann Nicholas (born, "Norbone," Dinwiddie County, Va., and died at "Eagle's Nest," King George County, Va.); died, "Eagle's Nest," King George County, Va., about 1803, with the following issue: Lucy Fitzhugh, born, "Eagle's Nest," King George County, Va., February 11, 1781, and died, King George County, Va., January 30, 1808 (married Abram Barnes Hooe, "Eagle's Nest," King George County, Va., January 2, 1804); William Fitzhugh, born and died at "Eagle's Nest," King George County, Va. (married Jane Pratt of King George County, Va.); Benjamin, born, "Eagle's Nest," King George County, Va., and died at "Somerset," King George County,

THE COMMANDER-IN-CHIEF'S GUARD.

Va. (married Margaret Pratt of King George County, Va.); George Nicholas, born, "Eagle's Nest," King George County, Va., October 9, 1785, and died, "Montchene," King George County, Va., November 10, 1853 (married Ann Eilbeck Mason, "Lexington," Fairfax County, Va., November 10, 1808); and Martha Carter, born, "Eagle's Nest," King George County, Va., and died at "Liberty," King George County, Va. (married John G. Stuart at "Eagle's Nest," King George County, Va.).

HAGERTY, HUGH: Enlisted August 10, 1776, for three years, a private, Pennsylvania Line; transferred, Valley Forge, Pa., March 19, 1778, to the Commander-in-Chief's Guard, commanded by Captain Caleb Gibbs; at battle of Monmouth, N. J., June 28, 1778; discharged, West Point, N. Y., August 10, 1779.

HALL, SILVANUS:* Enlisted, Kingston, Mass., January 1, 1776, for one year, a private, Captain Samuel Bradford's Company, Twenty-third Regiment, Continental Infantry, commanded by Colonel John Bailey; discharged, Peekskill, N. Y., December 31, 1776; re-enlisted March 12, 1777, for three years, Captain Joseph Wadsworth's Company, Fourteenth Massachusetts Regiment, commanded by Colonel Gamaliel Bradford; at battles of Stillwater, N. Y., September 19 and October 7, 1777; transferred, Valley Forge, Pa., March 19, 1778, to the Commander-in-Chief's Guard, commanded by Captain Caleb Gibbs; at battle of Monmouth, N. J., June 28, 1778; furloughed five weeks, November 6, 1779; discharged, Morristown, N. J., March 12, 1780.

Born[46] September 5, 1762; occupation, carpenter; married Hannah Bent (born March 11, 1756; died, Bridgewater, Mass., October 16, 1830); residing at Tamworth, N. H., February 14, 1828; issue: Sylvanus, born December 17, 1787, and died, Amelia, Ohio, May 31, 1846 (married, first, Almira Cushman in 1825; second, Serena Pease Dunham, Amelia, Ohio, 1828); Ebenezer, born October 16, 1789, and died, Bridgewater, Mass., April 29, 1874 (married Nancy

REVOLUTIONARY WAR.

Dunbar of Halifax, Mass., April 17, 1816); Asa, born February 8, 1791, and died, Bridgewater, Mass., February 10, 1817, unmarried; Lavinia, born February 16, 1793, and died, Bridgewater, Mass., June 8, 1862, unmarried; Reuben, born November 5, 1794; and Hannah, born November 12, 1795, and died, Bridgewater, Mass., May 9, 1827, unmarried.

HANCOCK, ELIHU :‡ Enlisted, Stonington, Conn., May 10, 1777, for the war, a private, Captain James Eldredge's Company, First Connecticut Regiment, commanded by Colonel Jedediah Huntington; transferred, Valley Forge, Pa., March 19, 1778, to the Commander-in-Chief's Guard, commanded by Captain Caleb Gibbs; at battle of Monmouth, N. J., June 28, 1778; battle of Connecticut Farms, N. J., June 7, 1780; skirmish of King's Bridge, N. Y., July 3, 1781; battle of Yorktown, Va., October 19, 1781; promoted 4th corporal, March 1, 1783; furloughed, Newburgh, N. Y., June 6, 1783, until the ratification of the definite treaty of peace; discharged November 3, 1783.

Died, Stonington, Conn., 1813; married, with the following surviving children residing in New London County, Conn., June 1, 1834: Elihu, Deborah and Edward.

HANSON, SAMUEL: Surgeon, March 1, 1778; assigned to the Commander-in-Chief's Guard, commanded by Captain Caleb Gibbs, March 19, 1778; at battle of Monmouth, N. J., June 28, 1778; on furlough from October, 1778, until resigned, March 26, 1779.

Born,[46] Charles County, Md., August 25, 1756, and died, Frederick County, Md., June 29, 1781, unmarried.

HARMON, THOMAS: Enlisted, Scarborough, Mass., January 1, 1777, for three years, a private, Captain Silas Burbank's Company, Twelfth Massachusetts Regiment, commanded by Colonel Samuel Brewer; transferred, Valley Forge, Pa., March 19, 1778, to the Commander-in-Chief's Guard, commanded by Captain Caleb Gibbs; at battle of

The Commander-in-Chief's Guard.

Monmouth, N. J., June 28, 1778; discharged, Morristown, N. J., January 1, 1780.

HARRIS, THOMAS:* Enlisted, Canterbury, Conn., May 17, 1775, for eight months, a private, Captain Obadiah Johnson's Company, Thirty-fourth Regiment, Continental Infantry, commanded by Colonel Israel Putnam; discharged December 16, 1775; re-enlisted June 20, 1776, Captain Asa Bacon's Company, Sixth Battalion, Connecticut State Troops, commanded by Colonel John Chester; at battle of Long Island, N. Y., August 27, 1776; battle of White Plains, N. Y., October 28, 1776; discharged December 25, 1776; re-enlisted April 22, 1777, for the war, a sergeant, Captain Nathaniel Webb's Company, Fourth Connecticut Regiment, commanded by Colonel John Durkee; at battle of Germantown, Pa., October 4, 1777; transferred, Valley Forge, Pa., March 19, 1778, to the Commander-in-Chief's Guard, commanded by Captain Caleb Gibbs, and assigned 5th sergeant; at battle of Monmouth, N. J., June 28, 1778; promoted 4th sergeant, August 2, 1778; promoted 3d sergeant, December 11, 1778; promoted 2d sergeant, August 25, 1779; on rolls to January 4, 1780, without remark.

Born,[47] New London, Conn., August 16, 1759; occupation, cabinetmaker; married Elizabeth Miner (born, New London, Conn., 1762; died, New London, Conn., March 15, 1842), New London, Conn., October 28, 1780, by Rev. Zadock Darrow; died, New London, Conn., May 9, 1802, with the following issue: Thomas, born, New London, Conn., January 10, 1782, and died, New London, Conn., January 17, 1866 (married Lucy Rogers, New London, Conn., August 25, 1805); Elizabeth, born, New London, Conn., October 11, 1784, and died at New London, Conn. (married William McCarthy at New London, Conn.); Fanny, born, New London, Conn., October 2, 1786, and died at Philadelphia, Pa. (married James Peters; no issue); Sally, born, New London, Conn., October 27, 1788, and died, New London, Conn., June 4, 1818, unmarried; Emelia, born, New London, Conn., October 30, 1790, and died at

REVOLUTIONARY WAR.

Philadelphia, Pa. (married William Butler, New London, Conn., September 11, 1810); Ezra, born, New London, Conn., January 19, 1794, and drowned at Key West, Fla. (married Sarah Rogers at New London, Conn.); Jessie, born, New London, Conn., April 14, 1796, and died in infancy; and Lucy, born, New London, Conn., March 2, 1798, and died, New London, Conn., January 17, 1873 (married Samuel Hobron, New London, Conn., February 14, 1819).

HARRIS, THOMAS: Enlisted, Rowley, Mass., April 19, 1775, a private, Captain Thomas Mighill's Company of Minute-men; re-enlisted April 24, 1775, for eight months, Captain Thomas Mighill's Company, Thirty-eighth Regiment, Continental Infantry, commanded by Lieutenant-Colonel Loammi Baldwin; re-enlisted January 1, 1776, for one year, Captain Thomas Mighill's Company, Twenty-sixth Regiment, Continental Infantry, commanded by Colonel Loammi Baldwin; transferred, Cambridge, Mass., March 12, 1776, to the Commander-in-Chief's Guard, commanded by Captain Caleb Gibbs; at battle of White Plains, N. Y., October 28, 1776; discharged, Newtown, Pa., December 14, 1776, and re-enlisted for three years, Captain George Lewis's Troop, Third Regiment, Continental Dragoons, commanded by Colonel George Baylor; assigned to the Cavalry of the Commander-in-Chief's Guard, commanded by Captain George Lewis, May 1, 1777; on rolls to August 1, 1777, without remark.

HARRIS, WILLIAM:* Enlisted April 19, 1775, a private, Captain Isaac Gates's Company of Minute-men, commanded by Colonel Asa Whitcomb; re-enlisted April 26, 1775, for eight months, Captain James Burt's Company, Twenty-third Regiment, Continental Infantry, commanded by Colonel Asa Whitcomb; at battle of Bunker Hill, Mass., June 17, 1775; re-enlisted January 1, 1776, for one year, Captain William H. Ballard's Company, Sixth Regiment, Continental Infantry, commanded by Colonel Asa Whitcomb; at battle of Trenton, N. J., December 26, 1776;

battle of Princeton, N. J., January 3, 1777; discharged, Morristown, N. J., February 10, 1777; re-enlisted, Harvard, Mass., April 1, 1777, for three years, Captain Benjamin Brown's Company, Eighth Massachusetts Regiment, commanded by Colonel Michael Jackson; at battles of Stillwater, N. Y., September 19 and October 7, 1777; transferred, Valley Forge, Pa., March 19, 1778, to the Commander-in-Chief's Guard, commanded by Captain Caleb Gibbs; at battle of Monmouth, N. J., June 28, 1778; discharged, Morristown, N. J., April 1, 1780.

Born, Harvard, Mass., October 8, 1754; married Mary Bradley (born 1769; died, Nelson, N. Y., July 31, 1848), Sunderland, Vt., March 17, 1793, by Rev. Jacob Sherwin; died, Sunderland, Vt., February 21, 1819.

HARRIS, WILLIAM:[*] Enlisted, Culpeper Court-House, Va., January 17, 1777, for three years, a private, Captain John Gillison's Company, Tenth Virginia Regiment, commanded by Colonel Edward Stevens; transferred, Morristown, N. J., May 1, 1777, to the Commander-in-Chief's Guard, commanded by Captain Caleb Gibbs; at battle of Brandywine, Del., September 11, 1777; battle of Germantown, Pa., October 4, 1777; battle of Monmouth, N. J., June 28, 1778; discharged, Morristown, N. J., January 17, 1780.

Born[48] 1752; occupation, farmer; married Sarah Lyon (born 1762-3; died, Wilkes County, N. C., 1831); died, Wilkes County, N. C., December 18, 1848, with the following issue: Lucy, born in Wilkes County, N. C., and died, Wilkes County, N. C., January, 1866 (married Daniel Fields); Squire, died, in Kentucky (married Marion Phillips); James, died in Surry County, N. C. (married Franky Fields); Mary, born, Wilkes County, N. C., 1790 (married Isom Dickerson); Peggy (married Joseph Fields); Jacob, died in Kentucky (married Jennie Kennedy); Susan, died in Kentucy (married Isaac Whitaker in Alleghany County, N. C.); and William, born and died in Wilkes County, N. C., unmarried.

REVOLUTIONARY WAR.

HARRISON, ANDREW: Enlisted August 29, 1776, for three years, a private, Captain Francis Taylor's Company, Second Virginia Regiment, commanded by Colonel Alexander Spotswood; transferred, White Plains, N. Y., August 1, 1778, to the Commander-in-Chief's Guard, commanded by Major Caleb Gibbs; discharged, West Point, N. Y., August 29, 1779.

HENDEE, CALEB:* Enlisted, Ashford, Conn., April 19, 1775, a private, Captain Thomas Knowlton's Company of Minute-men; discharged May 4, 1775; re-enlisted May 5, 1775, for eight months, Captain Thomas Knowlton's Company, Thirty-fourth Regiment, Continental Infantry, commanded by Lieutenant-Colonel Experience Storrs; discharged December 16, 1775; re-enlisted January 1, 1776, for one year, Captain John Keyes's Company, Twentieth Regiment, Continental Infantry, commanded by Colonel Benedict Arnold; transferred, Cambridge, Mass., March 12, 1776, to the Commander-in-Chief's Guard, commanded by Captain Caleb Gibbs; at battle of White Plains, N. Y., October 28, 1776; discharged, Newtown, Pa., December 14, 1776, and re-enlisted for three years, Captain George Lewis's Troop, Third Regiment, Continental Dragoons, commanded by Colonel George Baylor; assigned to the Cavalry of the Commander-in-Chief's Guard, commanded by Captain George Lewis, May 1, 1777; at battle of Brandywine, Del., September 11, 1777; battle of Germantown, Pa., October 4, 1777; battle of Monmouth, N. J., June 28, 1778; rejoined regiment, September 26, 1778; at skirmish of Tappan, N. Y., September 28, 1778; discharged, Schuylkill Barracks, Philadelphia Pa., December 13, 1779; re-enlisted May 21, 1781, for one year, a sergeant, Captain James Dana's Company, First Battalion, Connecticut State Troops, commanded by Major Edward Shipman; commissioned ensign, August 19, 1781.

Born, Ashford, Conn., August 24, 1756; occupation, shoemaker; residing at Ashford, Conn., June 20, 1820, with wife and son; died November 17, 1839.

THE COMMANDER-IN-CHIEF'S GUARD.

HENUSSEY, WILLIAM:‡ Private, First Pennsylvania Regiment, commanded by Colonel Daniel Broadhead; transferred, Philadelphia, Pa., January 11, 1782, to the Commander-in-Chief's Guard, commanded by Lieutenant-Commandant William Colfax; sick at New Windsor Hospital, N. Y., November 1, 1782, to February 1, 1783; furloughed, Newburgh, N. Y., June 6, 1783, until the ratification of the definite treaty of peace; discharged November 3, 1783.

Died, Berkley County, Va., about January, 1798.

HERRICK, JOHN: Enlisted, Brookfield, Mass., January 1, 1777, for the war, a private, Captain Thomas Fish's Company, Fourth Massachusetts Regiment, commanded by Colonel William Shepard; transferred, Valley Forge, Pa., March 19, 1778, to the Commander-in-Chief's Guard, commanded by Captain Caleb Gibbs; at battle of Monmouth, N. J., June 28, 1778; in arrest, Fredericksburg, N. Y., October 18, 1778; court-martialed October 22, 1778, and found guilty of a breach of article 21, section 13, of the articles of war, and sentenced to receive one hundred lashes; sentence approved by the Commander-in-Chief, October 23, 1778, who directed that the punishment be inflicted October 24, 1778, at 9 A. M.; sick-hospital, October 31, 1778; sick at Quaker Hill Hospital, November 26, 1778, to January 1, 1779; sick at Fishkill Hospital, N. Y., January 1, 1779, to March 31, 1779; at battle of Connecticut Farms, N. J., June 7, 1780; skirmish of King's Bridge, N. Y., July 3, 1781; battle of Yorktown, Va., October 19, 1781; promoted 4th corporal, April 1, 1782; promoted 3d corporal, October 23, 1782; promoted 2d corporal, March 1, 1783; furloughed, Newburgh, N. Y., June 6, 1783, until the ratification of the definite treaty of peace; discharged November 3, 1783.

HERRING, JOHN: See John Hurring.

HERSEY, DANIEL: Enlisted, Hingham, Mass., April 27, 1775, for eight months, a private, Captain Jothan Loring's Company, Thirty-sixth Regiment, Continental Infantry, commanded by Colonel John Greaton; re-enlisted, Newtown, Pa., December 14, 1776, for three years, Captain George Lewis's Troop, Third Regiment, Continental Dragoons, commanded by Colonel George Baylor; assigned to the Cavalry of the Commander-in-Chief's Guard, commanded by Captain George Lewis, May 1, 1777; at battle of Brandywine, Del., September 11, 1777; battle of Germantown, Pa., October 4, 1777; battle of Monmouth, N. J., June 28, 1778; rejoined regiment, September 26, 1778; at skirmish of Tappan, N. Y., September 28, 1778; discharged, Schuylkill Barracks, Philadelphia, Pa., December 13, 1779.

Born,[49] Hingham, Mass., November 18, 1754; married Abigail Stodder (born, Hingham, Mass., April 29, 1764; married Jeremiah Hobart December 17, 1797), Hingham, Mass., January 1, 1784; died, Hingham, Mass., June, 1794, with the following issue: Daniel, born, Hingham, Mass., December 14, 1784, and died, Hingham, Mass., August 24, 1786; Daniel, born, Hingham, Mass., December 14, 1786, and died, Boston, Mass., May 26, 1858 (married, first, Hannah Orrok, Boston, Mass., November 3, 1811, who died, Boston, Mass., July 12, 1834; second, Lydia G. Hearsey, Cambridge, Mass., May 30, 1826, who died, Boston, Mass., January 17, 1859); Juletta, born, Hingham, Mass., January, 1790, and died, Hingham, Mass., July 31, 1791; and Juletta, born, Hingham, Mass., October 20, 1793, and died, Hingham, Mass., September 5, 1795.

HETFIELD, STEPHEN:* Enlisted, Essex County, N. J., January 7, 1777, for the war, a private, Captain Abraham Lyon's (7th) Company, Fourth New Jersey Regiment, commanded by Colonel Ephraim Martin, Brigadier-General William Maxwell's Brigade; at battle of Short Hills, N. J., June 26, 1777; battle of Brandywine, Del., September 11, 1777; battle of Germantown, Pa., October 4, 1777; promoted drummer, October 12, 1777; sick-hospital, June, 1778; transferred, February 1, 1779, to Captain Bateman Lloyd's Company, Third New Jersey Regiment, commanded by Colonel Elias Dayton; assigned with Regiment and

THE COMMANDER-IN-CHIEF'S GUARD.

Brigade to Major General John Sullivan's Division, Continental Army, engaged in an expedition against the Six Nations of Indians in Western Pennsylvania and New York, May 26 to October 26, 1779; reduced to the ranks, January 1, 1780; transferred, Morristown, N. J., March 20, 1780, to the Commander-in-Chief's Guard, commanded by Major Caleb Gibbs; at battle of Connecticut Farms, N. J., June 7, 1780—wounded; skirmish of King's Bridge, N. Y., July 3, 1781; battle of Yorktown, Va., October 19, 1781; furloughed, Newburgh, N. Y., June 6, 1783, until the ratification of the definite treaty of peace; discharged November 3, 1783.

Born,[50] New Jersey, 1759; occupation, farmer; married Elizabeth Freeborn (born 1781; died, Waynesburg, Pa., July 19, 1861), Greene County, Pa., July 23, 1798; died, Waynesburg, Pa., May 19, 1824, with the following issue: Sarah, born, Greene County, Pa., April 3, 179—, and died, Waynesburg, Pa., May 2, 1879 (married Charles Adamson, Greene County, Pa., 1818); Mary, born, Greene County, Pa., 1802, and died, Greene County, Pa., January 15, 1834 (married John Clark); Elizabeth, born, Greene County, Pa., 1805, and died in Iowa (married Josiah Adamson); Charlotte, born, Greene County, Pa., April 30, 1807, and died, Greene County, Pa., May 3, 1890 (married Richard Areford, Greene County, Pa., 1829); Anthony, born, Greene County, Pa., 1810, and died in Kentucky (married ——— Black in Greene County, Pa.); Letitia, born, Greene County, Pa., 1814, and died at Connellsville, Pa. (married Cyrus Frakes in Greene County, Pa.); Jacob, born, Greene County, Pa., 1815, and died, Terre Haute, Ind., 1838; Maria, born, Greene County, Pa., June 24, 1818, and died, Sullivan County, Mo., May 4, 1902 (married R. C. Clark, Greene County, Pa., August 4, 1839); Andrew, born, Greene County, Pa., 1819, and died, Dayton, Ohio, 1896; and Sceny, born, Greene County, Pa., February 11, 1824, and died, Waynesburg, Pa., December 30, 1897 (married S. Rinehart in Greene County, Pa.).

Revolutionary War.

HICKEY, THOMAS: Private, Commander-in-Chief's Guard, commanded by Captain Caleb Gibbs; in arrest, New York, June 15, 1776; court-martialed June 26, 1776, and found guilty of a breach of the 5th and 30th articles of war, and sentenced to be hanged; sentence approved by the Commander-in-Chief, June 27, 1776, to take effect June 28, 1776, at 11 A. M.; hanged, June 28, 1776.

HILL, SPENCER: Private, Virginia Line; transferred. Valley Forge, Pa., March 1, 1778, to the Commander-in-Chief's Guard, commanded by Captain Caleb Gibbs; at battle of Monmouth, N. J., June 28, 1778; battle of Connecticut Farms, N. J., June 7, 1780; on rolls to January 15, 1781, without remark.

HILTON, JOSEPH: Enlisted November 16, 1776, for the war, a private, Captain Christian Staddle's Company, Second Pennsylvania Regiment, commanded by Colonel James Irvine; transferred, Valley Forge, Pa., March 19, 1778, to the Commander-in-Chief's Guard, commanded by Captain Caleb Gibbs; at battle of Monmouth, N. J., June 28, 1778; confined in the main guard, October, 1779; at battle of Connecticut Farms, N. J., June 7, 1780; on return dated April 8, 1781, with remark "Present."

HINCHER, WILLIAM: Enlisted July 12, 1777, for three years, a private, Captain George Lewis's Troop, assigned as the Cavalry of the Commander-in-Chief's Guard; on rolls to August 1, 1777, without remark.

HOLDEN, LEVI:* Enlisted, Cambridge, Mass., January 1, 1776, for one year, a private, Captain Micajah Gleason's Company, Fourth Regiment, Continental Infantry, commanded by Colonel John Nixon; promoted sergeant-major, November 9, 1776; discharged December 31, 1776; ensign, Captain Thomas Barnes's Company, Sixth Massachusetts Regiment, commanded by Colonel Thomas Nixon, January 1, 1777; promoted 2d lieutenant, December

22, 1777; transferred, New Windsor, N. Y., June 23, 1781, to the Commander-in-Chief's Guard, commanded by Lieutenant-Commandant William Colfax; at skirmish of King's Bridge, N. Y., July 3, 1781; battle of Yorktown, Va., October 19, 1781; promoted 1st lieutenant, May 17, 1782, to rank from December 22, 1777; furloughed February 27, 1783, until May 15, 1783; furloughed, Newburgh, N. Y., June 6, 1783, until the ratification of the definite treaty of peace; discharged November 3, 1783; commissioned captain, by brevet, October 19, 1786.

Born,[61] Sudbury, Mass., January 12, 1754; married Hannah Plympton (born, Sudbury, Mass., July 27, 1754; died, Newark, N. J., September 28, 1828), Sudbury, Mass., January 15, 1778; died, Newark, N. J., April 19, 1823, with the following issue: Thomas, born, Sudbury, Mass., September 5, 1779, and died, Newark, N. J., May 20, 1820 (married Ann Vose); Levi, born, Sudbury, Mass., December 27, 1780, and died, Lamington, N. J., December 28, 1847, unmarried; Mary, born, Sudbury, Mass., November 29, 1783, and died, New York City, December 23, 1844 (married Ward Richmond); George, born, Sudbury, Mass., July 21, 1785, and died, Newark, N. J., July 21, 1847 (married, first, Eliza Ogden Nicholds; second, Mary Halsey, nee Wheeler; third, Jane Eagles, nee Hardy); Henry, born, Sudbury, Mass., March 10, 1787, and died, Newark, N. J., July 22, 1846 (married, first, Eliza Plum; second, Mary Nutman; third, Susan Morgan); Warren, born, Sudbury, Mass., August 15, 1788, and died, Newark, N. J., February 16, 1816, unmarried; Hannah, born, Sudbury, Mass., January 30, 1790, and died, Lamington, N. J., July, 1867 (married Richard B. Duychinck, Boston, Mass., December 30, 1808); Emma, born, Sudbury, Mass., August 31, 1791, and died, Brooklyn, N. Y., March 21, 1863, unmarried; Horace, born, Sudbury, Mass., November 5, 1793, and died, New York City, March 21, 1862 (married, first, Bathsheba Sanford, New York City, August 8, 1816; second, Mary Cotton, New

REVOLUTIONARY WAR.

York City, February 19, 1824; third, Catherine P. Judson, Stratford, Conn., December 25, 1833); Otis, born, Sudbury, Mass., February 16, 1796, and died, Newark, N. J., November 24, 1825, unmarried; and Harriet, born, Sudbury, Mass., December 31, 1798, and died, Brooklyn, N. Y., February 7, 1867 (married Caleb Halsted Shipman, Newark, N. J., November 12, 1823).

HOLLAND, THOMAS: Enlisted June 28, 1776, a private, Captain Gross Scruggs's Company, Fifth Virginia Regiment, commanded by Colonel Charles Scott; transferred, Morristown, N. J., May 6, 1777, to the Commander-in-Chief's Guard, commanded by Captain Caleb Gibbs; promoted 2d corporal, June 4, 1777; on rolls to August 11, 1777, without remark.

HOLT, DANIEL: Enlisted, Wilton, N. H., February 27, 1781, for three years, a private, Ninth Company, First New Hampshire Regiment, commanded by Colonel Alexander Scammell; promoted corporal; transferred, Newburgh, N. Y,. June 16, 1783, to the Commander-in-Chief's Guard, commanded by Lieutenant-Commandant William Colfax, and assigned 2d sergeant; on return dated Rocky Hill, N. J., October 22, 1783, with remark "Present."

HOLT, JOEL:[*] Enlisted, Wilton, N. H., February 27, 1781, for three years, a private, Captain Isaac Frye's Company, First New Hampshire Regiment, commanded by Colonel Alexander Scammell; transferred, Newburgh, N. Y., June 16, 1783, to the Commander-in-Chief's Guard, commanded by Lieutenant-Commandant William Colfax, and assigned 3d corporal; detailed, Rocky Hill, N. J., November 9, 1783, wagonmaster to the Commander-in-Chief's baggage; discharged, West Point, N. Y., December 20, 1783.

Born,[52] Andover, Mass., 1764; married Polly Coburn (born, Wilton, N. H., September 2, 1765; died, Milford, N. H., July 4, 1858), Wilton, N. H., November 30, 1786, by Rev. Abel Fisk; died, Milford, N. H., June 16,

The Commander-in-Chief's Guard.

1848, with the following issue: Polly, born, Nelson, N. H., April 17, 1787 (married George Herrick November 17, 1808); Betsey, born, Nelson, N. H., September 6, 1789 (married Oliver Stone); Patty, born, Nelson, N. H., July 18, 1791, and died, Milford, N. H., July 4, 1858 (married Oliver Perham, Jr., November 22, 1810); Joel, born, Nelson, N. H., April 23, 1793, and died, Troy, N. Y., October, 1828 (married Lucinda Nelson); Daniel, born, Nelson, N. H., May 22, 1795, and died June 19, 1816, unmarried; Sally, born, Nelson, N. H., May 18, 1797, and died, Milford, N. H., March 25, 1853 (married Daniel Cram, Lyndeborough, N. H., December 18, 1822); Rachel, born, Nelson, N. H., July 31, 1801, and died, Ironton, Ohio, May 9, 1889 (married Phineas Stimpson, of Ashburnham, Mass., November, 1833); and Nehemiah, born, Nelson, N. H., May 9, 1803, and died, Milford, N. H., June 4, 1886 (married Jane Bent Brown, of Wayland, Mass., December 5, 1830).

HOLT, PETER: Enlisted, New London, Conn., February 26, 1777, for the war, a private, Captain Amos Stanton's Company, Colonel Henry Sherburne's Regiment, Continental Infantry; transferred, Morristown, N. J., March 20, 1780, to the Commander-in-Chief's Guard, commanded by Major Caleb Gibbs; at battle of Connecticut Farms, N. J., June 7, 1780; skirmish of King's Bridge, N. Y., July 3, 1781; battle of Yorktown, Va., October 19, 1781; furloughed forty days, December 21, 1782; furloughed, Newburgh, N. Y., June 6, 1783, until the ratification of the definite treaty of peace; discharged November 3, 1783.

HOLT, PHILIP: Private, Virginia Line; transferred, Morristown, N. J., May 1, 1777, to the Commander-in-Chief's Guard, commanded by Captain Caleb Gibbs; on rolls to August 11, 1777, with remark "In hospital."

HOWE, BEZALEEL:* Enlisted, Amherst, N. H., April 23, 1775, a private, Captain Josiah Crosby's Company, Third Regiment, Continental Infantry, commanded by Colonel

REVOLUTIONARY WAR.

James Reed; discharged July 8, 1775; 2d lieutenant, Captain Amos Morrill's Company, First New Hampshire Regiment, commanded by Colonel John Stark, November 8, 1776; wounded at battle of Stillwater, N. Y., September 19, 1777; transferred to Major William Scott's Company, December 1, 1778; promoted 1st lieutenant, June 24, 1779; detached and assigned to the command of the Commander-in-Chief's Guard, Newburgh, N. Y., September 5, 1783; promoted captain, by brevet, October 10, 1783; discharged, West Point, N. Y., December 20, 1783; 1st lieutenant, Second U. S. Infantry, March 4, 1791; captain, November 4, 1791; transferred to Second Sub-Legion, September 4, 1792; major, October 20, 1794; discharged November 1, 1796.

Born,[53] Marlborough, Mass., December 9, 1755; married, first, Hannah Merritt (born, Mamaroneck, N. Y.; died, New York, September 18, 1798), New York, September 16, 1787, by Rev. John Gano; issue: Maria, born January 6, 1789, and died 1852 (married John Guion November 23, 1805); second, Catherine Moffat (born, Little Britain, N. Y., March 3, 1755; died, New York, December 2, 1849), New York, February 15, 1800; died, New York, September 3, 1825, with the following issue: Eliza, born, New York, November 19, 1800, and died in infancy; George C., born, New York, September 23, 1802, and died, New York, December 4, 1841 (married Hester Ann Higgins, New York, May 24, 1832, who died, Brooklyn, N. Y., March 15, 1884); Margaretta, born, New York, February 27, 1804, and died, Brooklyn, N. Y., December 1, 1896 (married George W. Dupignac August 1, 1820); John Moffat, born, New York, January 23, 1806, and died, Passaic, N. J., February 5, 1885 (married, first, Mary Mason, New York, October 31, 1838, who died, New York, October 15, 1841; second, Ann W. Morgan, New York, September 14, 1843, who died, New York, October 19, 1844; third, Emeline Barnard Jenkins May 7, 1846); Oscar, born, New York, March 11, 1808, and died in infancy; Julia Ann, born, New York, October 4, 1810, and died in infancy; Catherine, born, New York, September 21, 1812, and died, Mamaroneck,

N. Y., March 4, 1883 (married Samuel R. Spelman, New York, October 11, 1831); and Bezaleel, born, New York, August 17, 1815, and died, Goshen, N. Y., January 18, 1858 (married Jane Cordelia Frank, New York, August 5, 1838).

HOWELL, ISAAC:* Enlisted, Philadelphia, Pa., May 27, 1777, for the war, a private, Captain James Taylor's Company Fifth Pennsylvania Regiment, commanded by Colonel Francis Johnston; at battle of Brandywine, Del., September 11, 1777—wounded in leg and taken prisoner; exchanged February, 1778, and rejoined regiment; transferred, Valley Forge, Pa., March 19, 1778, to the Commander-in-Chief's Guard, commanded by Captain Caleb Gibbs; at battle of Monmouth, N. J., June 28, 1778; battle of Connecticut Farms, N. J., June 7, 1780; transferred, August 16, 1780, to Lieutenant-Colonel Francis Mentges's Company, Fifth Pennsylvania Regiment, commanded by Colonel Francis Johnston; shortly after taken prisoner and confined on Jersey Prison Ship, at New York, for three months, when he enlisted in the British army; deserted, Harlem Heights, N. Y., two months after and reached American lines, when he received pass from General Heath to proceed home to Rhinebeck, N. Y.

Born May 12, 1762; residing at Hanley, N. Y., June, 1833.

HOWELL, THOMAS: Enlisted March 28, 1777, for three years, a private, Virginia Line; transferred, Morristown, N. J., May 6, 1777, to the Commander-in-Chief's Guard, commanded by Captain Caleb Gibbs; at battle of Brandywine, Del., September 11, 1777; battle of Germantown, Pa., October 4, 1777; battle of Monmouth, N. J., June 28, 1778; discharged, Morristown, N. J., March 28, 1780.

HOWL, THOMAS: See Thomas Howell.

HUGHES, JAMES: Enlisted, Pennsylvania, November 15, 1776, for the war, a private, Captain Thomas Pry's Com-

REVOLUTIONARY WAR.

pany, Colonel Moses Hazen's Regiment, Continental Infantry; transferred, Morristown, N. J., March 20, 1780, to the Commander-in-Chief's Guard, commanded by Major Caleb Gibbs; at battle of Connecticut Farms, N. J., June 7, 1780; skirmish of King's Bridge, N. Y., July 3, 1781; battle of Yorktown, Va., October 19, 1781; furloughed, Newburgh, N. Y., June 6, 1783, until the ratification of the definite treaty of peace; discharged, November 3, 1783.

HUNTER, WILLIAM: Enlisted March 11, 1777, for the war, a sergeant, Captain William Cross's Company, Fourth Pennsylvania Regiment, commanded by Colonel Lambert Cadwallader; transferred, Morristown, N. J., March 20, 1780, to the Commander-in-Chief's Guard, commanded by Major Caleb Gibbs, and assigned 5th sergeant; at battle of Connecticut Farms, N. J., June 7, 1780; promoted 4th sergeant, September 15, 1780; promoted 1st sergeant, July 1, 1781; at skirmish of King's Bridge, N. Y., July 3, 1781; battle of Yorktown, Va., October 19, 1781; furloughed, Newburgh, N. Y., June 6, 1783, until the ratification of the definite treaty of peace; discharged November 3, 1783.

HURRING, JOHN: Enlisted, Nantucket, Mass., January 13, 1776, for one year, a private, Captain Lemuel Trescott's Company, Sixth Regiment, Continental Infantry, commanded by Colonel Asa Whitcomb; re-enlisted January 1, 1777, for the war, Captain Abraham Tucker's Company, First Massachusetts Regiment, commanded by Colonel Joseph Vose; transferred, Valley Forge, Pa., March 19, 1778, to the Commander-in-Chief's Guard, commanded by Captain Caleb Gibbs; at battle of Monmouth, N. J., June 28, 1778; in arrest, Fredericksburg, N. Y., October 19, 1778; court-martialed October 22, 1778, and found guilty of a breach of article 21, section 13, of the articles of war, and sentenced to death; sentence approved by the Commander-in-Chief, October 23, 1778, who directed that he be hanged immediately in Baron DeKalb's Division; hanged October 23, 1778.

The Commander-in-Chief's Guard.

Huston, Samuel: Enlisted January 1, 1777, for three years, a private, Captain George Lewis's Troop, Third Regiment, Continental Dragoons, commanded by Colonel George Baylor; assigned to the Cavalry of the Commander-in-Chief's Guard, commanded by Captain George Lewis, May 1, 1777; on rolls to August 1, 1777, without remark.

Hutchinson, ————: Private, New Hampshire Line; transferred, Newburg, N. Y., June 16, 1783, to the Commander-in-Chief's Guard, commanded by Lieutenant-Commandant William Colfax; on return dated Rocky Hill, N. J., October 22, 1783, with remark "Present."

Hymer, Daniel: Enlisted February 2, 1777, for the war, a private, Fourth Pennsylvania Regiment, commanded by Colonel Lambert Cadwallader; transferred, Valley Forge, Pa., March 19, 1778, to the Commander-in-Chief's Guard, commanded by Captain Caleb Gibbs; at battle of Monmouth, N. J., June 28, 1778; battle of Connecticut Farms, N. J., June 7, 1780; skirmish of King's Bridge, N. Y., July 3, 1781; battle of Yorktown, Va., October 19, 1781; furloughed, Newburgh, N. Y., June 6, 1783, until the ratification of the definite treaty of peace; discharged November 3, 1783.

Isbell, Pendleton:* Enlisted October 7, 1775, for one year, a private, Captain Robert Ballard's Company, First Virginia Regiment, commanded by Colonel James Read; re-enlisted September 7, 1776, for three years; transferred, Morristown, N. J., May 1, 1777, to the Commander-in-Chief's Guard, commanded by Captain Caleb Gibbs; at battle of Brandywine, Del., September 11, 1777; battle of Germantown, Pa., October 4, 1777; sick-absent, June and July, 1778; re-enlisted and furloughed one hundred and ten days, January 18, 1779; deserted, Morristown, N. J., February 1, 1780.
Married Margaret Lahow (residing at Pickens, S. C., November 14, 1853), Pendleton District, S. C., March,

Revolutionary War.

1828, by Robert Holland, Esquire; died Pendleton District, S. C., March, 1829.

IVES, JOHN :* Enlisted, New Hartford, Conn., February 11, 1777, for three years, a private, Captain Solomon Strong's Company, Fifth Connecticut Regiment, commanded by Colonel Philip B. Bradley; at battle of Germantown, Pa., October 4, 1777; transferred, Valley Forge, Pa., March 19, 1778, to the Commander-in-Chief's Guard, commanded by Captain Caleb Gibbs; at battle of Monmouth, N. J., June 28, 1778; discharged, Morristown, N. J., February 12, 1780.
Born 1760; married; residing at Fabius, N. Y., September 1, 1820.

JACKSON, ZACHARIAH: Enlisted June 13, 1776, for three years, a private, Captain Benjamin Williams's Company Sixth North Carolina Regiment, commanded by Colonel John A. Lillington (also given Captain Tilman Dixon's Company, First North Carolina Regiment, commanded by Colonel Thomas Clark); transferred, Valley Forge, Pa., March 19, 1778, to the Commander-in-Chief's Guard, commanded by Captain Caleb Gibbs, and assigned private; at battle of Monmouth, N. J., June 28, 1778; discharged, New Windsor, N. Y., July 13, 1779.

JANET, SOLOMON: Enlisted February 1, 1777, for three years, a private, Captain Benjamin Williams's Company (also given Major Hardy Murfree's Company), Second North Carolina Regiment, commanded by Colonel Alexander Martin; transferred, Valley Forge, Pa., March 19, 1778, to the Commander-in-Chief's Guard, commanded by Captain Caleb Gibbs; at battle of Monmouth, N. J., June 28, 1778; discharged, West Point, N. Y., November 1, 1779.

JOHNSON, ASA: Enlisted January 1, 1777, for the war, a private, Captain Stephen Olney's Company, Second Rhode Island Regiment, commanded by Colonel Israel Angell; transferred, Valley Forge, Pa., March 19, 1778,, to the

Commander-in-Chief's Guard, commanded by Captain Caleb Gibbs; at battle of Monmouth, N. J., June 28, 1778; deserted December 1, 1779.

JOHNSON, JAMES: Fifer, Commander-in-Chief's Guard, commanded by Captain Caleb Gibbs; in arrest, New York, June 22, 1776; committed to prison in city hall, New York, July 12, 1776.

JOHNSON, JAMES: Enlisted November 16, 1776, for three years, a private, Virginia Line; transferred, Morristown, N. J., May 1, 1777, to the Commander-in-Chief's Guard, commanded by Captain Caleb Gibbs; at battle of Brandywine, Del., September 11, ,1777; battle of Germantown, Pa., October 4, 1777; battle of Monmouth, N. J., June 28, 1778; discharged, West Point, N. Y., November 16, 1779.

JOHNSON, LEVI: Enlisted, Readington, N. J., October 1, 1776, for one year, a private, Captain John Ross's (3d) Company, Third New Jersey Regiment, commanded by Colonel Elias Dayton; re-enlisted, Ticonderoga, N. Y., January 7, 1777, for three years, Captain John Ross's (3d) Company, Third New Jersey Regiment, commanded by Colonel Elias Dayton, Brigadier-General William Maxwell's Brigade; sick at Albany, N. Y., February 22, 1777; at battle of Short Hills, N. J., June 26, 1777; battle of Brandywine, Del., September 11, 1777; battle of Germantown, Pa., October 4, 1777; transferred, Valley Forge, Pa., March 19, 1778, to the Commander-in-Chief's Guard, commanded by Captain Caleb Gibbs; at battle of Monmouth, N. J., June 28, 1778; discharged, Morristown, N. J., February 16, 1780.

JONES, EPHRAIM: Enlisted, New Canaan, Mass., May 20, 1777, for the war, a private, Captain Jeremiah Miller's Company, First Massachusetts Regiment, commanded by Colonel Joseph Vose; born, 1760; height, five feet, seven inches; hair light; complexion, light; transferred, Valley Forge, Pa., March 19, 1778, to the Commander-in-Chief's

REVOLUTIONARY WAR.

Guard, commanded by Captain Caleb Gibbs; at battle of Monmouth, N. J., June 28, 1778; battle of Connecticut Farms, N. J., June 7, 1780; on rolls to January 15, 1781, without remark.

JONES, JOHN: Enlisted August 13, 1776, for three years, a private, Virginia Line; transferred, Morristown, N. J., May 1, 1777, to the Commander-in-Chief's Guard, commanded by Captain Caleb Gibbs; at battle of Brandywine, Del., September 11, 1777; battle of Germantown, Pa., October 4, 1777; promoted 1st corporal, March 1, 1778; reduced to 3d corporal, March 19, 1778; at battle of Monmouth, N. J., June 28, 1778; promoted 2d corporal, August 2, 1778; promoted 7th sergeant, September 1, 1778; promoted 6th sergeant, December 11, 1778; discharged, West Point, N. Y., August 13, 1779.

JONES, JOSEPH: Enlisted, Newcastle, Mass., December 20, 1776, for three years, a private, Captain George White's Company, Eleventh Massachusetts Regiment, commanded by Colonel Ebenezer Francis; transferred, Valley Forge, Pa., March 19, 1778, to the Commander-in-Chief's Guard, commanded by Captain Caleb Gibbs; sick-absent, June, 1778; discharged, Morristown, N. J., December 16, 1779.

JONES, WILLIAM: Enlisted August, 1776, for three years, a private, Virginia Line; transferred, Morristown, N. J., May 1, 1777, to the Commander-in-Chief's Guard, commanded by Captain Caleb Gibbs; at battle of Brandywine, Del., September 11, 1777; battle of Germantown, Pa., October 4, 1777; battle of Monmouth, N. J., June 28, 1778; re-enlisted and furloughed one hundred days, January 18, 1779; at battle of Connecticut Farms, N. J., June 7, 1780; skirmish of King's Bridge, N. Y., July 3, 1781; battle of Yorktown, Va., October 19, 1781; in hospital, January, 1782; discharged, Philadelphia, Pa., March 18, 1782, by General Washington.

JUSTICE, JOHN: Enlisted May 1, 1777, for the war, a sergeant, Captain James Carnahan's Company, Tenth Pennsylvania Regiment, commanded by Colonel Walter Stewart; born, Shippensburg, Pa., 1752; height, five feet, nine inches; occupation, yeoman; transferred to Major John Murray's Company; transferred, Morristown, N. J., March 20, 1780, to the Commander-in-Chief's Guard, commanded by Major Caleb Gibbs, and assigned 4th sergeant; at battle of Connecticut Farms, N. J., June 7, 1780; promoted 3d sergeant, September 15, 1780; reduced to 5th sergeant, July 1, 1781; at skirmish of King's Bridge, N. Y., July 3, 1781; battle of Yorktown, Va., October 19, 1781; on rolls to February 16, 1782, without remark.

KENNEY, JOHN :* Enlisted, Hampton Falls, N. H., May 31, 1782, for three years, a private, Second Company, Second New Hampshire Regiment, commanded by Lieutenant-Colonel George Reid; transferred, Newburgh, N. Y., June 16, 1783, to the Commander-in-Chief's Guard, commanded by Lieutenant-Commandant William Colfax; on return dated Rocky Hill, N. J., October 22, 1783, with remark "Present."

Married Betsey S. Mason (born 1762; died, Barnstead, N. H., November 24, 1841), Chichester, N. H., June 18, 1786, by Rev. William Parsons; presumed to have died in Michigan, about 1820; issue: Joseph; Susan; Betsey; Nancy; and John, residing at Barnstead, N. H., April 29, 1845.

KERNAHAN, WILLIAM :* Enlisted, Little York, Pa., January, 1777, for the war, a private, Captain Henry Miller's Company, First Pennsylvania Regiment, commanded by Colonel Edward Hand; at battle of Brandywine, Del., September 11, 1777; battle of Germantown, Pa., October 4, 1777; transferred, Valley Forge, Pa., March 19, 1778, to the Commander-in-Chief's Guard, commanded by Captain Caleb Gibbs; at battle of Monmouth, N. J., June 28, 1778; battle of Connecticut Farms, N. J., June 7, 1780; skirmish of King's Bridge, N. Y., July 3, 1781; battle of Yorktown, Va., October 19, 1781; furloughed, Newburgh, N. Y., June

Revolutionary War.

6, 1783, until the ratification of the definite treaty of peace; discharged November 3, 1783.

Born 1750; occupation, weaver; residing in Warrington Township, Bucks County, Pa., June 30, 1820, with wife Grissel (born 1746); issue: two children, married.

KIDDER, ISAAC: Enlisted, Townsend, Mass., April 19, 1775, a private, Captain James Hosley's Company of Minute-men, commanded by Colonel William Prescott; re-enlisted April 27, 1775, for eight months, Captain Henry Farwell's Company, Tenth Regiment, Continental Infantry, commanded by Colonel William Prescott; re-enlisted, Newtown, Pa., January 1, 1777, for three years, Captain George Lewis's Troop, Third Regiment, Continental Dragoons, commanded by Colonel George Baylor; assigned to the Cavalry of the Commander-in-Chief's Guard, commanded by Captain George Lewis, May 1, 1777; at battle of Brandywine, Del., September 11, 1777; battle of Germantown, Pa., October 4, 1777; battle of Monmouth, N. J., June 28, 1778; rejoined regiment, September 26, 1778; at skirmish of Tappan, N. Y., September 28, 1778; discharged, Schuylkill Barracks, Philadelphia, Pa., December 13, 1779.

KIDDER, JOHN: Enlisted, New Marlborough, Mass., April 21, 1775, a private, Captain Moses Soule's Company of Minute-men, commanded by Colonel John Fellows; re-enlisted May 7, 1775, for eight months, Captain Moses Soule's Company, Eighth Regiment, Continental Infantry, commanded by Colonel John Fellows; re-enlisted July 4, 1777, for three years, Captain Noah Allen's Company, Thirteenth Massachusetts Regiment, commanded by Colonel Edward Wigglesworth; born 1752; height, five feet, eight inches; complexion, dark; hair, dark; occupation, yeoman; transferred, Valley Forge, Pa., March 19, 1778, to the Commander-in-Chief's Guard, commanded by Captain Caleb Gibbs; at battle of Monmouth, N. J., June 28, 1778; furloughed fifteen days, West Point, N. Y., August 31, 1779; deserted September 16, 1779.

THE COMMANDER-IN-CHIEF'S GUARD.

KING, CHARLES:* Enlisted, Cambridge, Mass., May 2, 1775, for eight months, a private, Captain Abner Cranston's Company, Twenty-third Regiment, Continental Infantry, commanded by Colonel Asa Whitcomb; re-enlisted January 1, 1776, for one year, Captain Abner Cranston's Company, Sixth Regiment, Continental Infantry, commanded by Colonel Asa Whitcomb; transferred to Major-General Charles Lee's Guard, commanded by Ensign Benjamin Gould; transferred to Major-General Artemas Ward's Guard, March 17, 1776; rejoined regiment, August 1, 1776; transferred, New York, August, 1776, to the Commander-in-Chief's Guard, commanded by Captain Caleb Gibbs; at battle of White Plains, N. Y., October 28, 1776; discharged, Newtown, Pa., December 14, 1776, and re-enlisted for three years, a corporal, Captain George Lewis's Troop, Third Regiment, Continental Dragoons, commanded by Colonel George Baylor; assigned to the Cavalry of the Commander-in-Chief's Guard, commanded by Captain George Lewis, May 1, 1777, and appointed acting quartermaster sergeant; at battle of Brandywine, Del., September 11, 1777; battle of Germantown, Pa., October 4, 1777; battle of Monmouth, N. J., June 28, 1778; rejoined regiment, September 26, 1778, and promoted sergeant-major; at skirmish of Tappan, N. Y., September 28, 1778; discharged, Schuylkill Barracks, Philadelphia, Pa., December 13, 1779.

Born 1756; married; residing in Licking Township, Muskingum County, Ohio, October 23, 1832.

KING, JOHN:* Enlisted, Louisa County, Va., January 2, 1777, for three years, a private, Captain Moses Hawkins's Company, Fourteenth Virginia Regiment, commanded by Colonel Charles Lewis; transferred, Morristown, N. J., May 6, 1777, to the Commander-in-Chief's Guard, commanded by Captain Caleb Gibbs; at battle of Brandywine, Del., September 11, 1777; battle of Germantown, Pa., October 4, 1777; battle of Monmouth, N. J., June 28, 1778; discharged, Morristown, N. J., January 6, 1780.

Born,[54] Louisa County, Va., January 12, 1758; occupation, carpenter; married Sarah LeMaster (born, Amherst

Revolutionary War.

County, Va., September 17, 1774; died, Rich Hill, S. C., October, 1849), Spartanburg, S. C., March 2, 1790; died, Rich Hill, S. C., March 25, 1842, with the following issue: Edmund, born, Rich Hill, S. C., December 1, 1790 (married Nancy Emberson, Tennessee, January 30, 1830); William, born, Rich Hill, S. C., March 19, 1792 (married Rhoda Smith, Tennessee, 1825); Mary, born, Rich Hill, S. C., March 8, 1794, and died at Homer, Ga.; Ann, born, Rich Hill, S. C., November 7, 1796, and died at Rich Hill, S. C.; Lucy, born, Rich Hill, S. C., November 15, 1798, and died at Cedar Springs, S. C. (married James W. Cooper, Spartanburg, S. C., December 15, 1816); Elizabeth, born, Rich Hill, S. C., September 6, 1800, and died at Greenville, S. C. (married John Easley, Spartanburg, S. C., January 30, 1823); Martha, born, Rich Hill, S. C., October 2, 1801, and died at Pickens, S. C. (married John Gossett, Spartanburg, S. C., December 15, 1830); Philip W., born, Rich Hill, S. C., October 22, 1803 (married Dolly Browning, Tennessee, August 1, 1829); Sarah, born, Rich Hill, S. C., January 11, 1806, and died at Glenn Springs, S. C. (married Hiram White, Spartanburg, S. C., November 11, 1828); an infant, born, Rich Hill, S. C., December 8, 1808, and died January 30, 1809; Margaret, born, Rich Hill, S. C., November 2, 1809, and died, Spartanburg, S. C., June 27, 1895 (married David Reid, Spartanburg, S. C., October 11, 1827); John M., born, Rich Hill, S. C., March 28, 1812, and died at Homer, Ga. (married Sarah Hammett, Laurens, S. C., November 1, 1842); and Minerva, born, Rich Hill, S. C., May 25, 1815, and died February 5, 1817.

Knox, James:* Enlisted, Marblehead, Mass., May 19, 1775, for eight months, a private, Captain Samuel R. Trevett's Company, Colonel Richard Gridley's Massachusetts Artillery Regiment; at battle of Bunker Hill, Mass., June 17, 1775; transferred to Captain Abijah Child's Company; Thirty-seventh Regiment, Continental Infantry, commanded by Lieutenant-Colonel William Bond, August, 1775; re-enlisted January 1, 1776, for one year, Twelfth Regiment, Continental Infantry, commanded by Colonel Moses Little,

The Commander-in-Chief's Guard.

and transferred to Major-General Charles Lee's Guard, commanded by Ensign Benjamin Gould; transferred, March 17, 1776, to Major-General Artemas Ward's Guard; transferred, New York, August, 1776, to the Commander-in-Chief's Guard, commanded by Captain Caleb Gibbs; at battle of White Plains, N. Y., October 28, 1776; discharged, Newtown, Pa., December 30, 1776, and re-enlisted for three years, a corporal, Captain George Lewis's Troop, Third Regiment, Continental Dragoons, commanded by Colonel George Baylor; assigned to the Cavalry of the Commander-in-Chief's Guard, commanded by Captain George Lewis, May 1, 1777; at battle of Brandywine, Del., September 11, 1777; battle of Germantown, Pa., October 4, 1777; battle of Monmouth, N. J., June 28, 1778; rejoined regiment, September 26, 1778; at skirmish of Tappan, N. Y., September 28, 1778; discharged, Schuylkill Barracks, Philadelphia, Pa., December 13, 1779.

Born,[55] Ashford, Conn., June 20, 1755; married Lydia Stratton (born February 29, 1767; died, Windsor, N. Y., December 9, 1848), Northfield, Mass., February 21, 1786, by Rev. John Hubbard; died, Windsor, N. Y., February 23, 1839, with the following issue: Charles, born, Northfield, Mass., March 29, 1786, and died, Ouaquaga, N. Y., August 27, 1861 (married Malonia Badger); Patte, born, Windsor, N. Y., April 10, 1788, and died, Harpursville, N. Y., March 19, 1850 (married Dyer Chaffee at Ouaquaga, N. Y.); James, born, Windsor, N. Y., March 12, 1790, and died, Center Village, N. Y., April 15, 1871 (married Phebe Freeman); Caleb, born, Windsor, N. Y., January 11, 1792, and died, Center Village, N. Y., March 21, 1881 (married Julia Ann Lackey, Colesville, N. Y., August 26, 1824); William, born, Windsor, N. Y., August 24, 1793, and died, Windsor, N. Y., May 9, 1835 (married Elmira Stow, Windsor, N. Y., 1821); Elizabeth, born, Windsor, N. Y., July 14, 1795, and died, Center Village, N. Y., November 18, 1853 (married John Freeman); Henry, born, Windsor, N. Y., June 24, 1797, and died, Windsor, N. Y., March 10, 1845 (married Harriet Manville); Hezekiah, born, Windsor,

Revolutionary War.

N. Y., May 9, 1800, and died, Windsor, N. Y., February 4, 1883 (married Almedia Sonborger, North East, Dutchess County, N. Y., April 28, 1832); Ira, born, Windsor, N. Y., November 17, 1801, and died, Windsor, N. Y., March 10, 1871 (married Anna Doolittle, Colesville, N. Y., September 2, 1835); Sally, born, Windsor, N. Y., February 25, 1804, and died, Windsor, N. Y., June 5, 1877 (married David Hoadley, Windsor, N. Y., November 3, 1836); and Clarissa, born, Windsor, N. Y., March 16, 1806, and died, Deposit, N. Y., February 3, 1845 (married David Burrows, Windsor, N. Y., September 2, 1841).

LANDON, LABAN:* Enlisted, Hardwick, N. J., April 29, 1777, for three years, a private, Captain Nathaniel Tomm's Company, Colonel William Malcolm's Regiment, Continental Infantry; transferred, Valley Forge, Pa., February 1, 1778, to Captain Henry Luse's (9th) Company, Second New Jersey Regiment, commanded by Colonel Israel Shreve, Brigadier-General William Maxwell's Brigade; transferred, Valley Forge, Pa., March 19, 1778, to the Commander-in-Chief's Guard, commanded by Captain Caleb Gibbs; at battle of Monmouth, N. J., June 28, 1778; sick at Quaker Hill Hospital, November 26, 1778, to January 1, 1779; at battle of Connecticut Farms, N. J., June 7, 1780; skirmish of King's Bridge, N. Y., July 3, 1781; battle of Yorktown, Va., October 19, 1781; sick-hospital, September, 1782; furloughed, Newburgh, N. Y., June 6, 1783, until the ratification of the definite treaty of peace; discharged November 3, 1783.

Born,[56] Hardwick, N. J., January 13, 1759; occupation, farmer; married Elizabeth Gilless (born August 20, 1765; died, Le Roy, Pa., June 23, 1848), March 15, 1784; died, Troy, Pa., June 28, 1828, with the following issue: Laban, born September 2, 1785, and died April 28, 1869; Mahala, born March 29, 1787, and died April 5, 1787; Benjamin, born January 22, 1788, and died August 20, 1855 (married April 11, 1808); Ezra, born July 5, 1790, and died January 3, 1869; Levi D., born March 29, 1792, and died April 17, 1862; Elizabeth, born July 20, 1794 (married

THE COMMANDER-IN-CHIEF'S GUARD.

————— Ingram, January 30, 1821); Sarah, born October 5, 1796, and died October 5, 1796; Mercy, born October 5, 1796, and died October 5, 1796; Hannah, born August 9, 1797; Joshua G., born February 27, 1800, and died May 9, 1870 (married Diantha Rich, March 24, 1827); David S., born March 2, 1802 (married April 3, 1825); Catherine, born December 28, 1803; Nancy, born November 26, 1805 (married September 22, 1824); and Eldaah, born April 15, 1808.

LANGLEY, JASPER: Enlisted, Morristown, N. J., February 15, 1776, for one year, a private, Captain Peter Dickerson's (5th) Company, Third New Jersey Regiment, commanded by Colonel Elias Dayton; re-enlisted, Ticonderoga, N. Y., February 20, 1777, for three years, Captain Peter Dickerson's (1st) Company, Third New Jersey Regiment, commanded by Colonel Elias Dayton, Brigadier-General William Maxwell's Brigade; at battle of Short Hills, N. J., June 26, 1777; battle of Brandywine, Del., September 11, 1777; battle of Germantown, Pa., October 4, 1777; transferred, Valley Forge, Pa., March 19, 1778, to the Commander-in-Chief's Guard, commanded by Captain Caleb Gibbs; at battle of Monmouth, N. J., June 28, 1778; discharged, Morristown, N. J., February 16, 1780.

LARD, GEORGE: See George Layard.

LAW, JOSEPH:* Enlisted, Lebanon, Conn., June 20, 1776, for six months, a private, Captain James Clark's Company, Third Regiment, Connecticut State Troops, commanded by Colonel Comfort Sage; at skirmish of Harlem Plains, N. Y., Septembr 16, 1776; battle of White Plains, N. Y., October 28, 1776; discharged December 25, 1776; re-enlisted May 1, 1777, for three years, Captain Paul Brigham's Company, Eighth Connecticut Regiment, commanded by Colonel John Chandler; at battle of Germantown, Pa., October 4, 1777; defence of Fort Mifflin, Pa., November 12-16, 1777; transferred, Valley Forge, Pa., March 19, 1778, to the Commander-in-Chief's Guard, commanded by Captain Caleb

Revolutionary War.

Gibbs; at battle of Monmouth, N. J., June 28, 1778; promoted 3d corporal, September 1, 1778; promoted 2d corporal, March 1, 1780; discharged, Morristown, N. J., May 1, 1780.

Born[57] 1752; occupation, carpenter; married Dulana Fellows (born 1758; died, New Lebanon, N. Y., June, 1847), March 4, 1784; died, Canaan, N. Y., August 18, 1835, with the following issue: Joseph, born January 1, 1785, and died at Canaan, N. Y., unmarried; Wealthy, born February 22, 1787, and died, Canaan, N. Y., August 9, 1869 (married Collins Flint; born November 9, 1777, and died, Canaan, N. Y., June 17, 1855); Samuel, born May 2, 1789; Charles, born September 29, 1791 (married Lavica Pease); Laura, born October 17, 1793, and died at Richfield, N. Y. (married William Brown); Horace, born September 30, 1795; Anna P., born April 21, 1798, and died, Haydensville, Mass., October 12, 1885 (married Hezekiah Marks, Canaan, N. Y., March 25, 1821); and Mary Bethia, born July 4, 1803.

LAWELL, ABRAHAM: Enlisted January 1, 1777, for three years, a private, Captain George Lewis's Troop, Third Regiment, Continental Dragoons, commanded by Colonel George Baylor; assigned to the Cavalry of the Commander-in-Chief's Guard, commanded by Captain George Lewis, May 1, 1777; on rolls to August 1, 1777, without remark.

LAWRENCE, ELIJAH:* Enlisted, Stillwater, N. Y., March 1, 1780, for the war, a private, Colonel Seth Warner's Regiment, Continental Infantry; taken prisoner at battle of Fort George, N. Y., October 11, 1780, and confined two years at Montreal, Canada, when exchanged at Boston, Mass.; transferred, Newburgh, N. Y., December 24, 1782, from late Colonel Seth Warner's Regiment, Continental Infantry, to the Commander-in-Chief's Guard, commanded by Lieutenant-Commandant William Colfax; furloughed ninety-three days, December 29, 1782; furloughed, Newburgh, N. Y., June 6, 1783, until the ratification of the definite treaty of peace; discharged November 3, 1783.

Born,[58] Canaan, Conn., October 17, 1763; married, first,

The Commander-in-Chief's Guard.

Hannah Clark (died, Shefford, Canada East, 1796), Hinesburg, Vt., 1787; issue: Elijah, born March 22, 1789, and died unmarried; Alice, born October 17, 1790, and died unmarried; Clark, born December 12, 1793, and died unmarried; and Sallie, born April 5, 1795, and died unmarried; second, Lucinda Butterfield (married Daniel Benjamin November, 1820; residing at Claranceville, Canada East, 1852), Franklin, Vt., November, 1796, by Samuel Peckham, Esquire; died, West Shefford, Canada East, March 15, 1809, with the following issue: Lucretia B., born January 30, 1798, and residing at Claranceville, Canada East, 1852, unmarried; Samuel H., born October 16, 1799, and died, South Stukely, Canada East, August, 1878, unmarried; Sewell B., born July 20, 1801, and died, West Shefford, Canada East, June, 1878 (married, first, Lucena Davidson of St. Armand; second, Mrs. Almira D. Libbey January 7, 1847); Charles, born April 2, 1803, and died, Claranceville, Canada East, 1884, unmarried; Eliza B., born December 19, 1804, and died at South Stukely, Canada East, unmarried; Lucinda, born October 15, 1806, and died, Waterloo, Canada East, March, 1886 (married John Obart, South Stukely, Canada East, November 28, 1841); and Shepherd, born September 8, 1808, and died at South Stukely, Canada East, unmarried.

LAYARD, GEORGE: Enlisted, Newtown, Pa., January 1, 1777, for three years, a private, Captain George Lewis's Troop, Third Regiment, Continental Dragoons, commanded by Colonel George Baylor; residence, Massachusetts; assigned to the Cavalry of the Commander-in-Chief's Guard, commanded by Captain George Lewis, May 1, 1777; at battle of Brandywine, Del., September 11, 1777; battle of Germantown, Pa., October 4, 1777; battle of Monmouth, N. J., June 28, 1778; rejoined regiment, September 26, 1778; at skirmish of Tappan, N. Y., September 28, 1778; discharged, Schuylkill Barracks, Philadelphia, Pa., December 13, 1779.

LEARY, JOHN: Enlisted, Litchfield, N. H., January 1, 1776, for one year, a private, Captain Amos Morrill's Company, Fifth Regiment, Continental Infantry, commanded by Colonel John Stark; transferred, Cambridge, Mass., March 12, 1776, to the Commander-in-Chief's Guard, commanded by Captain Caleb Gibbs; at battle of White Plains, N. Y., October 28, 1776; battle of Trenton, N. J., December 26, 1776; discharged December 30, 1776; re-enlisted January, 1777, for three years, Captain Amos Morrill's Company, First New Hampshire Regiment, commanded by Colonel John Stark; on return dated Valley Forge, Pa., January 10, 1778, with remark "Left at Albany, and now sick on furlough; age, 24; height, five feet, seven inches; complexion, dark; hair, dark; eyes, dark; residence, Litchfield."

LESTER, BENJAMIN: Private, Virginia Line; transferred, Morristown, N. J., May 1, 1777, to the Commander-in-Chief's Guard, commanded by Captain Caleb Gibbs; on rolls to August 11, 1777, without remark.

LEVERICH, SAMUEL: Enlisted, Newtown, Pa., December 14, 1776, for three years, a private, Captain George Lewis's Troop, Third Regiment, Continental Dragoons, commanded by Colonel George Baylor; residence, Massachusetts; assigned to the Cavalry of the Commander-in-Chief's Guard, commanded by Captain George Lewis, May 1, 1777; at battle of Brandywine, Del., September 11, 1777; battle of Germantown, Pa., October 4, 1777; battle of Monmouth, N. J., June 28, 1778; rejoined regiment, September 26, 1778; at skirmish of Tappan, N. Y., September 28, 1778; discharged, Schuylkill Barracks, Philadelphia, Pa., December 13, 1779.

LEWIS, GEORGE: First Lieutenant, Commander-in-Chief's Guard, commanded by Captain Caleb Gibbs, March 12, 1776; at battle of White Plains, N. Y., October 28, 1776; detached, Newtown, Pa., December 14, 1776, to recruit a troop of cavalry; captain, Third Regiment, Continental Dragoons, commanded by Colonel George Baylor, January 1, 1777; detached and assigned to the command of the Cavalry of the Commander-in-Chief's Guard, May 1, 1777;

at battle of Brandywine, Del., September 11, 1777; battle of Germantown, Pa., October 4, 1777; battle of Monmouth, N. J., June 28, 1778; rejoined regiment, September 26, 1778; at skirmish of Tappan, N. Y., September 28, 1778; promoted major; served to close of war.

Born,[59] Fredericksburg, Va., March 14, 1757; married Catherine Daingerfield (born, "Coventry," Spottsylvania County, Va., June 25, 1764; died, "Marmion," King George County, Va., February 16, 1820), "Coventry," Spottsylvania County, Va., October 15, 1779; died, "Marmion," King George County, Va., November 13, 1821, with the following issue: Samuel, born, Berryville, Va., November 11, 1780, and died at "Shellfield," Westmoreland County, Va. (married Sarah Attaway Miller, Washington, D. C., September 15, 1803); Mary Willis, born, "Marmion," King George County, Va., June 24, 1782, and died, Pensacola, Fla., October 7, 1834 (married Colonel Byrd C. Willis, "Marmion," King George County, Va., November, 1810); and Daingerfield, born, "Marmion," King George County, Va., July 14, 1785, and died, "Marmion," King George County, Va., September 10, 1862 (married Lucy Pratt, "Smithfield," Spottsylvania County, Va., September 15, 1807).

LINTON, HEZEKIAH: Enlisted November, 1776, for three years, a private, Captain Charles Allen's Company, Second North Carolina Regiment, commanded by Colonel Alexander Martin; transferred, Valley Forge, Pa., March 19, 1778, to the Commander-in-Chief's Guard, commanded by Captain Caleb Gibbs; sick-absent, June and July, 1778; at battle of Connecticut Farms, N. J., June 7, 1780; on rolls to January 15, 1781, without remark.

LINTON, JESSE: Enlisted November, 1776, for three years, a private, Captain James Martin's Company, Second North Carolina Regiment, commanded by Colonel Alexander Martain; transferred, Valley Forge, Pa., March 19, 1778, to the Commander-in-Chief's Guard, commanded by Captain Caleb Gibbs; at battle of Monmouth, N. J., June 28, 1778; discharged, New Windsor, N. Y., October 31, 1779.

Revolutionary War.

Livingston, Henry Phillip: First Lieutenant, Commander-in-Chief's Guard, commanded by Captain Caleb Gibbs, June 2, 1777; at battle of Brandywine, Del., September 11, 1777; battle of Germantown, Pa., October 4, 1777; battle of Monmouth, N. J., June 28, 1778; promoted captain, December 4, 1778; on furlough from November, 1778, until resigned, March 26, 1779.

Logan, William: Private, Virginia Line; transferred, Morristown, N. J., May 1, 1777, to the Commander-in-Chief's Guard, commanded by Captain Caleb Gibbs; at battle of Brandywine, Del., September 11, 1777; battle of Germantown, Pa., October 4, 1777; on rolls to March 31, 1778, without remark.

Lothrop, Simeon: Enlisted, Bridgewater Mass., February 8, 1777, for three years, a private, Captain Noah Allen's Company, Thirteenth Massachusetts Regiment, commanded by Colonel Edward Wigglesworth; transferred, New Windsor, N. Y., July 5, 1779, to the Commander-in-Chief's Guard, commanded by Major Caleb Gibbs; deserted July 5, 1779; rejoined, Newburgh, N. Y., May 19, 1782; discharged, Newburgh, N. Y., December 23, 1782, by General Washington.

Born,[60] Bridgewater, Mass., May 4, 1760; married, first, Keziah Lothrop (born, Bridgewater, Mass., September 23, 1767), August 11, 1785; second, Margaret Nevens of Salem, Mass., 1807; died, Bridgewater, Mass., February 3, 1808, with the following issue: Hannah (married William Miller); and Keziah (married Ezekiel Wilson of Methuen, Mass., 1808).

Lovejoy, John: Enlisted, Andover, Mass., February 19, 1777, for three years, a private, Captain Benjamin Farnum's Company, Eleventh Massachusetts Regiment, commanded by Colonel Ebenezer Francis; transferred, Valley Forge, Pa., March 19, 1778, to the Commander-in-Chief's Guard, commanded by Captain Caleb Gibbs; at battle of Monmouth, N. J., June 28, 1778; killed by a horse October 17, 1778.

Born,[61] Andover, Mass., July 24, 1743, and died unmarried.

LOVELL, SETH: Enlisted, Mansfield, Mass., March 28, 1777, for three years, a private, Captain Moses Knapp's Company, Fourth Massachusetts Regiment, commanded by Colonel William Shepard; transferred, Valley Forge, Pa., March 19, 1778, to the Commander-in-Chief's Guard, commanded by Captain Caleb Gibbs; rejoined company and regiment March 30, 1778; discharged March 28, 1780.

Low, JEREMIAH: Enlisted, Newtown, Pa., December 14, 1776, for three years, a saddler, Captain George Lewis's Troop, Third Regiment, Continental Dragoons, commanded by Colonel George Baylor; assigned to the Cavalry of the Commander-in-Chief's Guard, commanded by Captain George Lewis, May 1, 1777; at battle of Brandywine, Del., September 11, 1777; battle of Germantown, Pa., October 4, 1777; killed at battle of Monmouth, N. J., June 28, 1778.

LUCAS, EPHRAIM: Enlisted, Wellfleet, Mass., January 1, 1776, for one year, a private, Captain Wentworth Stewart's Company, Eighteenth Regiment, Continental Infantry, commanded by Colonel Edmund Phinney; transferred, Cambridge, Mass., March 12, 1776, to the Commander-in-Chief's Guard, commanded by Captain Caleb Gibbs; at battle of White Plains, N. Y., October 28, 1776; battle of Trenton, N. J., December 26, 1776; battle of Princeton, N. J., January 3, 1777; discharged, Morristown, N. J., February 10, 1777.

LYNCH, MICHAEL: Private, Commander-in-Chief's Guard, commanded by Captain Caleb Gibbs; in arrest, New York, June 15, 1776; committed to prison in city hall, New York, July 12, 1776.

Revolutionary War.

Macomber, Zenas :* Enlisted, Plymouth, Mass., April 20, 1775, a private, Captain Abraham Hammatt's Company of Minute-men; re-enlisted May 1, 1775, for eight months, Captain Thomas Mayhew's Company, Sixteenth Regiment, Continental Infantry, commanded by Colonel Theophilus Cotton; re-enlisted January 1, 1776, for one year, Captain Thomas Mayhew's Company, Twenty-fifth Regiment, Continental Infantry, commanded by Colonel William Bond; transferred, Cambridge, Mass., March 12, 1776, to the Commander-in-Chief's Guard, commanded by Captain Caleb Gibbs; at battle of White Plains, N. Y., October 28, 1776; battle of Trenton, N. J., December 26, 1776; discharged, Newtown, Pa., December 30, 1776, and re-enlisted for three years, Captain George Lewis's Troop, Third Regiment, Continental Dragoons, commanded by Colonel George Baylor; assigned to the Cavalry of the Commander-in-Chief's Guard, commanded by Captain George Lewis, May 1, 1777; at battle of Brandywine, Del., Septembr 11, 1777; battle of Germantown, Pa., October 4, 1777; battle of Monmouth, N. J., June 28, 1778; rejoined regiment, September 26, 1778; at skirmish of Tappan, N. Y., September 28, 1778 —severely wounded and taken prisoner to New York; exchanged, and rejoined regiment; discharged, Schuylkill Barracks, Philadelphia, Pa., December 13, 1779.

Born 1754; occupation, physician; married, second(?), Hannah Huff (born 1786; residing in York County, Pa., June 22, 1843), York County, Pa., August 26, 1829, by Rev. Samuel Parke; died, York County, Pa., June 2, 1831, with issue.

Manning, Diah :* Enlisted, Norwich, Conn., July 10, 1775, a drummer, Captain Asa Kingsbury's Company, Twenty-ninth Regiment, Continental Infantry, commanded by Colonel Jedediah Huntington; at battle of Bunker Hill, Mass., June 17, 1775; discharged December 16, 1775; re-enlisted January 1, 1777, for the war, Fourth Connecticut Regiment, commanded by Colonel John Durkee; transferred, Valley Forge, Pa., March 1, 1778, to the Commander-in-Chief's Guard, commanded by Captain Caleb Gibbs; at battle of Monmouth, N. J., June 28, 1778; on furlough July and August, 1778; at battle of Connecticut Farms, N. J., June 7, 1780; skirmish of King's Bridge, N. Y., July 3, 1781; battle of Yorktown, Va., October 19, 1781; furloughed twenty days, March 4, 1782; promoted drum-major, July 1, 1782; furloughed twenty-five days, November 22, 1782; furloughed, Newburgh, N. Y., June 6, 1783, until the ratification of the definite treaty of peace; discharged November 3, 1783.

Born,[62] Norwich, Conn., August 24, 1780; married Anna Gifford (born October 14, 1762; died, Norwich, Conn., September 30, 1851), Norwich, Conn., April 27, 1784, by Rev. Joseph Strong, D. D.; died, Norwich, Conn., August 25, 1815, with the following issue: Samuel, born, Norwich, Conn., April 12, 1785, and died, Norwich, Conn., May 2, 1828 (married Polly Sisson, Norwich, Conn., November 14, 1809); Eunice, born, Norwich, Conn., December 28, 1786, and died, Brooklyn, Conn., December, 1823 (married De Lafayette Wilcox May 11, 1811); Joanna, born, Norwich, Conn., December 25, 1788, and died 1877 (married Jacob Lillie February 14, 1813); William Lord, born, Norwich, Conn., April 4, 1791, and died, East Hartford, Conn., April 22, 1856 (married Mrs. Betsey Guliver Roberts March 27, 1823); Asa, born, Norwich, Conn., August 31, 1793, and died September 10, 1793; Asa, born, Norwich, Conn., November 26, 1795, and died, Norwich, Conn., July 5, 1879 (married Betsey Butler November 26, 1817); Almira, born, Norwich, Conn., June 8, 1798, and died February 21, 1875 (married Henry M. Spencer May 5, 1824); and Joseph Terry, born, Norwich, Conn., November 12, 1801, and died, Hartford, Conn., February 7, 1852 (married Cynthia B. Storey).

MANNING, ISAAC:* Enlisted, Tewksbury, Mass., May 27, 1775, for eight months, a fifer, Captain Benjamin Walker's Company, Twenty-seventh Regiment, Continental Infantry, commanded by Colonel Ebenezer Bridge; at battle of Bunker Hill, Mass., June 17, 1775; re-enlisted January 1, 1776, for one year, Captain William Hull's Company,

REVOLUTIONARY WAR.

Nineteenth Regiment, Continental Infantry, commanded by Colonel Charles Webb; transferred, New York, July 16, 1776, to the Commander-in-Chief's Guard, commanded by Captain Caleb Gibbs; at battle of White Plains, N. Y., October 28, 1776; battle of Trenton, N. J., December 26, 1776; battle of Princeton, N. J., January 3, 1777; battle of Brandywine, Del., September 11, 1777; battle of Germantown, Pa., October 4, 1777; battle of Monmouth, N. J., June 28, 1778; furloughed sixty days, October 10, 1778; deserted December 10, 1778; rejoined, Ramapo, N. Y., July 1, 1780; at skirmish of King's Bridge, N. Y., July 3, 1781; battle of Yorktown, Va., October 19, 1781; furloughed thirty days, March 4, 1782; furloughed eighty days, November 26, 1782; furloughed, Newburgh, N. Y., June 6, 1783, until the ratification of the definite treaty of peace; discharged November 3, 1783.

Born,[62] Tewksbury, Mass., January 20, 1755; occupation, shoemaker; married Sarah Pike (born 1765; residing at Mt. Vernon, N. H., November 22, 1849), Amherst, N. H., April 13 (also given June 13), 1786; died, Tewksbury, Mass., June 27, 1825, with the following issue: Betsey (married Micajah Harrison); John Tyng, born 1789 (married Charlotte Baker, Boston, Mass., March 25, 1815); Rachel, died at Goffstown, N. H., unmarried; Lydia, born, Amherst, N. H., October 22, 1794 (married Samuel Worthley January 22, 1815); Benjamin, born, Amherst, N. H., March 28, 1798 (married Abigail B. Smith April 1, 1821); Henry, died, Topsham, Vt., March 1, 1880 (married Harriet ——————); Woodbury; and William, born, Mt. Vernon, N. H., about 1810, and died, Togus, Me., August 6, 1885 (married, first, Mary Ann Walker; second, Mary Caroline Kidder).

MANNING, ROGER: Enlisted, Norwich, Conn., February 19, 1777, for three years, a drummer, First Connecticut Regiment, commanded by Colonel Jedediah Huntington; at battle of Germantown, Pa., October 4, 1777; transferred, Valley Forge, Pa., March 19, 1778, to the Commander-in-Chief's Guard, commanded by Captain Caleb Gibbs; at

THE COMMANDER-IN-CHIEF'S GUARD.

battle of Monmouth, N. J., June 28, 1778; on furlough, October, 1778; discharged, Morristown, N. J., February 19, 1780.

Born,[62] Norwich, Conn., May 15, 1758; died spring of 1780, unmarried.

MAPES, PHINEAS: Enlisted May 11, 1777, for the war, a private, Captain John Santford's Company, Colonel William Malcolm's Regiment, Continental Infantry; transferred, March 1, 1779, with company to Colonel Oliver Spencer's Regiment, Continental Infantry, Brigadier-General William Maxwell's Brigade; assigned with Regiment and Brigade to Major-General John Sullivan's Division, Continental Army, engaged in an expedition against the Six Nations of Indians in Western Pennsylvania and New York, May 11 to October 26, 1779; transferred, Morristown, N. J., March 20, 1780, to the Commander-in-Chief's Guard, commanded by Major Caleb Gibbs; rejoined company and regiment, April 1, 1780; at battle of Connecticut Farms, N. J., June 7, 1780; battle of Springfield, N. J., June 23, 1780; transferred, January 1, 1781, to Captain James Gregg's Company, First New York Regiment, commanded by Colonel Goose Van Shaick; furloughed, New Windsor, N. Y., June 5, 1783, until the ratification of the definite treaty of peace; discharged November 3, 1783.

MARTIN, PETER:* Enlisted, Andover, Mass., February 19, 1777, for three years, a private, Captain Benjamin Farnum's Company, Eleventh Massachusetts Regiment, commanded by Colonel Ebenezer Francis; at battle of Stillwater, N. Y., October 7, 1777; transferred, Valley Forge, Pa., March 19, 1778, to the Commander-in-Chief's Guard, commanded by Captain Caleb Gibbs; at battle of Monmouth, N. J., June 28, 1778; furloughed thirty days, November 25, 1778; discharged, Morristown, N. J., April 1, 1780; re-enlisted, West Point, N. Y., March 12, 1781, for three years, Captain Seth Drew's Company, Second Massachusetts Regiment, commanded by Lieutenant-Colonel Ebenezer Sprout; at battle of Yorktown, Va., October 19, 1781; dis-

Revolutionary War.

charged, New Windsor, N. Y., June 9, 1783, by procuring a substitute, William Trout.

Born,[63] Andover, Mass., February 22, 1759; occupation, farmer; married Hannah Dean (born November 3, 1764; died, Newbury, Vt., March 15, 1840), Andover, Mass., March 7, 1786; died, Newbury, Vt., June 23, 1820, with the following issue: Peter, born, Andover, Mass., March 25, 1787, and died, Newbury, Vt., December 24, 1864 (married Catherine McKeith of Topsham, Vt.); Hannah, born August 17, 1789, and died, Bradford, Vt., August 30, 1872 (married Asher Hunkins of Bradford, Vt.); Elizabeth Wyman, born June 29, 1791, and died, Newbury, Vt., December 2, 1863 (married James Abbott, Newbury, Vt., July 6, 1820); Dorcas, born November 19, 1795, and died, Newbury, Vt., November 1, 1847 (married John F. Johnston, Newbury, Vt., January 6, 1827); Clarissa, born February 27, 1798, and died in 1800; and Samuel, born, Claremont, N. H., April 2, 1800, and died, Newbury, Vt., August 13, 1866 (married Anna Burroughs, Newbury, Vt., December 28, 1826).

MARTIN, WILLIAM :*‡ Enlisted, Monmouth, N. J., March 29, 1777, for the war, a private, Captain Abraham Lyon's (7th) Company, Fourth New Jersey Regiment, commanded by Colonel Ephraim Martin, Brigadier-General William Maxwell's Brigade; at battle of Short Hills, N. J., June 26, 1777; missing at battle of Brandywine, Del., September 11, 1777; rejoined October 1, 1777; at battle of Germantown, Pa., October 4, 1777; battle of Monmouth, N. J., June 28, 1778; transferred to Captain Richard Cox's (7th) Company, Third New Jersey Regiment, commanded by Colonel Elias Dayton, February 1, 1779; assigned with Regiment and Brigade to Major-General John Sullivan's Division, Continental Army, engaged in an expedition against the Six Nations of Indians in Western Pennsylvania and New York, May 26 to October 26, 1779; transferred, Morristown, N. J., March 20, 1780, to the Commander-in-Chief's Guard, commanded by Captain Caleb Gibbs; at battle of Connecticut Farms, N. J., June 7, 1780; skirmish of King's Bridge,

THE COMMANDER-IN-CHIEF'S GUARD.

N. Y., July 3, 1781—wounded in the neck by musket ball; battle of Yorktown, Va., October 19, 1781; furloughed, Newburgh, N. Y., June 6, 1783, until the ratification of the definite treaty of peace; discharged November 3, 1783.

Born November 15, 1760; married Susanna Buckingham (born December 9, 1766; residing at Plattekill, N. Y., November, 1841); Newburgh, N. Y., June 24, 1783, by Abel Belknap, Esquire; died, Ulster County, N. Y., March 31, 1807, with the following issue: Sarah, born July 1, 1784; Elijah, born August 31, 1787; Sophia, born April 30, 1792; Rachel, born January 5, 1794; James, born August 13, 1797; Solomon, born July 12, 1800; David, born January 22, 1803; and Stephen, born April 2, 1805.

McCARTHY, THOMAS: Enlisted, Newtown, Pa., January 14, 1776, for three years, a farrier, Captain George Lewis's Troop, Third Regiment, Continental Dragoons, commanded by Colonel George Baylor; assigned to the Cavalry of the Commander-in-Chief's Guard, commanded by Captain George Lewis, May 1, 1777; on rolls to August 1, 1777, without remark.

McCOWN, WILLIAM: Enlisted, New Windsor, N. Y., January 16, 1781, a private, Commander-in-Chief's Guard, commanded by Lieutenant-Commandant William Colfax; at skirmish of King's Bridge, N. Y., July 3, 1781; battle of Yorktown, Va., October 19, 1781; deserted, Philadelphia, Pa., February 11, 1782.

McCULLOCH, ALEXANDER: Private, Third Regiment, Continental Dragoons, commanded by Colonel George Baylor; assigned to the Cavalry of the Commander-in-Chief's Guard, commanded by Captain George Lewis, May 1, 1777; on rolls to August 1, 1777, without remark.

McDONALD, JAMES: Private, Seventh Maryland Regiment; transferred, New Windsor, N. Y., January 1, 1781, to the Commander-in-Chief's Guard, commanded by Lieutenant-Commandant William Colfax; at skirmish of

Revolutionary War.

King's Bridge, N. Y., July 3, 1781; battle of Yorktown, Va., October 19, 1781; deserted, Philadelphia, Pa., March 22, 1782.

McIntire, William:* Enlisted, Caroline County, Va., October 10, 1775, for one year, a private, Captain William Talifaferro's Company, Second Virginia Regiment, commanded by Colonel William Woodford; discharged, Williamsburg, Va., August 27, 1776; re-enlisted September 20, 1776, for three years, Captain John Willis's Company, Second Virginia Regiment, commanded by Colonel Alexander Spotswood; transferred, Morristown, N. J., May 1, 1777, to the Commander-in-Chief's Guard, commanded by Captain Caleb Gibbs; promoted 1st corporal, June 4, 1777; at battle of Brandywine, Del., September 11, 1777; battle of Germantown, Pa., October 4, 1777; promoted 4th sergeant, March 1, 1778; reduced to the ranks, March 19, 1778; at battle of Monmouth, N. J., June 28, 1778; discharged, West Point, N. Y., September 19, 1779.

Born 1753; occupation, farmer; married ——— Ford; residing in Gallatin County, Ky., August, 1826; issue: Wesley (married Eliza Gossett); Julia; Louis; and James.

Melsom, James: See James Milsom.

Milsom, James:* Enlisted, Haddonfield, N. J., June 14, 1776, for five months, a private, Captain Joseph Matlack's Company, Colonel Silas Newcomb's Battalion, Brigadier-General Nathaniel Heard's Brigade, New Jersey State Troops, assigned to Major-General Nathaniel Greene's Division, Continental Troops, on Long Island, N. Y., August 12, 1776; at battle of Long Island, N. Y., August 27, 1776; battle of White Plains, N. Y., October 28, 1776; discharged December 1, 1776; re-enlisted May 17, 1777, for the war, Captain Jonathan Pierson's Company, Colonel Oliver Spencer's Regiment, Continental Infantry, Brigadier-General Thomas Conway's Brigade; age, twenty; height, five feet five inches; complexion, dark; hair, brown; occupation, tanner; at battle of Short Hills, N. J., June 26, 1777; battle of Brandywine, Del., September 11, 1777; battle of Germantown, Pa., October 4, 1777—wounded in right shoulder by musket ball before the Chew House, and remained in hospital to January 1, 1778; on furlough to June 1, 1778; regiment assigned to Brigadier-General William Maxwell's Brigade, May, 1778; at battle of Monmouth, N. J., June 28, 1778; transferred to Captain Benjamin Weatherby's Company, March 1, 1779; assigned with Regiment and Brigade to Major-General John Sullivan's Division, Continental Army, engaged in an expedition against the Six Nations of Indians in Western Pennsylvania and New York, May 26 to October 26, 1779; transferred, Morristown, N. J., March 20, 1780, to the Commander-in-Chief's Guard, commanded by Major Caleb Gibbs; rejoined Company, Regiment and Brigade, April 1, 1780; at battle of Connecticut Farms, N. J., June 7, 1780; battle of Springfield, N. J., June 23, 1780; transferred to Captain Jonathan Holmes's Company, Second New Jersey Regiment, commanded by Colonel Elias Dayton, January 1, 1781; at battle of Yorktown, Va., October 19, 1781; transferred to Captain Nathaniel Bowman's Company, August 23, 1782; transferred to Captain Jonathan Holmes's (2d) Company, New Jersey Battalion, commanded by Lieutenant-Colonel Commandant John N. Cumming, Brigadier-General Elias Dayton's Brigade, March 1, 1783; furloughed, New Windsor, N. Y., June 5, 1783, until the ratification of the definite treaty of peace; discharged November 3, 1783.

Born, England, 1753 (also given 1757); married; residing in Gloucester County, N. J., April 8, 1818; died, February 19, 1826.

MITCHEL, REAPS:‡ Enlisted January, 1777, for three years, a private, Captain Buller Claiborne's Company, Second Virginia Regiment, commanded by Colonel Alexander Spotswood; transferred, White Plains, N. Y., August 1, 1778, to the Commander-in Chief's Guard, commanded by Major Caleb Gibbs; re-enlisted and furloughed one hundred days, January 18, 1779; at battle of Connecticut Farms, N. J., June 7, 1780; promoted 4th corporal, August 1, 1780; promoted 2d corporal, July 1, 1781; at skirmish of King's Bridge, N. Y., July 3, 1781; battle of Yorktown, Va., October 19, 1781; reduced to the ranks, March 1, 1782; promoted 1st corporal, October 23, 1782; sick, New Windsor Hospital, N. Y., December, 1782 and January, 1783; promoted 5th sergeant, March 1, 1783; furloughed, Newburgh, N. Y., June 6, 1783, until the ratification of the definite treaty of peace; discharged November 3, 1783.

Will dated February 28, 1803, admitted to probate, Sussex County, Va., August 4, 1803; heirs-at-law: wife, Susanna, and the following children: Martha (married Benjamin Turner), residing in King and Queen County, Va., June 10, 1844; Paul M.; Thomas B.; Henry; and Peggy (married William Elder), residing in King and Queen County, Va., June 10, 1844.

MONTGOMERY, JOHN:* Enlisted, Carlisle, Pa., January, 1776, for one year, a private, Captain Abraham Smith's Company, Sixth Pennsylvania Battalion, commanded by Colonel William Irvine; at battle of Three Rivers, Canada, June 8, 1776; re-enlisted March 3, 1777, for the war, Captain Herman Stout's Company, Tenth Pennsylvania Regiment, commanded by Colonel Joseph Penrose; at battle of Brandywine, Del., September 11, 1777; battle of Germantown, Pa., October 4, 1777; transferred, Valley Forge, Pa., March 19, 1778, to the Commander-in-Chief's Guard, commanded by Captain Caleb Gibbs; at battle of Monmouth, N. J., June 28, 1778; battle of Connecticut Farms, N. J., June 7, 1780; skirmish of King's Bridge, N. Y., July 3, 1781; battle of Yorktown, Va., October 19, 1781; furloughed, Newburgh, N. Y., June 6, 1783, until the ratification of the definite treaty of peace; discharged November 3, 1783.

Born 1756; residing near Blairsville, Pa., November 11, 1829.

MOOR, HEZEKIAH: Private, Commander-in-Chief's Guard, commanded by Captain Caleb Gibbs; deserted, New

York, June 17, 1776; age, twenty-two; height, five feet eight inches; complexion, dark; hair, black; residence, Salisbury, Mass.

MOORE, JONATHAN :* Enlisted, New York, N. Y., June 28, 1775, for six months, a private, Captain William Goforth's Company, First New York Regiment, commanded by Colonel Alexander McDougall; discharged, Albany, N. Y., December 28, 1775; re-enlisted, Hopewell, N. J., April, 1776, for one year, Captain Thomas Paterson's (2d) Company, Third New Jersey Regiment, commanded by Colonel Elias Dayton, assigned to Brigadier-General John Sullivan's Brigade, at New York, N. Y., May 2, 1776, and Major-General Philip Schuyler's Division, at Albany, N. Y., May 7, 1776; re-enlisted, Ticonderoga, N. Y., January 13, 1777, for the war, Captain Thomas Paterson's (2d) Company, Third New Jersey Regiment, commanded by Colonel Elias Dayton, assigned to Brigadier-General William Maxwell's Brigade, at Morristown, N. J., March 19, 1777; at battle of Short Hills, N. J., June 26, 1777; battle of Brandywine, Del., September 11, 1777; sick-absent, October and November, 1777; transferred, Valley Forge, Pa., March 19, 1778, to the Commander-in-Chief's Guard, commanded by Captain Caleb Gibbs; at battle of Monmouth, N. J., June 28, 1778; battle of Connecticut Farms, N. J., June 7, 1780; skirmish of King's Bridge, N. Y., July 3, 1781; battle of Yorktown, Va., October 19, 1781; furloughed, Newburgh, N. Y., June 6, 1783, until the ratification of the definite treaty of peace; discharged November 3, 1783.

Born[65] 1754; occupation, tailor; married Elizabeth Long (born, Germany, 1760; died, Bartholomew County, Ind.; September 1, 1855), Berkley County, Va., July 8, 1790, by Rev. Mr. Kemp; died, Bartholomew County, Ind., September 25, 1853, with the following issue: Hannah, born, Virginia, May 8, 179—, and died, Bartholomew County, Ind., 1859 (married Thomas Rogers at Lebanon, Ohio); Hugh, born, Virginia, August 2, 1795, and died at Marysville, Ohio (married Margaret Loux at Lebanon, Ohio); Mar-

REVOLUTIONARY WAR.

garet, born, Virginia, December 7, 1799, and died at Lebanon, Ohio, unmarried; Hosea, born, Virginia, February 11, 1803, and killed at Alamo, Tex. (married ——— Loux at Lebanon, Ohio); and Jonathan, born, Virginia, July 24, 1808, and died, Mooney, Ind., June 13, 1858 (married Barbara Hester, Lebanon, Ohio, 1833).

MORIARITY, DENNIS: Enlisted April 3, 1778, for the war, a private, Captain Michael Simpson's Company, First Pennsylvania Regiment, commanded by Colonel James Chambers; transferred, Morristown, N. J., March 20, 1780, to the Commander-in-Chief's Guard, commanded by Major Caleb Gibbs; at battle of Connecticut Farms, N. J., June 7, 1780; skirmish of King's Bridge, N. Y., July 3, 1781; battle of Yorktown, Va., October 19, 1781; sick in hospital at Philadelphia, Pa., March 1 to May 1, 1782; furloughed, Newburgh, N. Y., June 6, 1783, until the ratification of the definite treaty of peace; discharged November 3, 1783.

MORRILL, ———: Private, New Hampshire Line; transferred, Newburgh, N. Y., June 16, 1783, to the Commander-in-Chief's Guard, commanded by Lieutenant-Commandant William Colfax; on return dated Rocky Hill, N. J., October 22, 1783, with remark "Present."

MORRIS, JOHN: Corporal, New Hampshire Line; transferred, Newburgh, N. Y., June 16, 1783, to the Commander-in-Chief's Guard, commanded by Lieutenant-Commandant William Colfax, and assigned 3d sergeant; on return dated Rocky Hill, N. J., October 22, 1783, with remark "Present."

MORRISON, DAVID:* Enlisted, Londonderry, N. H., February 15, 1781, for three years, a private, Captain Caleb Robinson's Company, Second New Hampshire Regiment, commanded by Lieutenant-Colonel George Reid; transferred to Captain Joseph Potter's Company; transferred, Newburgh, N. Y., June 16, 1783, to the Commander-in-Chief's Guard, commanded by Lieutenant-Commandant

The Commander-in-Chief's Guard.

William Colfax; discharged, West Point, N. Y., December 20, 1783.

Born,[66] Londonderry, N. H., August 27, 1763; occupation, farmer; married Mary Kimball (born, Rochester, N. H., June 9, 1784; died, Alton, N. H., January 9, 1839), Rochester, N. H., March 27, 1788, by Rev. Joseph Haven; died, Alton, N. H., December 9, 1831, with the following issue: Daniel, born, Rochester, N. H., October 26, 1788, and died, Alton, N. H., October 31, 1869 (married Joanna McNiel); Isabella, born, Rochester, N. H., February 7, 1790, and died, Barrington, N. H., June 24, 1870 (married Daniel Caverly, Alton, N. H., January 27, 1831); Martha, born, Rochester, N. H., April 1, 1792, and died, Northwood, N. H., February, 1864 (married Daniel Dudley); Nehemiah, born, Rochester, N. H., August 21, 1794, and died, Candia, N. H., January, 1871 (married Mary French, New Durham, N. H., January 2, 1817); Mary, born, Rochester, N. H., July 10, 1796, and died, Alton, N. H., June 26, 1814, unmarried; Lydia, born, Alton, N. H., March 30, 1800, and died, Alton, N. H., August 17, 1897 (married Benjamin Bennett, Alton, N. H., January 10, 1822); David, born, Alton, N. H., October 6, 1803, and died, Alton, N. H., October 21, 1855 (married Sophia Nutter of Farmington, N. H.); and Jane, born, Alton, N. H., November 23, 1806, and died, Alton, N. H., January 9, 1879 (married Richard Furber October 25, 1827).

NICHOLAS, JOHN:*‡ Captain, First Virginia State Regiment, commanded by Colonel George Gibson, February 1, 1777; detached and assigned 1st lieutenant to the Commander-in-Chief's Guard, commanded by Captain Caleb Gibbs, May 1, 1777; rejoined regiment June 1, 1777; resigned September 30, 1778.

Born, Buckingham County, Va., 1757; married; died, Richmond, Va., April 29, 1836.

NORRIS, ———: Private, New Hampshire Line; transferred, Newburgh, N. Y., June 16, 1783, to the Commander-in-Chief's Guard, commanded by Lieutenant-Commandant William Colfax; on return dated Rocky Hill, N. J., October 22, 1783, with remark "Present."

Nott, Jesse: Enlisted, Walpole, N. H., March 2, 1777, for three years, a private, Captain Jason Wait's Company, First New Hampshire Regiment, commanded by Colonel John Stark; transferred, Valley Forge, Pa., March 19, 1778, to the Commander-in-Chief's Guard, commanded by Captain Caleb Gibbs; at battle of Monmouth, N. J., June 28, 1778; died, White Plains, N. Y., July 15, 1778.

Odell, Reuben: Enlisted January 24, 1777, for the war, a private, Captain Jonathan Langdon's Company, Twelfth Virginia Regiment, commanded by Colonel James Wood; transferred, Morristown, N. J., May 1, 1777, to the Commander-in-Chief's Guard, commanded by Captain Caleb Gibbs; at battle of Brandywine, Del., September 11, 1777; battle of Germantown, Pa., October 4, 1777; transferred, Valley Forge, Pa., April 1, 1778, to Captain Benjamin Casey's Company, Twelfth Virginia Regiment, commanded by Colonel James Wood; transferred, June, 1778, to Captain Michael Boyer's Company, Eighth Virginia Regiment, commanded by Colonel James Wood; transferred, May, 1779, to Captain Robert Gamble's Company; on rolls to December 1, 1779, without remark.

Odiorne, Samuel: Enlisted, Portsmouth, N. H., January 1, 1780, a fifer, Lieutenant-Colonel's Company, Third New Hampshire Regiment, commanded by Colonel Alexander Scammell; transferred, January 1, 1781, to Captain John Dennett's Company, Second New Hampshire Regiment, commanded by Lieutenant-Colonel George Reid; transferred, Newburgh, N. Y., June 16, 1783, to the Commander-in-Chief's Guard, commanded by Lieutenant-Commandant William Colfax; on return dated Rocky Hill, N. J., October 22, 1783, with remark "Present."

The Commander-in-Chief's Guard.

O'NEIL, WILLIAM: Enlisted, August, 1776, for three years, a private, Virginia Line; transferred, Valley Forge, Pa., May 1, 1778, to the Commander-in-Chief's Guard, commanded by Captain Caleb Gibbs; at battle of Monmouth, N. J., June 28, 1778; re-enlisted and furloughed one hundred and five days, January 18, 1779; deserted May 3, 1779.

PACE, WILLIAM: Enlisted January 23, 1777, for three years, a private, Captain Henry Conway's Company, Fourteenth Virginia Regiment, commanded by Colonel Charles Lewis; transferred, Morristown, N. J., May 6, 1777, to the Commander-in-Chief's Guard, commanded by Captain Caleb Gibbs; sick-hospital, June and July, 1777; at battle of Brandywine, Del., September 11, 1777; battle of Germantown, Pa., October 4, 1777; battle of Monmouth, N. J., June 28, 1778; re-enlisted and furloughed one hundred and ten days, January 18, 1779; rejoined September 1, 1779; at battle of Connecticut Farms, N. J., June 7, 1780; skirmish of King's Bridge, N. Y., July 3, 1781; battle of Yorktown, Va., October 19, 1781; promoted sergeant, June 4, 1783; furloughed, Newburgh, N. Y., June 6, 1783, until the ratification of the definite treaty of peace; discharged November 3, 1783.

PADDINGTON, JOHN: Enlisted, Pembroke, Mass., January 4, 1777, for the war, a private, Captain Isaiah Stetson's Company, Fourteenth Massachusetts Regiment, commanded by Colonel Gamaliel Bradford; transferred to the Commander-in-Chief's Guard, commanded by Lieutenant-Commandant William Colfax, June 23, 1781; deserted and captured August 31, 1781, and remained in hospital until June 26, 1782; deserted July 13, 1782.

PALMER, WILLIAM: Enlisted January 6, 1777, for three years, a private, Captain James Gray's Company, Fifteenth Virginia Regiment, commanded by Lieutenant-Colonel James Innes; transferred, Morristown, N. J., May 1, 1777, to the Commander-in-Chief's Guard, commanded by Captain Caleb

Gibbs; sick-hospital, June and July, 1777; at battle of Brandywine, Del., September 11, 1777; battle of Germantown, Pa., October 4, 1777; battle of Monmouth, N. J., June 28, 1778; discharged, Morristown, N. J., January 6, 1780.

PARKER, JOSEPH :* Enlisted, Fauquier County, Va., August 3, 1776, for three years, a private, Captain William Blackwell's Company, Eleventh Virginia Regiment, commanded by Colonel Daniel Morgan; transferred, Morristown, N. J., May 6, 1777, to the Commander-in-Chief's Guard, commanded by Captain Caleb Gibbs; at battle of Brandywine, Del., September 11, 1777; battle of Germantown, Pa., October 4, 1777; battle of Monmouth, N. J., June 28, 1778; discharged, West Point, N. Y., August 3, 1779.

Born March 25, 1756; occupation, farmer; married; residing in Fauquier County, Va., July 1, 1820; died September 18, 1821.

PARKS, FREDERICK :‡ Enlisted, Groton, Conn., December 16, 1776, for three years, a fifer, Captain Elisha Lee's Company, Fourth Connecticut Regiment, commanded by Colonel John Durkee; at battle of Germantown, Pa., October 4, 1777; defence of Fort Mifflin, Pa., November 12-16, 1777; battle of Monmouth, N. J., June 28, 1778; transferred, Middlebrook, N. J., February 1, 1779, to the Commander-in-Chief's Guard, commanded by Major Caleb Gibbs; re-enlisted for the war, August 25, 1779; at battle of Connecticut Farms, N. J., June 7, 1780; skirmish of King's Bridge, N. Y., July 3, 1781; battle of Yorktown, Va., October 19, 1781; furloughed, Newburgh, N. Y., June 6, 1783, until the ratification of the definite treaty of peace; discharged November 3, 1783.

Died, Delaware County, N. Y., about 1818, unmarried.

PATTON, JOHN :* Enlisted July 27, 1777, for the war, a private, Lieutenant David Zeigler's Company, First Pennsylvania Regiment, commanded by Colonel John Chambers; transferred, Morristown, N. J., March 20, 1780, to the

THE COMMANDER-IN-CHIEF'S GUARD.

Commander-in-Chief's Guard, commanded by Major Caleb Gibbs; at battle of Connecticut Farms, N. J., June 7, 1780; skirmish of King's Bridge, N. Y., July 3, 1781; battle of Yorktown, Va., October 19, 1781; furloughed, Newburgh, N. Y., June 6, 1783, until the ratification of the definite treaty of peace; discharged November 3, 1783.

Born 1754; occupation, tailor; residing at Doylestown, Pa., November 7, 1820, with wife Sarah; died January, 1840-1.

PEASE, JOHN: Enlisted, Londonderry, N. H., February 17, 1781, for three years, a private, Third Company, Second New Hampshire Regiment, commanded by Lieutenant-Colonel George Reid; transferred, Newburgh, N. Y., June 16, 1783, to the Commander-in-Chief's Guard, commanded by Lieutenant-Commandant William Colfax; on return dated Rocky Hill, N. J., October 22, 1783, with remark "Present."

PERRY, HENRY: Enlisted January, 1777, for three years, a private, Virginia Line; transferred, Valley Forge, Pa., March 19, 1778, to the Commander-in-Chief's Guard, commanded by Captain Caleb Gibbs; at battle of Monmouth, N. J., June 28, 1778; discharged, Morristown, N. J., January 31, 1780.

PHILLIPS, JOHN :* Enlisted, Bridgewater Mass., May 22, 1777, for three years, a corporal, Captain Judah Allen's Company, Second Massachusetts Regiment, commanded by Colonel John Bailey; at battle of Bemus Heights, N. Y., September 19, 1777; reduced to the ranks, October 10, 1777; transferred, Valley Forge, Pa., March 19, 1778, to the Commander-in-Chief's Guard, commanded by Captain Caleb Gibbs; at battle of Monmouth, N. J., June 28, 1778; furloughed fifty days, May 15, 1779; promoted 4th corporal, November 1, 1779; promoted 3d corporal, March 1, 1780; promoted 2d corporal, May 1, 1780; promoted 1st corporal, June 1, 1780; at battle of Connecticut Farms, N. J., June 7, 1780; promoted 3d sergeant, July 1, 1781; at skirmish

Revolutionary War.

of King's Bridge, N. Y., July 3, 1781; battle of Yorktown, Va., October 19, 1781; furloughed twenty days, March 4, 1782; promoted 2d sergeant, February 1, 1783; reappointed 2d sergeant, June 16, 1783; discharged, Rocky Hill, N. J., November 3, 1783.

Born,[67] Bridgewater Mass., 1756; married Jenett Young (born, Bridgewater, Mass., 1765; died, Bridgewater Mass., 1823), Bridgewater, Mass., 1784; died, Bridgewater, Mass., April 23, 1833, with the following issue: George Young, born, Bridgewater, Mass., February 7, 1788, and died, Ellenville, N. Y., August 14, 1861 (married Mrs. Bethia Lazell Mitchell December 29, 1812); Jenett, born, Bridgewater, Mass., 1790, and died, New York State, 1868, unmarried; Marquis Lafayette, born, Bridgewater, Mass., 1792, and died, Poughkeepsie, N. Y., 1875 (married, first, Jane Pell; second, Margaret Pitcher); Eunice Bass, born, Bridgewater, Mass., 1797, and died, Newark, N. J., 1890, unmarried; and Robert, born, Bridgewater, Mass., 1802, and died, Newburgh, N. Y., 1883 (married, first, Sarah Harris; second, Maria Merritt; third, ———— ————).

Pierce, Benjamin:[*] Enlisted, Wilton, N. H., February 27, 1781, for three years, a private, Captain Isaac Frye's Company, First New Hampshire Regiment, commanded by Colonel Alexander Scammell; transferred, Newburgh, N. Y., June 16, 1783, to the Commander-in-Chief's Guard, commanded by Lieutenant-Commandant William Colfax; discharged, West Point, N. Y., December 20, 1783.

Born,[68] Wilton, N. H., May 18, 1762; occupation, shoemaker; married, first, Dorcas Lovejoy (born, Wilton, N. H., April 16, 1762; died, Andover, Vt., August 15, 1817), Wilton, N. H., October 27, 1785; issue: Dorcas, born, Wilton, N. H., January 22, 1786, and died, South Londonderry, Vt., September 7, 1853 (Married Thomas Hall January 15, 1809); Polly, born, Wilton, N. H., April 29, 1787, and died, Londonderry, Vt., December 20, 1857 (married Daniel Dodge, Andover, Vt., July 26, 1810); James, born, Wilton, N. H., August 17, 1789, and died April 12,

1813 (married Mary Walker December 5, 1811); Abiel, born, Wilton, N. H., March 21, 1791, and died, Dodge's Corners, Wis., November 30, 1871 (married, first, Nancy Holt July 20, 1818; second, Hannah K. Manning April 13, 1830); Asa, born, Wilton, N. H., March 17, 1793, and died, Fort Wayne, Ind., December 7, 1858 (married Betsey Dodge, Andover, Vt., January 29, 1818); Alvah, born, Andover, Vt., October 6, 1796, and died, Andover, Vt., September 22, 1818 (married Dolly Baker September 21, 1817); Nancy, born, Andover, Vt., December 2, 1798, and died August 4, 1862 (married, first, Israel Jewett December 30, 1830; second, David Putnam); Alanson, born, Andover, Vt., August 27, 1801, and died, Weathersfield, Vt., April 20, 1851 (married Hannah Burton May 1, 1825); and Abel, born, Andover, Vt., April 1, 1803, and died June 25, 1832 (married Harriet Dodge, Andover, Vt., May 8, 1825); second, Mrs Nabby F. Dodge (born, Andover, Vt., 1785; died, Weathersfield, Vt., June 28, 1865), Andover, Vt., February 8, 1820, by Jonathan Putnam, Esquire; died, Londonderry, Vt., May 9, 1847, with the following issue: Abigail, born, Andover, Vt., November 25, 1820, and died at Farmer, Ohio (married George C. Mason April 7, 1842); James, born, Andover, Vt., December 22, 1822, and died October 21, 1842, unmarried; Lucy, born, Andover, Vt., June 17, 1825, and died, Weathersfield, Vt., February 7, 1896 (married Daniel P. Chittenden, Clarenden, Vt., September 11, 1851); and Benjamin Franklin, born, Andover, Vt., February 7, 1828, and died at Bethlehem, Pa. (married Julia Ely May 8, 1851).

PILLAR, JOHN: Private, Pennsylvania Line; transferred, Valley Forge, Pa., March 19, 1778, to the Commander-in-Chief's Guard, commanded by Captain Caleb Gibbs; at battle of Monmouth, N. J., June 28, 1778; sick-hospital, July 1, 1778; rejoined from hospital November 1, 1778; deserted, West Point, N. Y., November 14, 1779.

PINKSTONE, SHADRACK: Enlisted November 26, 1776, for three years, a corporal, Captain William Smith's Com-

REVOLUTIONARY WAR.

pany, Eleventh Virginia Regiment, commanded by Colonel Daniel Morgan; transferred, Morristown, N. J., May 1, 1777, to the Commander-in-Chief's Guard, commanded by Captain Caleb Gibbs, and assigned private; sick-absent, June, 1777; at battle of Brandywine, Del., September 11, 1777; battle of Germantown, Pa., October 4, 1777; sick-absent, June, 1778; discharged, Morristown, N. J., December 16, 1779.

PIPER, THOMAS: Enlisted, Gilmanton, N. H., May 24, 1777, for three years, a private, Captain James Gray's Company, Third New Hampshire Regiment, commanded by Colonel Alexander Scammell; transferred, Valley Forge, Pa., March 19, 1778, to the Commander-in-Chief's Guard, commanded by Captain Caleb Gibbs; at battle of Monmouth, N. J., June 28, 1778; furloughed sixty days, November 1, 1779; deserted April 1, 1780.
Born,[49] Stratham, N. H., April 4, 1756; died, Wolfboro, N. H., December 24, 1787; married; issue, four children.

PITCHER, ABNER:* Enlisted, Norwich, Conn., March 1, 1777, for three years, a private, Captain Benjamin Throop's Company, First Connecticut Regiment, commanded by Colonel Jedediah Huntington; at battle of Germantown, Pa., October 4, 1777; transferred, Valley Forge, Pa., March 19, 1778, to the Commander-in-Chief's Guard, commanded by Captain Caleb Gibbs; at battle of Monmouth, N. J., June 28, 1778; deserted, White Plains, N. Y., August 17, 1778.
Born 1754; occupation, farmer; residing with wife Abigail (born 1755) in Chautauqua County, N. Y., March, 1832; died April 16, 1832.

POLLOCK, ELIJAH:* Enlisted, Brookfield, Mass., May 1, 1775, for eight months, a private, Captain Peter Herod's Company, Fourth Regiment, Continental Infantry, commanded by Colonel Ebenezer Learned; re-enlisted, Hartford, Conn., January 1, 1776, for one year, Captain Ozias Bissell's Company, Seventeenth Regiment, Continental Infantry,

The Commander-in-Chief's Guard.

commanded by Colonel Jedediah Huntington; at siege of Boston; battle of Long Island, N. Y., August 27, 1776; battle of White Plains, N. Y., October 28, 1776; re-enlisted, Lyme, Conn., January 1, 1777, for the war, Captain Elisha Lee's Company, Fourth Connecticut Regiment, commanded by Colonel John Durkee; at battle of Germantown, Pa., October 4, 1777; defence of Fort Mifflin, Pa., November 12-16, 1777; transferred, Valley Forge, Pa., March 19, 1778, to the Commander-in-Chief's Guard, commanded by Captain Caleb Gibbs; at battle of Monmouth, N. J., June 28, 1778; battle of Connecticut Farms, N. J., June 7, 1780; skirmish of King's Bridge, N. Y., July 3, 1781; battle of Yorktown, Va., October 19, 1781; deserted, Newburgh, N. Y., May 20, 1782.

Born 1757; married; residing at Huron, Ohio, October 27, 1820; died August 25, 1824.

Pope, ———: Private, New Hampshire Line; transferred, Newburgh, N. Y., June 16, 1783, to the Commander-in-Chief's Guard, commanded by Lieutenant-Commandant William Colfax; on return dated Rocky Hill, N. J., October 22, 1783, with remark "Present."

Potter, Nathaniel: Enlisted, Newtown, Pa., December 14, 1776, for three years, a private, Captain George Lewis's Troop, Third Regiment, Continental Dragoons, commanded by Colonel George Baylor; assigned to the Cavalry of the Commander-in-Chief's Guard, commanded by Captain George Lewis, May 1, 1777; residence, Freetown, Mass.; at battle of Brandywine, Del., September 11, 1777; battle of Germantown, Pa., October 4, 1777; battle of Monmouth, N. J., June 28, 1778; rejoined regiment, September 26, 1778; at skirmish of Tappan, N. Y., September 28, 1778; discharged, Schuylkill Barracks, Philadelphia, Pa., December 13, 1779.

Prentiss, Thomas:* Enlisted, Cambridge, Mass., May 23, 1775, for eight months, a private, Captain Job Cushing's

REVOLUTIONARY WAR.

Company, Thirty-sixth Regiment, Continental Infantry, commanded by Colonel William Heath; at battle of Bunker Hill, Mass., June 17, 1775; re-enlisted, Dorchester, Mass., January 1, 1776, for one year, Captain Daniel Barnes's Company, Twenty-first Regiment, Continental Infantry, commanded by Colonel Jonathan Ward; transferred, Cambridge, Mass., March 12, 1776, to the Commander-in-Chief's Guard, commanded by Captain Caleb Gibbs, and assigned sergeant; at battle of White Plains, N. Y., October 28, 1776; battle of Trenton, N. J., December 26, 1776; discharged, Newtown, Pa., December 30, 1776.

Born[70] May 29, 1755; occupation, shoemaker; married Alice Parker (born, South Kingston, R. I., February 12, 1769; died, Huron County, Ohio, February 1, 1825), 1791; died, Watervliet, N. Y., June, 1838-9, with the following issue: John Sherman, born, Milo, N. Y., October 3, 1792, and died, Monroeville, Ohio, June 23, 1853 (married Margaret Fulton, Seneca, Ohio, February 12, 1818); Thomas I., born, Richelieu, Canada East, October 3, 1794, married; Susan, born, Richelieu, Canada East, October 15, 1796; Oliver, born, Stanbridge, Canada East, September 1, 1798, and died, Mt. Lebanon, N. Y., May 14, 1885, unmarried; Alice, born, Stanbridge, Canada East,, June 3, 1801, and died, Watervliet, N. Y., March 29, 1871, unmarried; Eliza, born, Highgate, Vt., May 9, 1803; Chauncey, born, St. Armand, Canada East, May 2, 1805, and died, Watervliet, N. Y., September 26, 1859, unmarried; Angeline, born, St. Armand, Canada East, September 26, 1807, and died, Watervliet, N. Y., March 7, 1839, unmarried; and Laura, born, Milo, N. Y., September 5, 1809, and died, Watervliet, N. Y., May 7, 1882 (married Abram Remar).

PRESTON, ROBERT :* Enlisted, Alexandria, Va., September 9, 1775, a private, Captain George Johnston's Company, Second Virginia Regiment, commanded by Colonel William Woodford; at battle of Great Bridge, Va., December 9, 1775; discharged, Williamsburg, Va., October, 1776, and re-enlisted for three years, Captain Peyton Harrison's Company, Second Virginia Regiment, commanded by Lieutenant-Colonel Alexander Spotswood; transferred, Morristown, N. J., May 6, 1777, to the Commander-in-Chief's Guard, commanded by Captain Caleb Gibbs; at battle of Brandywine, Del., September 11, 1777; battle of Germantown, Pa., October 4, 1777; battle of Monmouth, N. J., June 28, 1778; rejoined regiment, White Plains, N. Y., August 1, 1778; at siege of Charleston, S. C., March 29 to May 12, 1780; taken prisoner and released on parole.

Born 1748-9; occupation, farmer; married Nancy ——— (born 1761; died, Funkstown, Md., July 4, 1845), Protestant Episcopal Church, Pohick, Va.; died, Fairfax County, Va., May 2, 1827, with the following issue: Delilah, born 1786, and died, Virginia, 1830; John; Nancy; and Catherine, born 1791, and residing at Baltimore, Md., May 4, 1852, unmarried.

PRICE, WILLIAM: Private, Virginia Line; transferred, Morristown, N. J., May 1, 1777, to the Commander-in-Chief's Guard, commanded by Captain Caleb Gibbs; on rolls to August 11, 1777, without remark.

PRITCHETT, ANDREW: Enlisted December 9, 1776, for two years, a private, Captain George Stubblefield's Company, Fifth Virginia Regiment, commanded by Colonel Charles Scott; transferred, Morristown, N. J., May 6, 1777, to the Commander-in-Chief's Guard, commanded by Captain Caleb Gibbs; on rolls to August 11, 1777, without remark.

PULLEN, HENRY: Enlisted August, 1776, for two years, a private, Captain Burgess Ball's Company, Fifth Virginia Regiment, commanded by Colonel Charles Scott; transferred, Morristown, N. J., May 1, 1777, to the Commander-in-Chief's Guard, commanded by Captain Caleb Gibbs; at battle of Brandywine, Del., September 11, 1777; battle of Germantown, Pa., October 4, 1777; re-enlisted for three years, March, 1778; at battle of Monmouth, N. J., June 28, 1778; battle of Connecticut Farms, N. J., June 7, 1780; on rolls to January 15, 1781, without remark.

Revolutionary War.

PUSHEE, NATHAN: Enlisted, Lunenburg, Mass., June 27, 1775, for eight months, a private, Captain Phineas Cook's Company, Thirty-Seventh Regiment, Continental Infantry, commanded by Lieutenant-Colonel William Bond; re-enlisted, Newtown, Pa., January 1, 1777, for three years, a trumpeter, Captain George Lewis's Troop, Third Regiment, Continental Dragoons, commanded by Colonel George Baylor; assigned to the Cavalry of the Commander-in-Chief's Guard, commanded by Captain George Lewis, May 1, 1777; at battle of Brandywine, Del., September 11, 1777; battle of Germantown, Pa., October 4, 1777; battle of Monmouth, N. J., June 28, 1778; rejoined regiment, September 26, 1778; at skirmish of Tappan, N. Y., September 28, 1778; discharged, Schuylkill Barracks, Philadelphia, Pa., December 13, 1779.

PUTNAM, JOHN :*‡ Enlisted, Lyndeborough, N. H., March 1781, for three years, a private, Captain Isaac Farwell's Company, First New Hampshire Regiment, commanded by Colonel Alexander Scammell; transferred, New Windsor, N. Y., May 1, 1781, to the Commander-in-Chief's Guard, commanded by Lieutenant-Commandant William Colfax; rejoined regiment, June 1, 1781; transferred, Valentine's Hill, N. Y., August, 1781, to Captain Enoch Chase's Company; at battle of Yorktown, Va., October 19, 1781; transferred, October 31, 1781, to Captain Henry Bedkin's Troop, Colonel Charles T. Armand's Partisan Corps, Continental Troops; discharged, York, Pa., October, 1783.

Born,[71] Lyndeborough, N. H., 1763; married Olive Barron (born, Tyngsborough, Mass., February 24, 1765; died, Hartford, Vt., May 24, 1858), Lyndeborough, N. H., November 30, 1784, by Rev. Sewell Goodridge; died, Hyde Park, Vt., November 5, 1837, with the following issue: Olive, born, Lyndeborough, N. H., January 28, 178—, and died in Michigan (married Moses Collins of Bradford, Vt.); Sarah, born, Lyndeborough, N. H., October 5, 1786, and died, Emerald Grove, Wis., August 31, 1854 (married Ebenezer Chapin of Newbury, Vt., September 5, 1803);

The Commander-in-Chief's Guard.

Jonathan, born, Bradford, Vt., June 19, 1789, and died, Bradford, Vt., May 21, 1855 (married Mary Stockwell); Rebecca, born, Bradford, Vt., July 8, 1791, and died, Danville, Canada East, May 9, 1865 (married Isaac Stockwell); John, born, Bradford, Vt., May 22, 1793, and died, Johnstown, Wis., August 18, 1857 (married Mary Pickett of Bradford, Vt., March 28, 1819); Micah B., born, Bradford, Vt., 1795, and died, Bradford, Vt., 1797; Hannah, born, Bradford, Vt., March 17, 1797, and died, Holyoke, Mass., August 10, 1892 (married John Pearsons of Bradford, Vt., 1817); Ephraim, born, Bradford, Vt., July 30, 1799, and died, Bradford, Vt., September, 1837 (married Rachel Stoddard); Elizabeth, born, Bradford, Vt., February 22, 1802, and died, East Boston, Mass., March 8, 1850 (married Israel Prescott, Bradford, Vt., March 8, 1826); Lucy B., born, Bradford, Vt., May 14, 1803, and died, New Oregon, Iowa, September 17, 1871 (married Samuel Phelps Bliss of Fairlee, Vt., December 7, 1826); and William B., born, Bradford, Vt., August 8, 1807, and died, Cartwright, Wis., January 9, 1887 (married, first, Esther Brown of Fairlee, Vt., who died, Bloomer, Wis., February 6, 1869; second, Mrs. Eunice Wheeler Winship, Tunnel City, Wis., September, 1870).

RANDOLPH, HENRY :* Enlisted, Portsmouth, Va., November 3, 1776, for three years, a private, Captain Wiliam Grymes's Company, Fifteenth Virginia Regiment, commanded by Lieutenant-Colonel James Innis; transferred, Morristown, N. J., May 1, 1777, to the Commander-in-Chief's Guard, commanded by Captain Caleb Gibbs; at battle of Brandywine, Del., September 11, 1777; battle of Germantown, Pa., October 4, 1777; battle of Monmouth, N. J., June 28, 1778; promoted 5th corporal, September 1, 1778; sick-absent, October, 1778; discharged, Morristown, N. J., December 7, 1779.

Born January 18, 1757; married Polly Peterson Poythress; residing in Fayette County, Tenn., October 1, 1832, late of Amelia County, Va.

REVOLUTIONARY WAR.

RANDOLPH, ROBERT: Cornet, Captain George Lewis's Troop, Third Regiment, Continental Dragoons, commanded by Colonel George Baylor, February 2, 1777; assigned to the Cavalry of the Commander-in-Chief's Guard, commanded by Captain George Lewis, May 1, 1777; 1st lieutenant June 15, 1777, to rank May 1, 1777; at battle of Brandywine, Del., September 11, 1777; battle of Germantown, Pa., October 4, 1777; battle of Monmouth, N. J., June 28, 1778; rejoined regiment, September 26, 1778; wounded and taken prisoner at skirmish of Tappan, N. Y., September 28, 1778; final record unknown.

Born,[72] "Chatsworth," Henrico County, Va., 1755; married Elizabeth Carter (born, "Shirley," Charles City County, Va., 1761; died, "Eastern View," Fauquier County, Va., 1832), "Shirley," Va., 1785; died, "Eastern View," Va., September 12, 1825, with the following issue: Peter Beverly, born, "Eastern View," Va., 1786, and died, "Norwood," Powhatan County, Va., 1840 (married Lavinia Heth, "Black Heth," Powhatan County, Va., 1809-10); Eliza, born, "Eastern View," Va., 1787, and died, "Kinloch," Fauquier County, Va., 1864 (married Thomas Turner, "Eastern View," Va., 1803); Nancy, born, "Eastern View," Va., 1789, and died, Alexandria, Va., 1810 (married James L. McKenna, "Eastern View," Va., 1809); Charles, born, "Eastern View," Va., 1792, and died, "Kinloch," Va., December 20, 1863 (married Mary Mortimer, "Lisconny Cottage," Spotslyvania County, Va., 1825); Robert, born, "Eastern View," Va., 1794, and died, "Eastern View," Va., December 26, 1857 (married Mary Magill, Winchester, Va., 1829); Lucy, born, "Eastern View," Va., 1796, and died, "Shirley," Va., 1862 (married Dr. Richard C. Mason, "Eastern View," Va., 1820); Landonia, born, "Eastern View," Va., 1798, and died, "Norwood," Va., September, 1863, unmarried; and Mary Braxton, born, "Eastern View," Va., November 26, 1800, and died, "Shirley," Va., June, 1864 (married Hill Carter, "Eastern View," Va., November 20, 1817).

THE COMMANDER-IN-CHIEF'S GUARD.

RAYMOND, SAMUEL:[7] Enlisted, Middleborough, Mass., January 1, 1776, for one year, a private, Captain Isaac Dean's Company (also given Lieutenant Joshua Benson's Company), Twenty-first Regiment, Continental Infantry, commanded by Colonel Jonathan Ward; transferred, Cambridge, Mass., March 12, 1776, to the Commander-in-Chief's Guard, commanded by Captain Caleb Gibbs; at battle of White Plains, N. Y., October 28, 1776; discharged, Newtown, Pa., December 14, 1776, and re-enlisted for three years, Captain George Lewis's Troop, Third Regiment, Continental Dragoons, commanded by Colonel George Baylor; assigned to the Cavalry of the Commander-in-Chief's Guard, commanded by Captain George Lewis, May 1, 1777; at battle of Brandywine, Del., September 11, 1777; battle of Germantown, Pa., October 4, 1777; battle of Monmouth, N. J., June 28, 1778; rejoined regiment, September 26, 1778; at skirmish of Tappan, N. Y., September 28, 1778; discharged, Schuylkill Barracks, Philadelphia, Pa., December 13, 1779.

Born 1756; occupation, millstone-maker; residing in Lawrence Township, Hunterdon County, N. J., August 4, 1820; died March 2, 1823.

REDINGTON, ASA: Enlisted, Wilton, N. H., June 16, 1778, a private, Captain Samuel Dearborn's Company, Colonel Stephen Peabody's Regiment, New Hampshire Militia; discharged January 4, 1779; re-enlisted June 28, 1779, for one year, Lieutenant-Colonel's Company, Third New Hampshire Regiment, commanded by Colonel Alexander Scammell; discharged, West Point, N. Y., June 28, 1780; re-enlisted February 27, 1781, for three years, Fourth Company, First New Hampshire Regiment, commanded by Colonel Alexander Scammell; at skirmish of King's Bridge, N. Y., July 3, 1781; battle of Yorktown, Va., October 19, 1781; transferred, Newburgh, N. Y., June 16, 1783, to the Commander-in-Chief's Guard, commanded by Lieutenant-Commandant William Colfax, and assigned 1st corporal; discharged, West Point, N. Y., December 20, 1783.

Born,[78] Boxford, Mass., December 22, 1761; occupation, farmer and merchant; married, first, Mary Getchell, Vassalboro, Me., September 2, 1787; issue: Asa, born, Vassalboro,

REVOLUTIONARY WAR.

Me., July 4, 1789, and died, Lewistown, Me., June 5, 1874 (married, first, Caroline Sherwin, Ohio, September, 1817; second, Mrs. Sophia Longfellow at Portland, Me.); Samuel, born, Vassalboro, Me., April 27, 1791, and died, Waterville, Me., February 21, 1868 (married Nancy Parker at Waterville, Me.); Silas, born, Vassalboro, Me., May 12, 1793, and died, Waterville, Me., February 19, 1876 (married, first, Bethulah Stevens, Waterville, Me., December 24, 1820; second, Mrs. Caroline M. Phillips, Waterville, Me., March 20, 1844); William, born, Waterville, Me., November 22, 1794, and died, Waterville, Me., February 17, 1865 (married, first, Sophia Parker at Waterville, Me.; second, Harriet Pearson at Waterville, Me.); Harriet, born, Waterville, Me., April 8, 1796, and died, Waterville, Me., September 15, 1868, unmarried; Mary, born, Waterville, Me., February 20, 1799, and died, Waterville, Me., February 13, 1870 (married Elah Esty, Waterville, Me., January 9, 1820); George, born, Waterville, Me., November 20, 1800, and died at Waterville, Me., unmarried; Isaac, born, Waterville, Me., March 13, 1803, and died at Waterville, Me. (married Eliza Gilman at Waterville, Me.); and Emily, born, Waterville, Me., November 18, 1804, and died, Waterville, Me., December 3, 1880 (married Solomon Heath, Waterville, Me., November 13, 1831); second, Mrs. Hannah Hobby, Portland, Me., February 9, 1806; died, Waterville, Me., March 31, 1846, with above issue.

REED, DANIEL: Rank, private; transferred, Valley Forge, Pa., March 19, 1778, to the Commander-in-Chief's Guard, commanded by Captain Caleb Gibbs; on rolls to June 30, 1778, with remark "Sick-absent."

REEVES, SAMUEL:* Enlisted, Surry County, N. C., May 10, 1776, for two and a half years, a private, Captain Joseph Phillips's Company, Fourth North Carolina Regiment, commanded by Colonel Thomas Polk; at battle of Brandywine, Del., September 11, 1777; battle of Germantown, Pa., October 4, 1777; transferred, Valley Forge, Pa., March 19,

1778, to the Commander-in-Chief's Guard, commanded by Captain Caleb Gibbs; at battle of Monmouth, N. J., June 28, 1778; discharged December 9, 1778.

Born 1753; occupation, farmer; married Susannah Brack (born 1758; residing in Lincoln County, Tenn., September 16, 1843), Wake County, N. C., November 20, 1785, by Harry Mekins; died, Lincoln County, Tenn., October 12, 1834; issue: Malichi, born July 23, 1796, and residing in Lincoln County, Tenn., December 14, 1840.

REID, SAMUEL:* Enlisted, Cambridge, Mass., January 1, 1776, for one year, a private, Twelfth Regiment, Continental Infantry, commanded by Colonel Moses Little, and transferred to Major-General Charles Lee's Guard, commanded by Ensign Benjamin Gould; transferred to Major-General Artemas Ward's Guard, March 17, 1776; transferred, Fort Washington, N. Y., August, 1776, to Captain Edward Burbeck's Company, Colonel Henry Knox's Regiment, Continental Artillery; at battle of White Plains, N. Y., October 28, 1776; transferred, White Plains, N. Y., October 30, 1776, to the Commander-in-Chief's Guard, commanded by Captain Caleb Gibbs; at battle of Trenton, N. J., December 26, 1776; battle of Princeton, N. J., January 3, 1777; discharged, Morristown, N. J., February 10, 1777.

Born,[74] Fall River, Mass., August 4, 1756-7; occupation, farmer and tanner; married Charity Bourne (born, Swansea, Mass., 1754; died, Colchester, Conn., January 5, 1816), Swansea, Mass., 1778-9; died, Fall River, Mass., December 29, 1832, with the following issue: Mary, born September 12, 1779, and died, Assonet, Mass., February 15, 1848 (married Samuel Bragg); Samuel, born, Assonet, Mass., November 25, 1780, and died, Suffield, Conn., December 4, 1852 (married, first, Hopey Chance, born June 22, 1786, and died June 26, 1817—no issue; second, Endocia Taintor, Colchester, Conn., April 29, 1818, who died September 7, 1849); Elizabeth, born January 15, 1782, and died, Fall River, Mass., 1876-7 (married Edward Smith); Anna, born November 3, 1783, and died, Fall River, Mass., September

REVOLUTIONARY WAR.

8, 1866, unmarried; Charity E., born March 7, 1785, and died February 14, 1827 (married Nathan Swift, Colhcester, Conn., February 14, 1827); Jared, born February 29, 1788, and died June 16, 1854 (married Sallie Bigelow); Sarah, born March 7, 1790 (married Dudley Worthington October 12, 1814); Phebe, born December 20, 1791, and died, Fall River, Mass., December 19, 1889 (married William R. Shaw, Fall River, Mass., October, 1829); and Darius, born March 1, 1797, and died, Kentucky, March 30, 1849 (married, first, Caroline Roach, Kentucky, May 30, 1820; second, Ann Muir, Kentucky, March 12, 1829).

REILEY, WILLIAM: Enlisted, Lancaster County, Pa., November 18, 1777, for the war, a private, Third Pennsylvania Regiment, commanded by Colonel Thomas Craig; transferred, Valley Forge, Pa., March 19, 1778, to the Commander-in-Chief's Guard, commanded by Captain Caleb Gibbs; at battle of Monmouth, N. J., June 28, 1778; battle of Connecticut Farms, N. J., June 7, 1780; skirmish of King's Bridge, N. Y., July 3, 1781; battle of Yorktown, Va., October 19, 1781; deserted, Philadelphia, Pa., March 22, 1782.

REYNOLDS, SAMUEL: Enlisted, Boston, Mass., June 3, 1775, for eight months, a private, Captain Silas Ward's Company, Thirty-sixth Regiment, Continental Infantry, commanded by Colonel John Greaton; re-enlisted January 1, 1776, for one year, Captain Lemuel Trescott's Company, Sixth Regiment, Continental Infantry, commanded by Colonel Asa Whitcomb; "on command" with General Lee, November 27, 1776; re-enlisted, Newtown, Pa., January 1, 1777, for three years, Captain George Lewis's Troop, Third Regiment, Continental Dragoons, commanded by Colonel George Baylor; assigned to the Cavalry of the Commander-in-Chief's Guard, commanded by Captain George Lewis, May 1, 1777; at battle of Brandywine, Del., September 11, 1777; battle of Germantown, Pa., October 4, 1777; battle of Monmouth, N. J., June 28, 1778; rejoined regiment,

September 26, 1778; at skirmish of Tappan, N. Y., September 28, 1778; discharged, Schuylkill Barracks, Philadelphia, Pa., December 13, 1779.

RICE, DAVID: Sergeant, Virginia Line; transferred, Morristown, N. J., May 1, 1777, to the Commander-in-Chief's Guard, commanded by Captain Caleb Gibbs; promoted 1st sergeant, June 4, 1777; at battle of Brandywine, Del., September 11, 1777; battle of Germantown, Pa., October 4, 1777; reduced to 4th corporal, March 1, 1778; reduced to the ranks, April 1, 1778; on rolls to April 30, 1778, without remark.

RICHARDS, PETER: Sergeant, Captain Thomas Willington's Company, Sixth Regiment, Continental Infantry, commanded by Colonel Asa Whitcomb; transferred, Cambridge, Mass., March 12, 1776, to the Commander-in-Chief's Guard, commanded by Captain Caleb Gibbs; court-martialed, New York, September 11, 1776, and found guilty of abusing and striking Captain Gibbs, and sentenced to be reduced to the ranks and whipped thirty-nine lashes; sentence approved by the Commander-in-Chief, who ordered the punishment to be inflicted September 12, 1776, at 8 o'clock, A. M.; "on command" with General Washington by return dated November 27, 1776.

RICHMOND, ZEBULON:* Enlisted, Pelham, Mass., May 12, 1775, for eight months, a private, Captain Isaac Gray's Company, Sixth Regiment, Continental Infantry, commanded by Colonel Jonathan Brewer; re-enlisted January 1, 1776, for one year, Twelfth Regiment, Continental Infantry, commanded by Colonel Moses Little, and transferred to Major-General Charles Lee's Guard, commanded by Ensign Benjamin Gould; transferred to Major-General Artemas Ward's Guard, March 17, 1776; transferred, New York, August, 1776, to the Commander-in-Chief's Guard, commanded by Captain Caleb Gibbs; at battle of White Plains, N. Y., October 28, 1776; battle of Trenton, N. J., December

REVOLUTIONARY WAR.

26, 1776; battle of Princeton, N. J., January 3, 1777; discharged, Morristown, N. J., February 10, 1777.

Born,[75] Taunton, Mass., 1758; occupation, carpenter; married Susannah Beswick (born, Chesterfield, Mass., April, 1759; died, Springfield, Mass., October 17, 1845), Chesterfield, Mass., September 20, 1779, by Rev. Squire Mills; died, Springfield, Mass., February 5, 1832, with the following issue: Lucinda, born, Chesterfield, Mass., April 9, 1780, and died, Hinsdale, Mass., February 28, 1845 (married Jacob Booth, Peru, Mass., May, 1797); Wealthy, born, Chesterfield, Mass., 1782 (married Edward Hall of Hinsdale, Mass.); John, born, Chesterfield, Mass., December 11, 1784, and died, White Lake, Mich., November 29, 1869 (married Chloe McLouth of Cheshire, Mass., June 9, 1808); Ezra, born, Goshen, Mass., February 19, 1786, and died, Springfield, Mass., December 20, 1869 (married Mrs. Cynthia Lombard Dale, of Springfield, Mass., January 25, 1816); Emily, born, Goshen, Mass., May 24, 1789, and died, Springfield, Mass., September 12, 1838 (married Thomas Rodgers of Dalton, Mass., January 19, 1809); Betsey, born, Goshen, Mass., 1791, and died in Michigan (married William Smith of Dalton, Mass.); Zimri, born, Goshen, Mass., August 20, 1793, and died, Springfield, Mass., March 2, 1868 (married Sophia Vanhorn of Springfield, Mass., April, 1819); Susannah, born, Goshen, Mass., and died, Dalton, Mass., 1831 (married Waterman Smith of Dalton, Mass.); and Polly, who died in infancy.

RICKER, TIMOTHY:* Enlisted, Rochester, N. H., May 22, 1777, for three years, a private, Captain Frederick M. Bell's Company, Second New Hampshire Regiment, commanded by Colonel Nathan Hale; transferred to Captain James Carr's Company, October, 1777; transferred, Valley Forge, Pa., March 19, 1778, to the Commander-in-Chief's Guard, commanded by Captain Caleb Gibbs; sick-absent, June and July, 1778; sick-hospital, October, 1778; sick at Quaker Hill Hospital, November 26, 1778, to January 1,

1779, sick at Fishkill Hospital, January 1 to April 1, 1779; furloughed sixty days, May 15, 1779; deserted July 14, 1779.

Born 1753; occupation, farmer; residing at Milton, N. H., July 1, 1820, with wife Louisa (born 1761), and the following children: Louisa (born 1802), and George (born 1806).

ROACH, WILLIAM: Enlisted March 8, 1776, for three years, a private, Captain John Chilton's Company, Third Virginia Regiment, commanded by Colonel Thomas Marshall; transferred, Morristown, N. J., May 1, 1777, to the Commander-in-Chief's Guard, commanded by Captain Caleb Gibbs; at battle of Brandywine, Del., September 11, 1777; battle of Germantown, Pa., October 4, 1777; promoted 2d corporal, April 1, 1778; at battle of Monmouth, N. J., June 28, 1778; promoted 1st corporal, August 2, 1778; promoted 6th sergeant, September 1, 1778; promoted 5th sergeant, December 11, 1778; promoted 4th sergeant, August 25, 1779; promoted 3d sergeant, November 1, 1779; promoted 2d sergeant, January 1, 1780; promoted 1st sergeant, March 14, 1780; at battle of Connecticut Farms, N. J., June 4, 1780; on rolls to January 15, 1781, without remark.

ROBERTSON, JOHN: See John Robinson.

ROBINSON, DIXON: Private, Virginia Line; transferred, Morristown, N. J., May 1, 1777, to the Commander-in-Chief's Guard, commanded by Captain Caleb Gibbs; on rolls to August 11, 1777, without remark.

ROBINSON, JOHN: Enlisted December 22, 1776, for the war, a private, Captain Dirck Hanson's Company, Colonel James Livingston's Regiment, Continental Infantry; transferred, Morristown, N. J., March 20, 1780, to the Commander-in-Chief's Guard, commanded by Major Caleb Gibbs; at battle of Connecticut Farms, N. J., June 7, 1780; skirmish of King's Bridge, N. Y., July 3, 1781; battle of

REVOLUTIONARY WAR.

Yorktown, Va., October 19, 1781; furloughed, Newburgh, N. Y., June 6, 1783, until the ratification of the definite treaty of peace; discharged November 3, 1783.

RODAMER, CHRISTOPHER :* Enlisted, Reading, Pa., March, 1777, for the war, a private, Captain Peter Scull's Company, Third Pennsylvania Regiment, commanded by Lieutenant-Colonel Thomas Craig; at battle of Brandywine, Del., September 11, 1777; battle of Germantown, Pa., October 4, 1777; transferred, Valley Forge, Pa., March 19, 1778, to the Commander-in-Chief's Guard, commanded by Captain Caleb Gibbs; transferred to the Wagonmaster-General's Department, and assigned teamster to the Commander-in-Chief's baggage wagons, commanded by Wagonmaster Subert Cain, March 20, 1778; wounded by sabre-cut in face at the battle of Yorktown, Va., October 19, 1781; furloughed, Newburgh, N. Y., June 5, 1783, until the ratification of the definite treaty of peace; discharged November 3, 1783.

Born, Potts Grove, Pa., 1750; occupation, carpenter; residing at Montgomery, N. Y., October 31, 1828.

RUNDLETT, JONATHAN :* Enlisted, Epping, N. H., May 9, 1782, for three years, a private, Captain William Rowell's Company, Second New Hampshire Regiment, commanded by Lieutenant-Colonel George Reid; transferred, Newburgh, N. Y., June 16, 1783, to the Commander-in-Chief's Guard, commanded by Lieutenant-Commandant William Colfax; transferred,, November 9, 1783, to Colonel Henry Jackson's Regiment, Continental Infantry; discharged June 30, 1784.

Born 1763; occupation, farmer; residing at Gilmanton, N. H., August 3, 1820, with wife Rhoda, (born 1762) and daughter Rhoda (born 1807) ; died July 22, 1825.

SANBORN, ———: Private, New Hampshire Line; transferred, Newburgh, N. Y., June 16, 1783, to the Commander-in-Chief's Guard, commanded by Lieutenant-Commandant William Colfax; on return dated Rocky Hill, N. J., October 22, 1783, with remark "Present."

The Commander-in-Chief's Guard.

SANDERSON, ELNATHAN:* Enlisted, Deerfield, Mass., March 28, 1777, for three years, a private, Captain James Keith's Company, Eighth Massachusetts Regiment, commanded by Colonel Michael Jackson; at battles of Stillwater, N. Y., September 19 and October 7, 1777; transferred, Valley Forge, Pa., March 19, 1778, to the Commander-in-Chief's Guard, commanded by Captain Caleb Gibbs; at battle of Monmouth, N. J., June 28, 1778; discharged, Morristown, N. J., March 28, 1780.

Born 1759; occupation, baker; married Sarah Strickland (born 1759; residing at Whately, Mass., September 4, 1846), Greenfield, Mass., September 18, 1783, by Rev. Roger Newton; died, Sandgate, Vt., June 26, 1831; issue: Lyman, married.

SARGENT, ABLE: Enlisted, Hudson, N. H., May 15, 1782, for three years, a private, Captain Isaac Farwell's Company, First New Hampshire Regiment, commanded by Lieutenant-Colonel Henry Dearborn; age, 16; transferred, Newburgh, N. Y., June 16, 1783, to the Commander-in-Chief's Guard, commanded by Lieutenant-Commandant William Colfax; on return dated Rocky Hill, N. J., October 22, 1783, with remark "Present."

SAVORY, JOHN: Enlisted, Coventry, Conn., May 24, 1777, for three years, a private, Captain Paul Brigham's Company, Eighth Connecticut Regiment, commanded by Colonel John Chandler; transferred, Valley Forge, Pa., March 19, 1778, to the Commander-in-Chief's Guard, commanded by Captain Caleb Gibbs; at battle of Monmouth, N. J., June 28, 1778; discharged, Morristown, N. J., May 19, 1780.

SCHRIVER, JACOB: Enlisted April 19, 1777, for the war, a sergeant, Captain Samuel Sackett's Company, Fourth New York Regiment, commanded by Colonel Henry B. Livingston; reduced to the ranks, December 10, 1777; transferred, Valley Forge, Pa., March 19, 1778, to the Commander-in-Chief's Guard, commanded by Captain Caleb

Revolutionary War.

Gibbs; at battle of Monmouth, N. J., June 28, 1778; furloughed fifteen days, August 31, 1779;; at battle of Connecticut Farms, N. J., June 7, 1780; skirmish of King's Bridge, N. Y., July 3, 1781; battle of Yorktown, Va., October 19, 1781; furloughed, Newburgh, N. Y., June 6, 1783, until the ratification of the definite treaty of peace; discharged November 3, 1783.

SHERMAN, SAMUEL:* Enlisted, Coventry, R. I., May 3, 1775, for eight months, a private, Captain Edmund Johnson's Company, Twelfth Regiment, Continental Infantry, commanded by Colonel James M. Varnum; re-enlisted January 1, 1776, for one year, Captain ——— Gibbs's Company, Ninth Regiment, Continental Infantry, commanded by Colonel James M. Varnum; transferred, Cambridge, Mass., March 12, 1776, to the Commander-in-Chief's Guard, commanded by Captain Caleb Gibbs; at battle of White Plains, N. Y., October 28, 1776; discharged, Newtown, Pa., December 14, 1776, and re-enlisted for three years, Captain George Lewis's Troop, Third Regiment, Continental Dragoons, commanded by Colonel George Baylor; assigned to the Cavalry of the Commander-in-Chief's Guard, commanded by Captain George Lewis, May 1, 1777; at battle of Brandywine, Del., September 11, 1777; battle of Germantown, Pa., October 4, 1777; battle of Monmouth, N. J., June 28, 1778; rejoined regiment, September 26, 1778; at skirmish of Tappan, N. Y., September 28, 1778; discharged, Schuylkill Barracks, Philadelphia, Pa., December 13, 1779.

Born[16] October 23, 1756; married, first, ——— ———; issue: Olive (married Stephen Brunson); Abigail (married David Mann); Bashabee (married Mr. Mabee); Benson, born September 5, 1794, and died, McHenry, Ill., December 27, 1859 (married Wealthy Gates, Chittenango, N. Y., 1817); Betsey Elviva, born December 14, 1797, and died, Chicago, Ill., September 27, 1853 (married Hiram H. Scoville, Manlius, N. Y., March 23, 1819); and Samuel, died at McHenry, Ill. (married Elizabeth Dwelly); second, ——— ———; died, Manlius, N. Y., November 19, 1834, with the following issue: Jefferson Thomas; Thomas Jefferson, died unmarried; William Henry Harrison, died in California (married Catherine Pickle); and Sally (married Mr. Johnson).

SHERWOOD, MICAJAH: Enlisted November 21, 1776, for the war, a private, Captain Benjamin Walker's Company, Fourth New York Regiment, commanded by Colonel Henry B. Livingston; transferred, Valley Forge, Pa., March 19, 1778, to the Commander-in-Chief's Guard, commanded by Captain Caleb Gibbs; at battle of Monmouth, N. J., June 28, 1778; battle of Connecticut Farms, N. J., June 7, 1780; died December 1, 1780.

SHIPMAN, JOSEPH: Enlisted, Pequanac, N. J., November 12, 1775, for one year, a private, Captain Silas Howell's (2d) Company, First New Jersey Regiment, commanded by Colonel William Alexander (Lord Stirling), assigned to Brigadier-General John Sullivan's Brigade, at New York, N. Y., May 2, 1776; at battle of Three Rivers, Canada, June 8, 1776; re-enlisted, Morristown, N. J., January 5, 1777, for three years, Captain Silas Howell's (2d) Company, First New Jersey Regiment, commanded by Colonel Matthias Ogden, General William Maxwell's Brigade; at battle of Short Hills, N. J., June 26, 1777; battle of Brandywine, Del., September 11, 1777; battle of Germantown, Pa., October 4, 1777; transferred to Captain John Flahaven's Company, November 30, 1777; transferred, Valley Forge, Pa., March 19, 1778, to the Commander-in-Chief's Guard, commanded by Captain Caleb Gibbs; at battle of Monmouth, N. J., June 28, 1778; discharged, Morristown, N. J., February 16, 1780.

Born,[77] Springfield, N. J., May 8, 1757; married Annie Gillam (born Springfield, N. J., April 4, 1760; died, Springfield, N. J., March 18, 1813) died, Springfield, N. J., September 25, 1828, with the following issue: Matilda, born, Springfield, N. J., October 20, 1782, and died at Elizabeth, N. J. (married Jehiel Force); Susan W., born, Springfield,

Revolutionary War.

N. J., August 2, 1786, and died, Newark, N. J., January 22, 1842, unmarried; Charles Townley, born, Springfield, N. J., March 19, 1789, and died, Newark, N. J., December 11, 1864 (married Eliza Pierson Ross, Springfield, N. J., October 6, 1814); Eliakim, born, Springfield, N. J., March 29, 1791, and died at New Orleans, La.; Aaron, born, Springfield, N. J., May 5, 1794, and died, Newark, N. J., October 3, 1831 (married, first, Sarah Roberts, Newark, N. J., April 8, 1817; second, Sarah K. Druce, Newark, N. J., September 26, 1819); and Caleb Halsted, born, Springfield, N. J., 1797, and died, Brooklyn, N. Y., October 9, 1873 (married Harriet Holden, Newark, N. J., November 12, 1823).

SHOREY, JOHN:* Enlisted, Berwick, Mass., May 5, 1775, for eight months, a private, Captain Philip Hubbard's Company, Thirtieth Regiment, Continental Infantry, commanded by Colonel James Scammon; at battle of Bunker Hill, Mass., June 17, 1775; re-enlisted, Cambridge, Mass., January 1, 1776, for one year, Captain Jonathan Nowell's Company, Seventh Regiment, Continental Infantry, commanded by Colonel William Prescott; at battle of White Plains, N. Y., October 28, 1776; discharged, Peekskill, N. Y., January 1, 1777; re-enlisted May 21, 1777, for three years, Captain Daniel Pillsbury's Company, Thirteenth Massachusetts Regiment, commanded by Colonel Edward Wigglesworth; age, 24 years; height, five feet seven and three-quarters inches; complexion, dark; residence, Berwick; transferred, Valley Forge, Pa., March 19, 1778, to the Commander-in-Chief's Guard, commanded by Captain Caleb Gibbs; at battle of Monmouth, N. J., June 28, 1778; furloughed sixty days, November 1, 1779; deserted March 11, 1780.

Born,[18] Berwick, Me., 1755; married Mary Piper (born, Pembroke, N. H., May 30, 1762; residing at Wolfboro, N. H., July 11, 1820); died, Wolfboro, N. H., 1842, with the following issue: John, born, Wolfboro, N. H., January 10, 1780, and died, Jonesport, Me., January 16, 1861 (married Margaret Wilkins, Middleton, Mass., February 22, 1818); Lyford, died at Wolfboro, N. H. (married, first,

THE COMMANDER-IN-CHIEF'S GUARD.

Mercy Wiggin; second, Betsey Willey); Samuel; Susannah, died at Alfred, Me. (married John Lewis); Sarah, died at Tuftonborough, N. H. (married Samuel W. Hersey); Joseph, born, Wolfboro, N. H., June 15, 1792, and died, Lynn, Mass., July 3, 1865 (married Sylvia Howland Hall, Jonesboro, Me., September 10, 1818); Betsey, born, Wolfboro, N. H., July 26, 1796, and died, Jonesboro, Me., April 1, 1847 (married William Marston, Jonesboro, Me., 1822); and Mary, born, Wolfboro, N. H., March 20, 1799, and died, Jonesboro, Me., December 26, 1892 (married Thomas Flaherty at Jonesboro, Me.).

SIMMONS, WILLIAM: Enlisted May 10, 1777, for the war, a private, Colonel Thomas Hartley's Regiment, Continental Infantry; transferred, Sunbury, Pa., December 16, 1778, to Captain Andrew Walker's (5th) Company, Eleventh Pennsylvania Regiment, commanded by Colonel Thomas Hartley; transferred, Morristown, N. J., March 20, 1780, to the Commander-in-Chief's Guard, commanded by Major Caleb Gibbs; at battle of Connecticut Farms, N. J., June 7, 1780; on return dated April 8, 1781, with remark "Sick at Norristown, Pa."

SIMPSON, WILLIAM: Enlisted, Nottingham, N. H., May 27, 1781, for three years, a drummer, Fifth Company, First New Hampshire Regiment, commanded by Colonel Alexander Scammell; transferred, Newburgh, N. Y., June 16, 1783, to the Commander-in-Chief's Guard, commanded by Lieutenant-Commandant William Colfax; on return dated Rocky Hill, N. J., October 22, 1783, with remark "Present."

SLOCUM, JOHN :* Enlisted, Newport, R. I., May 7, 1777, for the war, a private, Captain William Tew's Company, Second Rhode Island Regiment, commanded by Colonel Israel Angell; transfered, Valley Forge, Pa., March 19, 1778, to the Commander-in-Chief's Guard, commanded by Captain Caleb Gibbs; at battle of Monmouth, N. J., June 28,

Revolutionary War.

1778; furloughed fifty days, May 15, 1779; at battle of Connecticut Farms, N. J., June 7, 1780—shot in knee and had leg amputated; transferred to the Invalid Regiment, commanded by Colonel Lewis Nicola, June 19, 1781; discharged at close of war.

Born,[79] Portsmouth, R. I., July 1, 1755; married Mrs. Sarah Callam Beard (died, Providence, R. I., November 30, 1835), Providence, R. I., March 19, 1783, by Rev. James Manning; died, Providence, R. I., October 8, 1828, with the following issue: Hannah, born, Providence, R. I., September 1, 1783, and died, Providence, R. I., 1869 (married John Peterson); William, born, Providence, R. I., November 24, 1784; Elizabeth, born, Providence, R. I., September 29, 1786, and died at Providence, R. I., married; Amasa Callam, born, Providence, R. I., August 10, 1789, and died, Providence, R. I., August 11, 1857, married; Samuel, born, Providence, R. I., January 26, 1791; Stephen, born, Providence, R. I., August 26, 1793, and drowned in Providence River, in 1820, unmarried; Mary Ann, born, Providence, R. I., July 13, 1795, and died, Providence, R. I., May 17, 1887 (married Charles A. Lake, Providence, R. I., June 14, 1812); Cyprian, born, Providence, R. I., July 13, 1795, and died, Providence, R. I., January 31, 1796; Charlotte, born, Providence, R. I., December 19, 1798, and died, Providence, R. I., July 18, 1864 (married Isaac Brown, Providence, R. I., January 12, 1821); and Alice, born, Providence, R. I., April 6, 1803, and died at Providence, R. I. (married George Bennett).

SMITH, FRANCIS: Enlisted December 22, 1776, for the war, a private, Captain Matthew Henderson's Company, Ninth Pennsylvania Regiment, commanded by Lieutenant-Colonel George Nagel; transferred, Morristown, N. J., March 20, 1780, to the Commander-in-Chief's Guard, commanded by Major Caleb Gibbs; at battle of Connecticut Farms, N. J., June 7, 1780; on return dated April 8, 1781 with remark "Present."

THE COMMANDER-IN-CHIEF'S GUARD.

SMITH, JESSE:[*] Enlisted, Newburyport, Mass., April 19, 1775, a private, Captain William Smith's Company of Minute-men; re-enlisted May 19, 1775, for eight months, Captain William Smith's Company, Fifth Regiment, Continental Infantry, commanded by Colonel John Nixon; re-enlisted January 1, 1776, for one year, Captain Adam Wheeler's Company, Fourth Regiment, Continental Infantry, commanded by Colonel John Nixon; transferred, Cambridge, Mass., March 12, 1776, to the Commander-in-Chief's Guard, commanded by Captain Caleb Gibbs; at battle of White Plains, N. Y., October 28, 1776; discharged, Newtown, Pa., December 14, 1776, and re-enlisted for three years, Captain George Lewis's Troop, Third Regiment, Continental Dragoons, commanded by Colonel George Baylor; assigned to the Cavalry of the Commander-in-Chief's Guard, commanded by Captain George Lewis, May 1, 1777; at battle of Brandywine, Del., September 11, 1777; battle of Germantown, Pa., October 4, 1777; battle of Monmouth, N. J., June 28, 1778; rejoined regiment, September 26, 1778; at skirmish of Tappan, N. Y., September 28, 1778; discharged, Schuylkill Barracks, Philadelphia, Pa., December 13, 1779.

Born,[50] Lexington, Mass., April 13, 1756; occupation, mariner; married Sarah Grant (born, Salem, Mass., January 15, 1761; died, Salem, Mass., August 21, 1840); died, Salem, Mass., June 4, 1844, with the following issue: Sarah, born at Salem, Mass., and died, Salem, Mass., May 9, 1835 (married Jeduthan Upton, Salem, Mass., May 12, 1807, who died, Havana, Cuba, August 21, 1815); Jesse, born, Salem, Mass., 1796—lieutenant U. S. Navy, and drowned on U. S. S. Hornet September 10, 1829 (married Hetty Smith at Salem, Mass.); and Abigail, died, Salem, Mass., 1856, unmarried.

SMITH, JOHN: Enlisted August, 1776, for three years, a private, Virginia Line; transferred, Morristown, N. J., May 1, 1777, to the Commander-in-Chief's Guard, commanded by Captain Caleb Gibbs; at battle of Brandywine,

REVOLUTIONARY WAR.

Del., September 11, 1777; battle of Germantown, Pa., October 4, 1777; battle of Monmouth, N. J., June 28, 1778; re-enlisted and furloughed one hundred days, January 18, 1779; deserted April 28, 1779.

SMITH, LUTHER:* Enlisted, Lyndeborough, N. H., February 28, 1781, for three years, a private, Captain Isaac Farwell's Company, First New Hampshire Regiment, commanded by Colonel Alexander Scammell; wounded in left leg by bayonet at skirmish of King's Bridge, N. Y., July 3, 1781; transferred, Newburgh, N. Y., June 16, 1783, to the Commander-in-Chief's Guard, commanded by Lieutenant-Commandant William Colfax; discharged, West Point, N. Y., December 20, 1783; served in war 1812-15.

Born,[51] Amherst, N. H., December 30, 1764; married Mrs. Azubah Smith (born November 24, 1770; died, Lewiston, N. Y., July 3, 1859), Lewiston, N. Y., January 1, 1822, by Rufus Spaulding, Esquire; died, Lewiston, N. Y., August 7, 1846.

SMITH, RANDOLPH: ‡ Enlisted January 1, 1777, for the war, a corporal, Captain Stephen Olney's Company, Second Rhode Island Regiment, commanded by Colonel Israel Angell; reduced to the ranks, October 1, 1778; transferred, Morristown, N. J., March 20, 1780, to the Commander-in-Chief's Guard, commanded by Major Caleb Gibbs; at battle of Connecticut Farms, N. J., June 7, 1780; skirmish of King's Bridge, N. Y., July 3, 1781; battle of Yorktown, Va., October 19, 1781; furloughed, Newburgh, N. Y., June 6, 1783, until the ratification of the definite treaty of peace; discharged November 3, 1783.

Residing at Ballston, N. Y., November 1, 1815.

SMITH, ROBINSON:* Enlisted, Deerfield, N. H., August 22, 1782, for three years, a private, Captain Samuel Cherry's Company, Second New Hampshire Regiment, commanded by Lieutenant-Colonel George Reid; transferred, March 1, 1783, to Captain Josiah Munson's Company; transferred,

The Commander-in-Chief's Guard.

Newburgh, N. Y., June 16, 1783, to the Commander-in-Chief's Guard, commanded by Lieutenant-Commandant William Colfax; transferred, November 9, 1783, to Captain Isaac Frye's Company, Colonel Henry Jackson's Regiment, Continental Infantry; discharged, West Point, N. Y., June 30, 1784.

Born[82] 1763; occupation, farmer; married Miriam ——— (born 1764; died, Murray, N. Y., 1837); died, Murray, N. Y., 1828, with the following issue: Nathaniel, died in Michigan (married Thankful Dodge); Isaac, died, Murray, N. Y., August 27, 1866 (married, first, Hannah ———; second, Sallie ———); Sarah, died in Michigan (married William Austin); Eunice (married Mr. Barclay); Joshua, born 1804, and died, Clarendon, N. Y., 1849 (married Jerusha Towsley); Nancy, born 1806, and died, Hindsburg, N. Y., 1885 (married Chauncey Burns); Lovinia, born 1808 (married Edwin Wansey); and Ezra, born 1810, and died at Vicksburg, Mich., married.

SMITH, SAMUEL:* Enlisted, Goffstown, N. H., April 23, 1775, for eight months, a private, Captain Samuel Richards's Company, Seventh Regiment, Continental Infantry, commanded by Colonel John Stark; discharged October 10, 1775; re-enlisted March 19, 1777, for three years, Captain Amos Morrill's Company, First New Hampshire Regiment, commanded by Colonel Joseph Cilley; transferred, Valley Forge, Pa., March 19, 1778, to the Commander-in-Chief's Guard, commanded by Captain Caleb Gibbs; at battle of Monmouth, N. J., June 28, 1778; re-enlisted for the war, September 26, 1779; at battle of Connecticut Farms, N. J., June 7, 1780; skirmish of King's Bridge, N. Y., July 3, 1781; battle of Yorktown, Va., October 19, 1781; furloughed, Newburgh, N. Y., June 6, 1783, until the ratification of the definite treaty of peace; discharged November 3, 1783.

Born,[83] Goffstown, N. H., December 21, 1757; occupation, shoemaker; married Margaret (born, Goffstown, N. H., November 13, 1764; died, Hartland, Vt., September 10, 1815); died, Gilsum, N. H., January 8, 1853, with the following issue: Abigail, born, Goffstown, N. H., March 10, 1785, and died, Hartland, Vt., March 17, 1852 (married ———— Jaquith); Sarah, born, New Boston, N. H., April 23, 1787; Betsey, born, New Boston, N. H., October 3, 1788, and died, Gilsum, N. H., January 8, 1837; Mary, born, Hartland, Vt., September 2, 1790, and died, Gilsum, N. H., April 6, 1851 (married David Ware); Abel, born, Hartland, Vt., November 27, 1793, and died, Hartland, Vt., September 30, 1803; Nancy, born, Hartland, Vt., March 13, 1796; John, born, Hartland, Vt., February 5, 1798, and died, Bangor, N. Y., March 24, 1841 (married Lucy Whitney May 27, 1824); Edith Clements, born, Hartland, Vt., January 20, 1800, and died April 8, 1827 (married ———— Bagley); Samuel, born, Hartland, Vt., November 9, 1801; Calista, born, Hartland, Vt., December 8, 1804, and died, Danville, Vt., April 24, 1842 (married Rev. George Fairbanks); William, born, Hartland, Vt., July 12, 1807, and died, Gilsum, N. H., April 1, 1870 (married Annis Eliza Newman June 9, 1835); and David McAllister, born, Hartland, Vt., May 29, 1809, and died, Springfield, Vt., November 1, 1881 (married, first, Lucy Barker Hemenway January 1, 1831, who died, Springfield, Vt., January 20, 1847; second, Sarah G. Burr, who died April 19, 1886, aged 57 years).

SMITH, TIMOTHY:* Enlisted, East Haddam, Conn., May 26, 1777, for three years, a private, Captain Christopher Darrow's Company, First Connecticut Regiment, Commanded by Lieutenant-Colonel Samuel Prentiss; at battle of Germantown, Pa., October 4, 1777; transferred, Valley Forge, Pa., March 19, 1778, to the Commander-in-Chief's Guard, commanded by Captain Caleb Gibbs; sick-absent, June and July, 1778; deserted August 7, 1779; shortly after, served one month on privateer sloop "Ranger" of New London; enlisted, Boston, Mass., October, 1779, on merchant ship bound for France; captured by British ships off Chesapeake Bay, taken to and confined on Jersey Prison Ship, New York, until exchanged, May, 1780; rejoined the Commander-in-Chief's Guard, April 22, 1782; discharged, Newburgh, N. Y., February 1, 1783, by General Washington.

Born 1758; residing at Tinmouth, Vt., June, 1820, with Lydia (born 1761), and daughter Sallie (born 1788).

SNOW, HENRY: Enlisted, Plymouth, N. H., February 6, 1777, for three years, a private, Captain Ebenezer Frye's Company, First New Hampshire Regiment, commanded by Colonel Joseph Cilley; transferred, Valley Forge, Pa., March 19, 1778, to the Commander-in-Chief's Guard, commanded by Captain Caleb Gibbs; at battle of Monmouth, N. J., June 28, 1778; died, Easton, Pa., October 1, 1779.

SPARK, HENRY:[*] Enlisted, Madison, Va., February 2, 1776, for two years, a private, Captain Oliver Towles's Company, Sixth Virginia Regiment, commanded by Lieutenant-Colonel James Hendricks; transferred, Morristown, N. J., May 6, 1777, to the Commander-in-Chief's Guard, commanded by Captain Caleb Gibbs; promoted 3d corporal, June 4, 1777; at battle of Brandywine, Del., September 11, 1777; battle of Germantown, Pa., October 4, 1777; discharged, Valley Forge, Pa., February 2, 1778; re-enlisted April, 1778, for six months, a private, Captain James Clark's Company, Colonel James Barbour's Regiment, Virginia Militia; re-enlisted March, 1780, for three months, Captain Edward Terrill's Company, Colonel James Barbour's Regiment, Virginia Militia.

Born,[84] Culpeper County, Va., June 16, 1753; married Lucy Clark (born 1761; residing in Owen County, Ky., May 29, 1839), Culpeper County, Va., January, 1776; died, Owen County, Ky., August 14, 1836, with the following issue: Elizabeth, born, Virginia, September 23, 1777, and died, Owen County, Ky., January 31, 1862 (married Leonard Smither in Owen County, Ky.); James, born, Virginia, December 11, 1779; Anthony, born, Virginia, January 7, 1781, and died, St. Joseph, Mo., 1865 (married Mary Sparks at Monterey, Ky.); William, born, Virginia, February 5, 1785; Thomas, born, Virginia, August 11, 1787; Mary, born,

REVOLUTIONARY WAR.

Virginia, December 14, 1790, and died, Owen County, Ky., about 1850 (married Joshua Wilboite in Owen County, Ky.); Reuben, born, Virginia, September 30,, 1792; Madison, born, Franklin County, Ky., August 10, 1795, and died, Owen County, Ky., August 13, 1873 (married Winnie Thomas in Owen County, Ky.); Rhoda, born at Monterey, Ky., and died, Henry County, Ky., about 1867 (married George Hill at Monterey, Ky.); John, born, Monterey, Ky., June 13, 1803, and died, Monterey, Ky., September 18, 1871, unmarried; A. Ivison, born, Monterey, Ky., January 8, 1807, and died, Greenup, Ky., June 28, 1879 (married, first, Mary A. Calvert in Franklin County, Ky.; second, Sallie A. Fades in Owen County, Ky.); and Henry, born and died at Monterey, Ky., unmarried.

STANDARD, JOHN: Private, Virginia Line; transferred, Morristown, N. J., May 1, 1777, to the Commander-in-Chief's Guard, commanded by Captain Caleb Gibbs; on rolls to August 11, 1777, without remark.

STOCKDELL, JOHN: Enlisted December 16, 1776, for three years, a private, Virginia Line; transferred, Morristown, N. J., May 1, 1777, to the Commander-in-Chief's Guard, commanded by Captain Caleb Gibbs; in hospital, August 11, 1777; at battle of Monmouth, N. J., June 28, 1778; discharged, Morristown, N. J., December 16, 1779.

STORM, JOHN: See John Sturm.

STOW, SIMEON: Enlisted January 1, 1777, for three years, a private, Captain George Lewis's Troop, Third Regiment, Continental Dragoons, commanded by Colonel George Baylor; assigned to the Cavalry of the Commander-in-Chief's Guard, commanded by Captain George Lewis, May 1, 1777; on rolls to August 1, 1777, without remark.

STRATTON, NEHEMIAH:[*] Enlisted, New Ipswich, N. H., June 29, 1777, a private, Captain Josiah Brown's Company,

Colonel Enoch Hale's Regiment, New Hampshire Militia; discharged July 12, 1777; re-enlisted July 12, 1777, Captain Stephen Parker's Company, Colonel Moses Nichols's Regiment, New Hampshire Militia; discharged September 20, 1777; re-enlisted August 10, 1778, Captain Robert Fletcher's Company, Colonel Enoch Hale's Regiment, New Hampshire Militia; discharged August 28, 1778; re-enlisted February 14, 1781, for three years, Captain David McGregor's Company, Second New Hampshire Regiment, commanded by Lieutenant-Colonel George Reid; promoted corporal, May 1, 1781; promoted sergeant, May 1, 1783; transferred, Newburgh, N. Y., June 16, 1783, to the Commander-in-Chief's Guard, commanded by Lieutenant-Commandant William Colfax, and assigned 1st sergeant; discharged, West Point, N. Y., December 20, 1783.

Born,[85] Concord, Mass., January 15, 1759; occupation, farmer; married, first, Sarah Pritchard (born, married and died at New Ipswich, N. H.); issue: Sally, born, New Ipswich, N. H., February 7, 1785, and died, Albion, Me., January 12, 1864 (married Benjamin Kidder, Albion, Me., 1808); and Hannah, born, New Ipswich, N. H., June 17, 1786, and died, New Ipswich, N. H., March 9, 1871 (married, first, Dr. Sprague of Boston, Mass.; second, Stephen Wheeler, New Ipswich, N. H., December 4, 1818); second, Lois Newhall (born, New Ipswich, N. H., 1769; died, Albion, Me., December 8, 1846), New Ipswich, N. H., 1787; died, Albion, Me., November 25, 1843, with the following issue: Ebenezer, born, New Ipswich, N. H., June 24, 1788, and died, Newport, Me., March 4, 1876 (married Prudelia White, Albion, Me., December 28, 1817); George, born, New Ipswich, N. H., February 10, 1790, and died at Kaskaskia, Ill., married—no issue; Charles, born, New Ipswich, N. H., December 24, 1792, and died, Clio, Pike County, Ill., August, 1846 (married Mrs. Harriet Beard Fulton); James, born, New Ipswich, N. H., November 21, 1794, and died, Albion, Me., January 20, 1864 (married Rachel Kidder); Onesimus, born, New Ipswich, N. H., November 16, 1796, and died, Albion, Me., 1813, unmarried; William, born January 14,

REVOLUTIONARY WAR.

1799, and died, Albion, Me., April 26, 1851 (married Jane Stratton); Nancy, born June 30, 1801, and died, Athens, Me., August 22, 1838 (married Joseph Tuck); Jonas, born, Albion, Me., June 1, 1803, and died, Plainville, Ill., January 5, 1888 (married, first, Malinda Hull; second, Sophia Boxley; third, Elizabeth Harvey; fourth, Mrs. Susan J. Elsworth); Roxy, born, Albion, Me., April 30, 1805, and died at Plainville, Ill. (married Benjamin Webb of Albion, Me.); Mehitable, born, Albion, Me., March 13, 1807 (married Rev. Joel Miller of Albion, Me.); Newell, born, Albion, Me., June 2, 1809, and died, Chicago, Ill., August 23, 1849 (married Abbie Dunham of Bangor, Me.); and Almon, born, Albion, Me., May 22, 1811, and died at Searsport, Me. (married Sarah Dow of Searsport, Me.).

STRIPE, JOSEPH: Private, Virginia Line; transferred, Morristown, N. J., May 1, 1777, to the Commander-in-Chief's Guard, commanded by Captain Caleb Gibbs; on rolls to August 11, 1777, without remark.

STURM, JOHN: Enlisted December 11, 1776, for three years, a sergeant, Captain Joseph Mitchell's Company, Twelfth Virginia Regiment, commanded by Colonel James Wood; transferred, Morristown, N. J., May 6, 1777, to the Commander-in-Chief's Guard, commanded by Captain Caleb Gibbs; promoted 4th sergeant, June 4, 1777; at battle of Brandywine, Del., September 11, 1777; battle of Germantown, Pa., October 4, 1777; promoted 3d sergeant, March 1, 1777; sick-absent, June and July, 1778; re-enlisted and furloughed ninety days, January 18, 1779; deserted April 18, 1779.

STURTEVANT, SETH :* Enlisted, Halifax, Mass., June 1, 1777, for three years, a private, Captain Amos Cogswell's Company, Ninth Massachusetts Regiment, commanded by Colonel James Wesson; at battle of Stillwater, N. Y., October 7, 1777; transferred, Valley Forge, Pa., March 19, 1778, to the Commander-in-Chief's Guard, commanded by

THE COMMANDER-IN-CHIEF'S GUARD.

Captain Caleb Gibbs; promoted 4th corporal, June 1, 1778; at battle of Monmouth, N. J., June 28, 1778; promoted 3d corporal, August 2, 1778; promoted 1st corporal, September 1, 1778; discharged, Morristown, N. J., June 1,, 1780.

Born,[86] Halifax, Mass., June 4, 1760; married Abigail Cushing of Duxbury, Mass.; died, Hartford, Me., July 11, 1852, with the following issue: Earl Pierce, born at Halifax, Mass., and died at Sumner, Me.; Sophia, born at Halifax, Mass., and died at Sumner, Me. (married Zenas Stetson); Martha, born, Sumner, Me., December 5, 1795, and died, Hartford, Me., November 28, 1893 (married Captain Hopestill Bisbee); and Abigail, born at Sumner, Me., and died at Hartford, Me. (married Jacob Brown).

SUTTON, MICHAEL: Enlisted, Canterbury, N. H., March 23, 1781, for three years, a private, First Company, First New Hampshire Regiment, commanded by Colonel Alexander Scammell; transferred, Newburgh, N. Y., June 16, 1783, to the Commander-in-Chief's Guard, commanded by Lieutenant-Commandant William Colfax; on return dated Rocky Hill, N. J., October 22, 1783, with remark "Present."

TALBOT, LEVI:* Enlisted September 9, 1775, for one year, a private, Captain George Johnston's Company, Second Virginia Regiment, commanded by Colonel William Woodford; re-enlisted September 3, 1776, for three years, a corporal, Captain Thomas Tebb's Company, Second Virginia Regiment, commanded by Colonel William Woodford; transferred, Morristown, N. J., May 6, 1777, to the Commander-in-Chief's Guard, commanded by Captain Caleb Gibbs; promoted 4th corporal, June 4, 1777; at battle of Brandywine, Del., September 11, 1777; battle of Germantown, Pa., October 4, 1777; promoted 2d corporal, March 1, 1778; reduced to the ranks, March 19, 1778; at battle of Monmouth, N. J., June 28, 1778; dismissed, White Plains, N. Y., August 1, 1778.

Born 1752; occupation, cooper; residing at Alexandria,

Revolutionary War.

Va., May 30, 1820, with wife Elizabeth (born 1765), and daughter Helen (born 1808).

TANNER, WILLIAM:‡ Enlisted May, 1777, for the war, a corporal, Captain Coggeshall Olney's Company, Second Rhode Island Regiment, commanded by Colonel Israel Angell; transferred, Valley Forge, Pa., March 19, 1778, to the Commander-in-Chief's Guard, commanded by Captain Caleb Gibbs, and assigned private; at battle of Monmouth, N. J., June 28, 1778; furloughed fifty days, May 15, 1779; at battle of Connecticut Farms, N. J., June 7, 1780; skirmish of King's Bridge, N. Y., July 3, 1781; battle of Yorktown, Va., October 19, 1781; furloughed, Newburgh, N. Y., June 6, 1783, until the ratification of the definite treaty of peace; discharged November 3, 1783.

THOMPSON, DANIEL:* Enlisted, Fishkill, N. Y., April 1, 1777, for three years, a private, Captain Charles Graham's Company, Second New York Regiment, commanded by Colonel Philip Van Cortlandt; at battles of Stillwater, N. Y., September 19 and October 7, 1777; transferred, Valley Forge, Pa., March 19, 1778, to the Commander-in-Chief's Guard, commanded by Captain Caleb Gibbs; at battle of Monmouth, N. J., June 28, 1778; discharged, Morristown, N. J., April 1, 1780.

Born 1754; married; residing at Reusselaerville, N. Y., August, 1820; died March 3, 1835.

THOMPSON, REUBEN: Enlisted January 13, 1777, for the war, a private, Captain William Tew's Company, Second Rhode Island Regiment, commanded by Colonel Israel Angell; transferred, Moristown, N. J., March 20, 1780, to the Commander-in-Chief's Guard, commanded by Major Caleb Gibbs; at battle of Connecticut Farms, N. J., June 7, 1780; skirmish of King's Bridge, N. Y., July 3, 1781; battle of Yorktown, Va., October 19, 1781; furloughed, Newburgh, N. Y., June 6, 1783, until the ratification of the definite treaty of peace; discharged November 3, 1783.

The Commander-in-Chief's Guard.

THURSTON, EZEKIEL: Enlisted, Deerfield, N. H., March 8, 1781, for three years, a private, Third Company, First New Hampshire Regiment, commanded by Colonel Alexander Scammell; transferred, Newburgh, N. Y., June 16, 1783, to the Commander-in-Chief's Guard, commanded by Lieutenant-Commandant William Colfax; on return dated Rocky Hill, N. J., October 22, 1783, with remark "Present."

Born,[87] Epping, N. H., May 28, 1765; occupation, sea-captain; married Mrs. Bray; died, Savannah, Ga., 1809, with the following issue: Samuel, born, Portland, Me., 1802, and died, Portland, Me., September 25, 1841 (married Mary Tucker of Cape Elizabeth, Me., May 6, 1824); John, died at Portland, Me. (married Susan Libby January 12, 1825); Eliza, born, Portland, Me., 1806, and died, Portland, Me., February 28, 1837 (married John Dela, Portland, Me., October 13, 1821); and Gilman, drowned near Portland, Me., September 13, 1860.

TIMBERLAKE, JOSEPH:‡ Enlisted, Louisa County, Va., February 28, 1776, for three years, a private, Captain Matthew Dewitt's Company, Seventh Virginia Regiment, commanded by Colonel Alexander McClenachan; transferred, Morristown, N. J., May 1, 1777, to the Commander-in-Chief's Guard, commanded by Captain Caleb Gibbs; at battle of Brandywine, Del., September 11, 1777; battle of Germantown, Pa., October 4, 1777; battle of Monmouth, N. J., June 28, 1778; in arrest, Fredericksburg, N. Y., October 8, 1778; court-martialed October 16, 1778, and found guilty of striking Lieutenant David Zeigler and sentenced to receive one hundred lashes; sentence approved by the Commander-in-Chief October 23, 1778, to take effect October 24, 1778, at 9 A. M.; re-enlisted and furloughed one hundred and five days, January 18, 1779; at battle of Connecticut Farms, N. J., June 7, 1780; skirmish of King's Bridge, N. Y., July 3, 1781; battle of Yorktown, Va., October 19, 1781; promoted sergeant, June 4, 1783; furloughed, Newburgh, N. Y., June 6, 1783, until the ratification of the definite treaty of peace; discharged November 3, 1783.

Revolutionary War.

Born,[88] Virginia, 1752; occupation, farmer; married Annie Douglass (born in Virginia, and died in Russell County, Ky); died, Hart County, Ky., 1841, with the following issue: Philip, born in Virginia, and died in Arkansas (married ———— Williams in Cumberland County, Ky.); Joseph, born, Virginia, 1788, and died, Hart County, Ky., 1860 (married Hannah Dye in Green County, Ky.); John; Charles, born in Virginia, and died in Tennessee, married; Annie, born in Virginia, and died in La Rue County, Ky. (married James Jackman in Cumberland County, Ky.); Douglass, born and died in Cumberland County, Ky., unmarried; Annie Mourning, born in Green County, Ky., and died in Hart County, Ky. (married James Williams in Green County, Ky.); Mary, born in Green County, Ky., and died in La Rue County, Ky. (married M. R. Dye in Green County, Ky.); and Robert Douglass, born, Green County, Ky., December 17, 1807, and died, Henry County, Ill., April 4, 1893 (married Jemima A. Simms, Sagamon County, Ill., October, 1833).

TIPPER, JOHN: Enlisted May 10, 1776, for two and a half years, a private, Captain James Williams's Company, Fourth North Carolina Regiment, commanded by Colonel Thomas Polk (also given the Colonel's Company, First North Carolina Regiment, commanded by Colonel Thomas Clark); transferred, Valley Forge, Pa., March 19, 1778, to the Commander-in-Chief's Guard, commanded by Captain Caleb Gibbs; at battle of Monmouth, N. J., June 28, 1778; discharged, Fredericksburg, N. Y., November 14, 1778.

TITCOMB, MICHAEL:* Enlisted, Newburyport, Mass., April 19, 1775, a private, Captain Moses Nowell's Company of Minute-men; re-enlisted May 9, 1775, for eight months, Captain Timothy Barnard's Company (also given Captain Benjamin Perkins's Company), Seventeenth Regiment, Continental Infantry, commanded by Colonel Moses Little; re-enlisted January 1, 1776, for one year, Captain Gideon Parker's Company, Twelfth Regiment, Continental Infantry,

THE COMMANDER-IN-CHIEF'S GUARD.

commanded by Colonel Moses Little; transferred, Cambridge, Mass., March 12, 1776, to the Commander-in-Chief's Guard, commanded by Captain Caleb Gibbs; at battle of White Plains, N. Y., October 28, 1776; discharged, Newtown, Pa., December 14, 1776, and re-enlisted for three years, Captain George Lewis's Troop, Third Regiment, Continental Dragoons, commanded by Colonel George Baylor; assigned to the Cavalry of the Commander-in-Chief's Guard, commanded by Captain George Lewis, May 1, 1777; at battle of Brandywine, Del., September 11, 1777; battle of Germantown, Pa., October 4, 1777; battle of Monmouth, N. J., June 28, 1778; rejoined regiment, September 26, 1778; at skirmish of Tappan, N. Y., September 28, 1778; discharged, Schuylkill Barracks, Philadelphia, Pa., December 13, 1779.

Born[80] October, 1750; married Lydia Hart (born, Portsmouth, N. H., September 24, 1748; died, Newburyport, Mass., July 26, 1820); died, Newburyport, Mass., June 9, 1819(?), with the following issue: Betsey, born, Newburyport, Mass., 1775, and died, Newburyport, Mass., February 22, 1843 (married Matthew Vincent); Anna Hart, born, Newburyport, Mass., 1777, and died, Newburyport, Mass., May 9, 1861 (married Asa Webster Chickering); Michael, born, Newburyport, Mass., October 20, 1780, and died, Newburyport, Mass., July, 1869 (married, first, Hannah C. Knapp, Newburyport, Mass., 1807; second, Jemima Giles, Newburyport, Mass., July, 1834); Sarah Little, born and died at Newburyport, Mass., unmarried; and Thomas, born, Newburyport, Mass., 1786, and died, Newburyport, Mass., 1836 (married Polly Sanborn of Kingston, N. H.).

TITCOMB, ZEBULON: Enlisted, Newburyport, Mass., April 19, 1775, a private, Captain Moses Nowell's Company of Minute-men; re-enlisted May 9, 1775, for eight months, Captain Benjamin Perkins's Company, Seventeenth Regiment, Continental Infantry, commanded by Colonel Moses Little; re-enlisted January 1, 1776, for one year, Twelfth

REVOLUTIONARY WAR.

Regiment, Continental Infantry, commanded by Colonel Moses Little; transferred, Cambridge, Mass., March 12, 1776, to the Commander-in-Chief's Guard, commanded by Captain Caleb Gibbs; at battle of White Plains, N. Y., October 28, 1776; discharged, Newtown, Pa., December 14, 1776, and re-enlisted for three years, Captain George Lewis's Troop, Third Regiment, Continental Dragoons, commanded by Colonel George Baylor; assigned to the Cavalry of the Commander-in-Chief's Guard, commanded by Captain George Lewis, May 1, 1777; at battle of Brandywine, Del., September 11, 1777; battle of Germantown, Pa., October 4, 1777; battle of Monmouth, N. J., June 28, 1778; rejoined regiment, September 26, 1778; at skirmish of Tappan, N. Y., September 28, 1778; discharged, Schuylkill Barracks, Philadelphia, Pa., December 13, 1779.

TOLBERT, LEVI: See Levi Talbot.

TOWNSEND, SOLOMON: Enlisted March 4, 1777, for the war, a private, Tenth Pennsylvania Regiment, commanded by Colonel Joseph Penrose; transferred, Valley Forge, Pa., March 19, 1778, to the Commander-in-Chief's Guard, commanded by Captain Caleb Gibbs; at battle of Monmouth, N. J., June 28, 1778; sick at Quaker Hill Hospital, November 26, 1778, to January 1, 1779; sick at Fishkill Hospital, January 1 to March 31, 1779; at battle of Connecticut Farms, N. J., June 7, 1780; on return dated April 8, 1781, with remark "Present."

TRASK, JOHN: Private, Massachusetts Line; transferred, West Point, N. Y., September 11, 1779, to the Commander-in-Chief's Guard, commanded by Major Caleb Gibbs; deserted, Morristown, N. J., February 28, 1780; age, 20; height, five feet nine inches; complexion, light; occupation, carpenter; residence, New Salem, Mass.

TUBBS, SIMON:* Enlisted, Canaan, Conn., April 24, 1777, for three years, a private, Captain Titus Watson's

THE COMMANDER-IN-CHIEF'S GUARD.

Company, Seventh Connecticut Regiment, commanded by Colonel Heman Swift; at battle of Germantown, Pa., October 4, 1777; transferred Valley Forge, Pa., March 19, 1778, to the Commander-in-Chief's Guard, commanded by Captain Caleb Gibbs; at battle of Monmouth, N. J., June 28, 1778; discharged, Morristown, N. J., April 24, 1780.

Born,[90] Canaan, Conn., January 16, 1756; occupation, farmer; married Rosina Lawrence (born May 4, 1761; died, Essex, Vt., January 28, 1832); died, Essex, Vt., April 2, 1824, with the following issue: Esther, born, Burlington, Vt., May 20, 1784, and died, Burlington, Vt., November 16, 1840 (married Truman Powell, M. D., June 5, 1803); John, born, Burlington, Vt., January 27, 1785, and died, Essex, Vt., April 12, 1845 (married Sally Tyler); Lucy, born, Burlington, Vt., March 8, 1787, and died, Essex, Vt., December 2, 1857 (married, first, Benjamin Thompson, December 29, 1808; second, Ebenezer Lyon); Remember, born, Essex, Vt., March 21, 1788, and died March 21, 1788; Ruth, born, Essex, Vt., March 21, 1788, and died March 21, 1788; Ira, born, Essex, Vt., March 19, 1789, and died, River Falls, Wis., June 5, 1863 (married Harriet Richards May 14, 1828); Phebe, born, Essex, Vt., October 28, 1791, and died October 28, 1791; Polly, born, Essex, Vt., October 28, 1791, and died October 28, 1791; Simon, born, Essex, Vt., March 2, 1793, and died, Essex, Vt., June 29, 1860 (married Wealthy Stevens); Lawrence Waite, born, Essex, Vt., December 29, 1794, and died, Oswego, N. Y., May 1, 1880 (married, first, Fanny Collins in 1820; second, Martha Tuttle in 1838); Rosina, born, Essex, Vt., April 29, 1797, and died, Essex, Vt., February 13, 1875 (married Oliver Bliss April 15, 1821); George, born, Essex, Vt., March 29, 1799, and died in infancy; and Thomas, born, Essex, Vt., May 3, 1801, and died, Essex, Vt., February 27, 1823, unmarried.

VAN SICKLE, ABRAHAM:* Enlisted, Berkley, Va., January 22, 1777, for three years, a private, Captain Joseph Mitchell's Company, Twelfth Virginia Regiment, com-

REVOLUTIONARY WAR.

manded by Colonel James Wood; at battle of Germantown, Pa., October 4, 1777; transferred, Valley Forge, Pa., March 19, 1778, to the Commander-in-Chief's Guard, commanded by Captain Caleb Gibbs; at battle of Monmouth, N. J., June 28, 1778; discharged, Morristown, N. J., January 22, 1780.

Born 1757; occupation, cooper; married Hannah (born 1757; residing in Somerset County, N. J., September 2, 1839), Baskinridge, N. J., January 31, 1779, by Rev. Mr. Kennedy; died, Somerset County, N. J., February 26, 1830-1.

VIBBART, JESSE:* Enlisted, East Hartford, Conn., August 22, 1777, for three years, a private, Captain James Watson's Company (also given Captain Samuel W. Williams's Company), Colonel Samuel B. Webb's Regiment, Continental Infantry; transferred, Morristown, N. J., March 20, 1780, to the Commander-in-Chief's Guard, commanded by Major Caleb Gibbs; at battle of Connecticut Farms, N. J., June 7, 1780; discharged September 1, 1780.

Born,[91] East Hartford, Conn., January 30, 1759; occupation, farmer; married Martha Abbey (born, East Hartford, Conn., August 19, 1759; died, East Hartford, Conn., June 9, 1823), East Hartford, Conn., August 7, 1783; died, Manchester, Conn., September, 1830, with the following issue: Jesse, born, East Hartford, Conn., March 3, 1784, and died, Glastonbury, Conn., December 16, 1833 (married Anna Risley at Glastonbury, Conn.); Clarissa, born, East Hartford, Conn., October 29, 1785, and died, East Hartford, Conn., June 29, 1857 (married Ambrose Beaumaux at East Hartford, Conn.); Olive, born, East Hartford, Conn., October 27, 1787, and died at East Hartford, Conn.; Eliphalet, born, East Hartford, Conn., September 16, 1789; Martha, born, East Hartford, Conn., September 28, 1791, and died, Vernon, Conn., June 17, 1887 (married Eli Millard at Vernon, Conn.); Triphenia, born, East Hartford, Conn., August 26, 1793, and died, Manchester, Conn., August 26, 1869 (married Selah Wilson); Stephen, born, East

THE COMMANDER-IN-CHIEF'S GUARD.

Hartford, Conn., September 20, 1795, and died, East Hartford, Conn., July 30, 1796; Mary, born, East Hartford, Conn., May 5, 1797, and died, Vernon, Conn., February 18, 1887 (married Chauncey Winchell, Manchester, Conn., January 26, 1816); and Alvin, born, East Hartford, Conn., January 26, 1801, and died, East Hartford, Conn., June 23, 1853 (married Emily Brewer, East Hartford, Conn., November 29, 1820).

VINAL, JOSEPH: Enlisted, Scituate, Mass., February 1, 1777, for three years, a private, Captain Jacob Wale's Company, Tenth Massachusetts Regiment, commanded by Colonel Thomas Marshall; transferred, Valley Forge, Pa., March 19, 1778, to the Commander-in-Chief's Guard, commanded by Captain Caleb Gibbs; at battle of Monmouth, N. J., June 28, 1778; furloughed fifty-five days, May 15, 1779; sick-absent, July 1 to September 22, 1779; at battle of Connecticut Farms, N. J., June 7, 1780; skirmish of King's Bridge, N. Y., July 3, 1781; battle of Yorktown, Va., October 19, 1781; furloughed, Newburgh, N. Y., June 6, 1783, until the ratification of the definite treaty of peace; discharged, November 3, 1783.

WADE, EDWARD. See Edward Weed.

WADSWORTH, ROBERT :* Enlisted, South Branch of Potomac River, Va., March 11, 1777, for two years, a private, Captain Abel Westfall's Company, Eighth Virginia Regiment, commanded by Colonel Abraham Bowman; transferred, Morristown, N. J., May 1, 1777, to the Commander-in-Chief's Guard, commanded by Captain Caleb Gibbs; at battle of Brandywine, Del., September 11, 1777; battle of Germantown, Pa., October 4, 1777; battle of Monmouth, N. J., June 28, 1778; re-enlisted and furloughed one hundred days, January 18, 1779; rejoined June 1, 1779; deserted, Morristown, N. J., February 1, 1780 (soldier claims subsequent and indefinite service at siege of Charleston, S. C.).

Revolutionary War.

Born,[92] England, 1750; occupation, cooper; married, first, Hannah ——————— near Cumberland, Md.; issue: Joseph, killed at Fort Meigs, War of 1812-15; Thomas; and Moses; second, Hannah Masters, near Cumberland, Md.; died, Harrison County, W. Va., about 1825, with the following issue: John; Elizabeth, died at Shinnston, W. Va. (married James Matson); Cornelius, died at Castleton, Ind. (married Cassander Leggin); Rebecca, died at Shinnston, W. Va. (married William Heldreth); Robert J., born 1804, and died at Shinnston, W. Va. (married Amelia Pigott); Mary, born 1805, and died at Shinnston, W. Va. (married Turner Shaw); Jesse, born 1806, and died at Shinnston, W. Va. (married Rebecca Pigott); Rachel, born 1808, and died in Preston County, W. Va. (married Samuel Menear); and Nancy, born 1810, and died near Shinnston, W. Va. (married Elisha Menear).

WAKELEE, HENRY:* Enlisted, Woodbury, Conn., October 1, 1779, for the war, a private, Captain Thomas Sill's Company, Colonel Seth Warner's Regiment, Continental Infantry; furloughed thirty days, November 11, 1779; promoted corporal, July 21, 1780; taken prisoner at battle of Fort George, N. Y., October 11, 1780, and confined two years at Montreal, Canada, when exchanged at Boston, Mass.; transferred, Newburgh, N. Y., December 20, 1782, from late Colonel Seth Warner's Regiment, Continental Infantry, to the Commander-in-Chief's Guard, commanded by Lieutenant-Commandant William Colfax, and assigned private; furloughed ninety-three days, December 28, 1782; furloughed, Newburgh, N. Y., June 6, 1783, until the ratification of the definite treaty of peace; discharged November 3, 1783.

Born, Woodbury, Conn., April 9, 1750; occupation, cooper; married, first, Lydia Ann (born January 7, 1765; died, Sandgate, Vt., August 18, 1787); second, Deborah Hurlburt (born 1771; residing at Sandgate, Vt., April 6, 1843), Sandgate, Vt., April 13, 1788, by Rev. James Murdock; died, Sandgate, Vt., September 22, 1835; issue: Lydia Ann, born June 13, 1793; and Deborah Eunice, born July 29, 1805, and died, Sandgate, Vt., December 1, 1829.

WALTON, MOSES: Enlisted, Westfield, Mass., January 1, 1777, for the war, a private, Captain Libbeus Ball's Company, Fourth Massachusetts Regiment, commanded by Colonel William Shepard; transferred, Valley Forge, Pa., March 19, 1778, to the Commander-in-Chief's Guard, commanded by Captain Caleb Gibbs; at battle of Monmouth, N. J., June 28, 1778; in arrest, Fredericksburg, N. Y., October 18, 1778; court-martialed October 22, 1778, and found guilty of a breach of article 21, section 13, of the articles of war, and sentenced to death; sentence approved by the Commander-in-Chief, October 23, 1778, who directed that he be hanged immediately in Major-General Gates's Division; escaped from the provost-guard October 23, 1778.

WARD, BENJAMIN: Enlisted, Brintwood, N. H., March 13, 1781, for three years, a private, Eighth Company, First New Hampshire Regiment, commanded by Colonel Alexander Scammell; age, 21; height, five feet seven inches; complexion, dark; transferred, Newburgh, N. Y., June 16, 1783, to the Commander-in-Chief's Guard, commanded by Lieutenant-Commandant William Colfax; on return dated Rocky Hill, N. J., October 22, 1783, with remark "Present."

WARNER, DANIEL:* Enlisted, Stockbridge, Mass., January 1, 1776, for one year, a private, Captain Jonathan Danforth's Company, Sixth Regiment, Continental Infantry, commanded by Colonel Asa Whitcomb; transferred, Cambridge, Mass., March 12, 1776, to the Commander-in-Chief's Guard, commanded by Captain Caleb Gibbs; at battle of White Plains, N. Y., October 28, 1776; battle of Trenton, N. J., December 26, 1776; battle of Princeton, N. J., January 3, 1777; discharged, Morristown, N. J., February 10, 1777.

Born, Great Barrington, Mass., August 19, 1757; married Rachel Lawrence (born July 31, 1763; married John Burleson April, 1824, who died September 6, 1839; residing at Almond, N. Y., January 19, 1844), Stockbridge, Mass., September 22, 1785, by Rev. Stephen West; died January 11, 1822; issue: Obedience Stone, born September 10, 1787; and Obedience, born March 11, 1789 (married Joseph C. Ferry; issue: Rachel, born October 22, 1805).

WARRINGTON, WILLIAM:* Enlisted, Accomack County, Va., February 14, 1776, for two years, a private, Captain Thomas Snead's Company, Ninth Virginia Regiment, commanded by Colonel Charles Fleming; transferred, Morristown, N. J., May 1, 1777, to the Commander-in-Chief's Guard, commanded by Captain Caleb Gibbs; at battle of Brandywine, Del., September 11, 1777; battle of Germantown, Pa., October 4, 1777; discharged, Valley Forge, Pa., February 14, 1778.

Born[98] 1755; married, first, name unknown; issue: eleven children, names unknown; second, Leah Townsend, in Accomack County, Va.; issue: John; Sallie; Polly; and William, born, Acomack County, Va., 1801, and died, Jones County, Iowa, 1857 (married Letitia Mershon, Flemingsburg, Ky., February 18, 1825); third, Nancy Holland (born 1771; died, Maysville, Ky., August 10, 1824), Accomack County, Va., 1803; issue: Julia Ann, born, Drummondtown, Va., August 16, 1806, and died, Davenport, Iowa, March 1, 1899 (married, first, David Fuller, Cincinnati, Ohio, November 9, 1828; second, John Weaver, Cincinnati, Ohio, June 30, 1837); Cosmore G., born, Drummondtown, Va., June, 1810, and died at Covington, Ky. (married Polly Conley at Covington, Ky.); George Washington, born and died at Drummondtown, Va., in infancy; and James, born and died at Drummondtown, Va., in infancy; fourth, Nancy Little (born 1791; residing in Sciota Township, Union County, Ohio, April 9, 1853), Cincinnati, Ohio, February 4, 1836, by Rev. William Burke; issue: Lottie, born, Cincinnati, Ohio, December 31, 1837; died, Delaware County, Ohio, May 25, 1851, with the above-named issue.

The Commander-in-Chief's Guard.

WASHINGTON, GEORGE AUGUSTINE: Second Lieutenant, Colonel William Grayson's Regiment, Continental Infantry, September 1, 1777; resigned November 16, 1777; cornet, Lieutenant-Colonel Henry Lee's Regiment, Partisan Corps, Continental Troops, April 20, 1778; resigned December 31, 1778; ensign, Second Virginia Regiment, commanded by Colonel Christian Febiger, April, 1780; assigned to the Commander-in-Chief's Guard, commanded by Major Caleb Gibbs, April 27, 1780; rejoined regiment, April 30, 1780; promoted lieutenant, May 26, 1781; aide-de-camp to General Lafayette, Yorktown campaign, 1781; served to close of war.

Born,[94] Stafford County, Va., 1763; married Frances Bassett (born December 19, 1767; married Tobias Lear), New Kent County, Va., October 15, 1785; died, Fairfax County, Va., February, 1793, with the following issue: George Fayette, born April 10, 1787, and died in infancy; Anna Maria, born April 3, 1788, and died, Fredericksburg, Va., 1814 (married Captain Reuben Thornton in 1810); George Fayette, born, "Mount Vernon," Va., January 17, 1790, and died "Waverly," Frederick County, Va., September, 1867 (married Maria Traner, Charlestown, W. Va., November 18, 1813); and Charles Augustine, born November 3, 1791, and died, Cadiz, Spain, unmarried.

WEED, EDWARD: Private, Third Maryland Regiment; transferred, New Windsor, N. Y., May 15, 1781, to the Commander-in-Chief's Guard, commanded by Lieutenant-Commandant William Colfax; at skirmish of King's Bridge, N. Y., July 3, 1781—wounded; battle of Yorktown, Va., October 19, 1781; furloughed, Newburgh, N. Y., June 6, 1783, until the ratification of the definite treaty of peace; discharged November 3, 1783.

WELLS, ENOCH: Enlisted February 1, 1777, for the war, a private, Third Pennsylvania Regiment, commanded by Colonel Joseph Wood; residence, Evesham, Burlington County, N. J.; transferred, Valley Forge, Pa., March 19,

Revolutionary War.

1778, to the Commander-in-Chief's Guard, commanded by Captain Caleb Gibbs; at battle of Monmouth, N. J., June 28, 1778; battle of Connecticut Farms, N. J., June 7, 1780; skirmish of King's Bridge, N. Y., July 3, 1781; battle of Yorktown, Va., October 19, 1781; promoted 4th corporal, October 23, 1782; promoted 3d corporal, March 1, 1783; furloughed, Newburgh, N. Y., June 6, 1783, until the ratification of the definite treaty of peace; discharged November 3, 1783.

WHELAN, EDWARD: Enlisted March 6, 1777, for the war, a private, Colonel John Patton's Regiment, Continental Infantry; at battle of Brandywine, Del., September 11, 1777; battle of Germantown, Pa., October 4, 1777; transferred, Sunbury, Pa., January 13, 1779, to Captain Abraham G. Claypoole's (6th) Company, Eleventh Pennsylvania Regiment, commanded by Colonel Thomas Hartley; promoted sergeant; transferred, Morristown, N. J., March 20, 1780, to the Commander-in-Chief's Guard, commanded by Major Caleb Gibbs, and assigned private; at battle of Connecticut Farms, N. J., June 7, 1780; skirmish of King's Bridge, N. Y., July 3, 1781—wounded in the left foot; battle of Yorktown, Va., October 19, 1781; discharged by reason of rheumatism, Philadelphia, Pa., March 20, 1782, by General Washington.

Born 1750; occupation, carpenter; residing in New York City, December 10, 1788.

WHITMARSH, SAMUEL:* Enlisted, Dighton, Mass., September 11, 1777, for three years, a private, Captain-Lieutenant John Hobby's Company, Colonel Henry Jackson's Regiment, Continental Infantry; height, five feet eleven inches; complexion, light; hair, brown; occupation, mason; at battle of Monmouth, N. J., June 28, 1778; assigned with Regiment to Major-General John Sullivan's Division, Continental Army, engaged in an expedition against the Six Nations of Indians in Western Pennsylvania and New York,

The Commander-in-Chief's Guard.

May 26 to October 26, 1779; transferred, Morristown, N. J., March 20, 1780, to the Commander-in-Chief's Guard, Commanded by Major Caleb Gibbs; at battle of Connecticut Farms, June 7, 1780; discharged September 11, 1780.

Born, Dighton, Mass., April, 1760 (?); occupation, mason; married Frances Burrell (born, Weymouth, Mass., July 15, 1761; died, Weymouth, Mass., about 1840), Weymouth, Mass, December 14, 1788; died, Weymouth, Mass., December 3, 1854, with the following issue: infant, died March 16, 1790; infant, died December 19, 1790; Mary, born May 14, 1793, and died, Weymouth, Mass., January 19, 1879, unmarried; Abigail, born November 6, 1796, and died, Weymouth, Mass., May 21, 1874, unmarried; Samuel, born May 6, 1798, and died, St. Jago, March 27, 1827, unmarried; Freeman, born July 27, 1800, and died, Weymouth, Mass., February 5, 1882 (married Lucy Phillips, Weymouth, Mass., May 9, 1824); and John, born October 18, 1804, and died, Braintree, Mass., October 1, 1902 (married Deborah Burrell, Weymouth, Mass., December 7, 1826).

WILEY, EDWARD: Enlisted January 1, 1777, for the war, a private, Captain Jacob Wright's Company, Second New York Regiment, commanded by Colonel Philip Van Cortlandt; transferred, Valley Forge, Pa., March 19, 1778, to the Commander-in-Chief's Guard, commanded by Captain Caleb Gibbs; absent, June, 1778; sick, July, 1778; sick at Quaker Hill Hospital, November 6, 1778, to January 1, 1779; at battle of Connecticut Farms, N. J., June 7, 1780; skirmish of King's Bridge, N. Y., July 3, 1781; battle of Yorktown, Va., October 19, 1781; furloughed, Newburgh, N. Y., June 6, 1783, until the ratification of the definite treaty of peace; discharged, November 3, 1783.

WILLIAMS, JOHN: Enlisted, Colchester, Conn., December 9, 1776, for three years, a private, Captain John McGregier's Company, Fourth Connecticut Regiment, commanded by Colonel John Durkee; transferred, Valley Forge,

REVOLUTIONARY WAR.

Pa., March 19, 1778, to the Commander-in-Chief's Guard, commanded by Captain Caleb Gibbs; at battle of Monmouth, N. J., June 28, 1778; deserted, White Plains, N. Y., August 17, 1778.

WILLS, ENOCH: See Enoch Wells.

WILSON, CORNELIUS: Enlisted, Philadelphia, Pa., February 21, 1782, a private, Commander-in-Chief's Guard, commanded by Lieutenant-Commandant William Colfax; promoted drummer, May 20, 1782; furloughed, Newburgh, N. Y., June 6, 1783, until the ratification of the definite treaty of peace; discharged, November 3, 1783.

WILSON, JOHN:* Enlisted, Woodstock, Conn., May 10, 1775, for eight months, a private, Captain Ephraim Manning's Company, Thirty-fourth Regiment, Continental Infantry, commanded by Lieutenant-Colonel Experience Storrs; at battle of Bunker Hill, Mass., June 17, 1775; discharged, December 14, 1775; re-enlisted January 1, 1776, for one year, Captain Ephraim Manning's Company, Twentieth Regiment, Continental Infantry, commanded by Colonel Benedict Arnold; transferred, Cambridge, Mass., March 12, 1776, to the Commander-in-Chief's Guard, commanded by Captain Caleb Gibbs; at battle of White Plains, N. Y., October 28, 1776; discharged, Newtown, Pa., December 30, 1776; re-enlisted January 1, 1777, for the war, Captain Samuel Talbot's Company, Second Pennsylvania Regiment, commanded by Colonel John P. DeHaas; reported in Captain Roger Stayner's Company; transferred, Valley Forge, Pa., March 19, 1778, to the Commander-in-Chief's Guard, commanded by Captain Caleb Gibbs, and assigned 3d sergeant; at battle of Monmouth, N. J., June 28, 1778—wounded in right arm by musket ball, and confined at Burlington (N. J.) Hospital; promoted 2d sergeant, August 2, 1778; discharged from hospital, unfit for service, December 11, 1778, by Major-General Arnold.

Born 1755; occupation, farmer; residing in Windsor County, Vt., 1795; pensioned by special act of Congress,

The Commander-in-Chief's Guard.

April 20, 1796; residing at Aurelius, N. Y., July, 1820; died January 4, 1823.

WINCH, JOSEPH: Enlisted, Packersfield, N. H., March 21, 1781, for three years, a private, Third Company, Second New Hampshire Regiment, commanded by Lieutenant-Colonel George Reid; transferred, Newburgh, N. Y., June 16, 1783, to the Commander-in-Chief's Guard, commanded by Lieutenant-Commandant William Colfax; on return dated Rocky Hill, N. J., October 22, 1783, with remark, "Deserted October 18, 1783."

WOOD, FRANCIS: Enlisted, Halifax, Mass., July 7, 1775, for eight months, a sergeant, Captain John Porter's Company, Twenty-eighth Regiment, Continental Infantry, commanded by Colonel Paul D. Sergent; re-enlisted January 1, 1776, for one year, Captain James Perry's Company, Sixteenth Regiment, Continental Infantry, commanded by Colonel Paul D. Sergent; transferred, Cambridge, Mass., March 12, 1776, to the Commander-in-Chief's Guard, commanded by Captain Caleb Gibbs; at the battle of White Plains, N. Y., October 28, 1776; discharged, Newtown, Pa., December 14, 1776, and re-enlisted for three years, Captain George Lewis's Troop, Third Regiment, Continental Dragoons, commanded by Colonel George Baylor; assigned to the Cavalry of the Commander-in-Chief's Guard, commanded by Captain George Lewis, May 1, 1777; on rolls to August 1, 1777, without remark.

WORTMAN, SAMUEL: Enlisted, Oxford, N. J., November 11, 1775, for one year, a private, Captain Daniel Piatt's (7th) Company, First New Jersey Regiment, commanded by Colonel William Alexander (Lord Sterling), assigned to Brigadier-General John Sullivan's Brigade, at New York, N. Y., May 2, 1776; at battle of Three Rivers, Canada, June 8, 1776; re-enlisted December 16, 1776, for the war, Captain John Flahaven's Company, First New Jersey Regiment, commanded by Colonel Matthias Ogden,

Revolutionary War.

Brigadier-General William Maxwell's Brigade; at battle of Short Hills, N. J., June 26, 1777; battle of Brandywine, Del., September 11, 1777; battle of Germantown, Pa., October 4, 1777; transferred, Valley Forge, Pa., March 19, 1778, to the Commander-in-Chief's Guard, commanded by Captain Caleb Gibbs; at battle of Monmouth, N. J., June 28, 1778; battle of Connecticut Farms, N. J., June 7, 1780; promoted 3d corporal, July 1, 1781; at Skirmish of King's Bridge, N. Y., July 3, 1781; battle of Yorktown, Va., October 19, 1781; promoted 2d corporal, April 1, 1782; reduced to the ranks, November 23, 1782; transferred, Newburgh, N. Y., March 1, 1783, to Captain William Piatt's (5th) Company, New Jersey Regiment, commanded by Colonel Matthias Ogden, Brigadier-General Elias Dayton's Brigade; furloughed, New Windsor, N. Y., June 5, 1783, until the ratification of the definite treaty of peace; discharged November 3, 1783.

WYMAN, WILLIAM: Enlisted, Lunenburgh, Mass., April 1, 1777, for three years, a private, Captain Sylvanus Smith's Company, Fifteenth Massachusetts Regiment, commanded by Colonel Timothy Bigelow; transferred, Valley Forge, Pa., March 19, 1778, to the Commander-in-Chief's Guard, commanded by Captain Caleb Gibbs; at battle of Monmouth, N. J., June 28, 1778; discharged, Morristown, N. J., April 1, 1780.

Born,[95] Lunenburgh, Mass., November 30, 1752; married Mary Gibson (born, Concord, Mass., February 2, 1764; died, Walpole, N. H., December 11, 1825), Lunenburgh, Mass., April 9, 1782; died, Grafton, Vt., February 15, 1809, with the following issue: Susanna, born, Lunenburgh, Mass., January 16, 1783, and died, Boston, Mass., May 31, 1829, unmarried; William, born, Rindge, N. H., March 15, 1785, and died, Fitchburg, Mass., August 16, 1852 (married Anna Palmer of Grafton, Vt., December 13, 1815, who died January, 1862); Francis, born, Rindge, N. H., May 17, 1787, and died, Boston, Mass., December 7, 1831 (married Sally Houghton January 1, 1812, who died November 6,

1819); Mary, born, Walpole, N. H., June 3, 1789, and died
June 9, 1875 (married ———— Williams); Sally, born,
Walpole, N. H., January 23, 1792, and died, Cambridge,
Mass., July 5, 1875 (married Captain Robert Clark of Acworth, N. H., July 4, 1816, who died April 4, 1842); Thomas
Bellows, born, Walpole, N. H., May 1, 1794, and died,
Charlestown, Mass., June 24, 1867 (married Mary Frothingham October 27, 1816, who died June 9, 1875); Willard,
born, Walpole, N. H., December 10, 1796, and died October
4, 1828, unmarried; Elnathan Winchester, born, Walpole,
N. H., January 31, 1799, and died in infancy; Abraham
Gibson, born, Walpole, N. H., August 5, 1801, and died,
Boston, Mass., June 24, 1868 (married Miranda Priest,
Boston, Mass., May 11, 1826, who died, Roxbury, Mass.,
March 11, 1869); John Fox, born, Walpole, N. H., March
23, 1804, and died, Tewksbury, Mass., October 11, 1882
(married Caroline E. Metcalf of Geneseo, N. Y., June 4,
1833); and George Washington, born, Walpole, N. H.,
February 21, 1806, and died, Cleveland, Ohio, August 30,
1858 (married Mary J. Moore of Rochester, N. Y., August,
1846).

YOUNG, FREDERICK: Enlisted August 25, 1776, for three
years, a private, Captain Buller Claiborne's Company, Second Virginia Regiment, commanded by Colonel Alexander
Spotswood; transferred, Morristown, N. J., May 6, 1777, to
the Commander-in-Chief's Guard, commanded by Captain
Caleb Gibbs; promoted 2d sergeant, June 4, 1777; at
battle of Brandywine, Del., September 11, 1777; battle of
Germantown, Pa., October 4, 1777; promoted 1st sergeant,
March 1, 1778; reduced to 4th sergeant, March 19, 1778;
at battle of Monmouth, N. J., June 28, 1778; promoted 3d
sergeant, August 2, 1778; promoted 2d sergeant, December 11, 1778; discharged, West Point, N. Y., August 25,
1779.

Revolutionary War.

ELIJAH FISHER'S DIARY.

(By Permission of Mrs. William B. Lapham, Augusta, Me.)

1778.

*   *   *   *

March 19th. There was orders that there should be three Men sent from each Reg't to jine His Excelences Gen. Washington's Life gard and Seth Lovil was sent out of our Company but after being there a fue Days and Did not like to be there he said, but I sepose that he was afeard that the Regt would go to Rhode island which they did afterward and he Could not go with them and he Come back to the Compeny and I was sent in the room of him.

The 30th. I jined the Life guard and liked being there much better than being in the Ridgment let them go where they would.

April 4th. There Come nuse that Gen. Lee was Come to the Lines and there was a Corpl. and Eight men sent to the Lines to guard his Baggage to Head Quarters.

The 5th. Gen. Washington with all his attendence went to the Lines to Meet Gen. Lee and to Accompany him to Head Quarters where they arrived at two of the Clock in the afternoon where they was receved with a kind salute of arms Drums fifes and Band of Musick.

May 6th. We had Rejoicing on the account of the French

declaring for us Independent and the howle of the Continental army was ordered to three larm posts in the senter and the army was all around us at there several stations (and there was a grand harber bilt and all the Commissioners were Envited to dine with His Exelency) our guard gave the first fire then thirteen Cannon then the fire began at the rite of the army and went through the howl line and fired three rouns apeace the Artillery Discharged forty-four Cannon and it was followed with three Chears for the King of France and three for the Friendly Powers of Europe and three Chears for the Thirteen United States of Amarica and His Exelency gave orders that every Prisoner should have his Freedom that belonged to the Continental army that they might taste the Pleasur of the Day.

The 15th. The Ingen Chief Come to Head Quarters to Congratelate with His Exelency and also Dined with him.

The 18th. One hundred and two of the Life guard and three thousands of the army was sent as a Detachment under the Command of the Right Honorable Maj. Gen. Delefiatee and we marched to Barronhill Chirch and there we made a halt and Formed a line of battle and our guard Lay in the Frunt of the Party by the Gen. Marques Quarters. Sixteen miles from Valleyford.

The 20. This Morning at Nine of the Clock there Come Express to the General Quarters and brought Entelegence that the howl of Gen. How's Army was Advansing upon us in three Colloms one Collom Coming in the senter to meet us one Collom Coming Round on our Left wing

REVOLUTIONARY WAR.

Marching up by Delwar river and through the Crooked hills and so Crossing the Country towards Schoolkills River to Cute off our Retreat, the other striving to flank us on our right wing. The Nuse alarmed us Enstently and we took a road that lead to Jones' Forde at Schoolkill river (for we were obliged to retreat Enstently) and the Enemy was so Nigh on our right flank that we Could see them Plain and our howl Party Crossed the river and the warter was up to our middle and run very swift so that we were obliged to hold to each other to keep the Corrent from sweeping us away and all in a fluster expecting the Enemy to fire in upon us for we could see them Plain but the reason was they Could not git thare Cannon to bare on us but we got all Safe across without the loss of any save fore or five of our party that the Enemy's Lite horse Cut to pieces and our flanks killed three of there Lite Draghoons and four of there Granadears. After we had Crossed the river we Retirred to the Gulf mills where we Remained till two in the afternoon and then we marched to Sweed's ford and there stayed all Night after a March of twelve miles.

The 21st. We Crossed Sweed's ford and Marching Down to the Same Place of ground where we was the Day before (barenhill Chirch) Nine miles.

The 22d. We at four of the Clock in the Morning, left barenhill Chirch and Marched Derect back to Sweed ford there stays till twelve of the Clock then returns to Camp after the March of twenty-two miles.

The 30th. I unhapely falls in to Schoolkill River and had

THE COMMANDER-IN-CHIEF'S GUARD.

Enliked to have been drowned one of my messmates havin gon over the River after some Milk and Comes and Calls for some one to Come with the Canew and fetch him acrost but none would go after him. I told them that if none of them would go I would trye but I being not used to a bote and the Current being very swift and as I shifted the setting Pole on the other side to keep the head of the bote up it happened to Catch on a side of a rock and as I shoved the Pole slipped off and pitches me out the other side and being surprised and current strong with all, made for the shore but the current was so swift it Carried me Down Stream and every little while I Could tuch bottom and the warter being up to my middle but I Could not stand in Compereson more than I could stand on the side of an house then I would trye for shore but the more I strove the faster the Current would sweep me down stream and at Length being tired of trying for shore I tries to tuch bottom but I could not then I tries to git to the top of the warter and it seames as if something held me and after struglen for some minnets I felt as easy as ever I did in my life and it seems as though I was going to sleep and the first that I knew I stood on my feet Clost to the shore and seemed as though I waked out of sleep. Blake the young man that I was going after Come as fast as he Could swim after me (and the Current Carried me down faster than he Could swim) and Come to me and soon a number was there and they helped me home to the barrack and the Doctor blooded but I was very unwell for several days.

Revolutionary War.

June 4th. There was a spye Hung on the grand parade from the Enemy he formerly belonged to our Army and was an Ensign in the Secund Pencelvania Ridgt. His name was Thomas Church.

The 9th. Lady Washington Left Head Quarters to Return to Virginey.

The 11th. Our army Left there huts and went into Tents.

The 18th. The Regelars Left Philadelphia and some Part of our army took possession of the City and Gen. Lee's Division Marched for the Eastward.

The 19th. The Remander of the army Left Valy forde and Marched and Crossed Solevan's Bridge over Schoolkill and Pitched tents.

The 20th. We Left Schoolkill and Marched and Come into Bucks County after Marching fifteen miles and Pitched our tents.

The 21st. We Left Buck's County at ten of the Clock in the four noon and after ten miles March we arrived at Carrell's ferrey and the Life guard crossed at four in the afternoon and Marched to Mr. Haises in Hunberton's County where his Excelency had his Quarters and Pitched our tents.

The 23d. Capt. Gibbs, Leut. Grimes, four Sarj. and four Corpl. and seventy-two men of the guard jined Col. Morgan's Party and went Down to the Lines and the rest of the guard went with the Baggage and Leut. Colfaxe had the Command and at four in the after noon We Left Mr. Haises and Marched all night and Mett with a good eal of Dificulty in giting along.

The Commander-in-Chief's Guard.

The 24th. We Come to Kittorn and Pitched our tents after a very fetigeing March.

We Left Kittorn at Nine of the Clock A. M. and Marched and Come to Rockey hill and Pitched our tents there a while.

The 28th. On Sunday our army had the Engagement with the British at Monmouth Court-house where Gen. Lee went Contrary to orders but our army Drove them and if that he had managed acording to his orders it was likely in all probability we should have taken the howl or the bigar Part of there army. It was a vary hot Day and a grate many died a drinking water.

July 1st. We Left Rockey hill and Marched and Come to Brumsick where Head Quarters was pitched our tents.

July 4th. We Selebrated the Independence of Amarica the howl army parraded and at the Right of Every Brigade there was a field peace placed, then was the signal given for the howl army to fire and they fired one round apiece and the artilery Discharged thirteen Cannon we gave three Chears &c. At Night his Exelency and the gentlemen and Ladys had a Bawl at Head Quarters with grate Pompe.

The 7th. We Left Brumswick and Come to Schots plains and there Capt. Gibbs and the rest of the guard that Left us at Carels farrey jined us again after a March of Nine miles from Brumswick.

The 8th. We Leaves the Schots Plains we marched in the Morning Marching through Springfield and the Township

REVOLUTIONARY WAR.

of York and Come to the Stone house Piket we pitched our tent after the march of twenty-six miles.

The 10th. We marched at three of the Clock in the morning and after Eighteen miles march we Come to Head Quarters two miles from Primmiss Chirch and there Pitched our tents.

The 14th. All the army but Gen. Marpue's Division Marched and Sargt. Edward and twenty-fore of the guard have still for his Excelency Remaned at Parmass; the rest of the guard Marched on and Come to Col. Haze's three miles from King's farry and Encamped after the March of twenty-fore miles from Parmass.

The 16th. His Exelency Come up with us and jined us.

The 19th. We Left Col. Hazes and Marched and Crossed the North river at King's farrey and Marches bye Crumford and after thirteen miles march we Pitched our tents Cotalan's manor.

The 20th. We marched at three of the Clock in the afternoon and Crossing Cotalan Bridge and after twelve miles March we Come to Mr. Right's mills on the age of the White Planes.

The 25th. Head Quarters moved Down to the White Planes and the guard likewise and pitched our tents and there Remaned some time.

Aug. 17th. There was a man shot Near Head Quarters for Enlisting seven times and taken bountys.

The 21st. There was sixteen men to be Executed some for Desarsion and some for Enlesting Nombers of times but for there former good Conduct and the Enterseding of there officers his Exelency was pleased to pardon them.

Sept 16. We Left the White planes and Marching through North Castel and after sixteen miles March we Come to Mr. Ragemand in Bedford.

The 18th. We Left Bedford and Marched and Come to Fredrexburg after the March of fifteen miles and Pitched our tents.

The 19th. We Left Fredericksburg and after thirteen miles march we pitched our tents at Mr. Reed's field in Oblong.

The 25th. Head Quarters and likewise the guard Left Oblong and Come to Mr. Cain's in Fredrexburg four miles and pitched tents.

The 2—th. A large Detachment under the Command of Gen. Lord starling Marched for the Jarseys Capt Levenston his addecamp.

The 30th. His Exelency with his addecamps went to Fishkills.

October 1st. I had a pass for five Days to go to New Millford (Mr. N. Fisher) to see a Relation of mine.

The 5th. As I was returning from New Milford, Missed my way which Detaned me.

The 6th. I Returned and jines the guard again and at my Return I finds an alteration in the Dress of my mates I asked one of them J. Herrick it seams as though there had been an alteration since I have been gon. He said that he had that Money sent to him that he sent for (Now

Revolutionary War.

I know that he had sent for som Money from his father) I said that I was glad off it for I hoped that we should not be so putout for money to bye things with now and that you will be able to pay me that trifill you owe me (Sixteen Dollars) he said he hoped he should. Presently in comes one or two more I said have you had money sent you from home too I fear that you have taken some other way to git it than that; then Herrick said that as J. Herrin was out after things for the General's famely (now Herrin was one that was sent after to bye things for the General's Famely and he had a horse and a pass to go where he Could git such things as was wanted for the General's Famely) he Come to an old Tory's house and they would not Let him have any thing and he see several things that he wanted so when he Come home he gos to his messmates and tales them and they gos and robed him of several things. I said that Whether he be a tory or not If it should be found out (which such things as Robery seldim is) some or all of you will be hung which surprised them Vary much but there was no more heard about it.

The 8th. His Exelency and Addecamp returned from Fishkill to Mr. Cane's.

The 17th. In Rememberance of Gen. Burgoin's Defeet the Day was selebrated with the firing of Canon and in throing of skilokets in the are thirteen Canon was fired then they begun to through the skilokets and a merry Day they had too at the Park of artilery. At night some of the Guard was a going to the park Col. Harrison's waiter was a coming from there under swift way run over one of them which hurt him so that he died the same Night.

The 18th. John Lovjoy the man that was killed by the horse was Desently Buried. There was them four that was said that Robed the Tory brought to an Exemanation Viz: John Herron, John Herrick Moses Walton and Elias Brown. The same Day John Stogdel one of the guard was to Mr. Howlens and he was a telling him how that he had been Robed so and so at such a time and that the liver that the men had on that Robed him was a round hatter with a peace of Bare skin on it but they ware all blacked and that he had made Enquirey through the army but Could not find any that wore such hats but the guard asked him if he had seen any of the guard more fuller of money than usuel he said he did not know but he had but Did not know how they Come by it. The man said that he Did not want any man hurt upon his account for he knew that they would be hung if they were found out and told Stogdal that if he would find the things and put them where he mite find them he would say no more about it. Stogdal gos home to the guard and was Consulting with one of his messmates about it for they had Destroyed a Part of the things and if they did anything about it it would bring it all out. In the meen while there Come Mr. Howage to the offisers of the guard on suspicion that some one had Robed him (for they Robed one on Friday Night and the other on Monday Night) and as they was a talking about it one of the waiters Come and told them that Stogdal knew something about them. He was Called and Exemened but he tryed to hide what he Could but they told him that if he Did not tell all he knew about it he would be taken up on suspicion and fare acordingly then he thought it would be known and if he Did not tell what he knew it would bring him into Difficulty so he up and tells all that he knew Consarning the affare then they sends and Confined Herrick and Brown and sends Sarjt. Harris with two Lite horse men into the Country after Walton that was not well and he was abed and asleep and they tells the wooman that they wanted a Candle and so they gos up Chamber and stands over him with there swords drawn in there hands and awakes him and told him that he was there prisoner and he gits up and had a pare of Dearskin Breeches that they had got to Mr. Howlens so they feches him to the gard and Confinds him with the others, and Herrin was out and having a general pass they ware afrade that he would hear of it so they sends to a Place where he Did sometimes Reside but he being not there they Returned.

The 19th. The Next Morning Leut. Livinstone was to the Park of artilery (Herrin in his return from the Country Come by there) sends a man with him for fear he would make his Escape so he was garded to Head Quarters and Confined with the others. The same Day they was Examend and Herrick said that he was loth to go after they had set out and gon a little way he would fane have had them gon back but they told him that if he did not go that they

THE COMMANDER-IN-CHIEF'S GUARD.

would Despach him for they would not have him Enform against them so he was obliged to go so he turned States Evedence aganst the others so after Examination was found gilty and what things that Could be found that they had not Desposed of was Restored to them again that they belonged too and where they had Payd any Dets they was obliged to Restore it to them again and they to the ones they got it from, then the Same Day they was all sent to the purvey guard.

The 22d. They all had ther Tryel and Herrin, Walton and Brown was sentenst to be hung and Herrick to have a hundred Lashes. Walton made his escape from the purvey gard and Herrin was hung at Fishkills and Brown made his escape from the gard that was sent to gard him to the Place of Execusion to New Millford to the part of the army that lay there. Herrick was Carried to Fredrixburg and had a hundred Lashes.

The 23d. Gen. Patesons, Gen. Huntington and Gen. Nixson's Brigades Marched to Hartford save Col. Parson's Regt and that went onward.

The 24th. The Gard Marcht down to Fredrixburg to see a man hung for Robing he was Executed at Eleven in the fournoon Thomas Glover by Name and there was five Whipt one hundred Lashes apeace all save one for Robing two of them belonged to the Gard Viz. John Harrick and Joseph Timberlek was for striking an offiser.

The 25th. The Pensilvania Troops Marcht for the Jarseys.

Revolutionary War.

The 26th. Gen. Nocks Parke of Artilery Marched for the Jarseys.

Nov. 28th. His Exelency and also his Gard Left Fredericksburg and Marched for the Jarseys and at Night we Pitcht our tents by Clane's Tavern in Philipespatten after the March of sixteen miles.

The 29th. We left the Patten at seven of the fournoon and at five in the afternoon we pitch our tents by Mr. Lents in Piekskill two miles from the King's farrey after the March of seventeen miles.

The 30th. Gen. Nock's Park of artilery Crossed at King's farrey. We lay still.

Dec. 1st. The guard Left Piekskill and Crossed at King's farrey Marched on to Col. Hazes and Encampt after Marching two and three is five miles.

The 2d. We left Col. Hazes and after seventeen miles March we Come to Mr. Jones Baggat in Romepawe and Pitcht our tents.

The 3d. We left Romepawe and after twenty miles March we Come to Mr. Goods in Prequannackit.

The 4th. We Left Mr. Goods and after twenty miles March we Come to Mr. Lott's in Troy and Pitcht our tents.

The 5th. We left Troy and Marched and Come to Morristown.

The 6th. We left Morristown and after twenty-three miles March we Come to Mr. Wallases where His Exelency had his winter Quarters and likewise the guard built huts and had there winter Quarters in Barringtown.

THE COMMANDER-IN-CHIEF'S GUARD.

The 9th. We begun to git the timber for the huts and to work on them.

The 16th. We finished our huts and we left our tents and moved into them.

The 30th. There was a Continentall thanksgiving Day ordered by Congress.

1779

Feb. 10th. I makes an agreament with Mr. J. Wallais for to Clear a peace of Land for him, the Condishons are as follows, I was to clear so much land fitt for mooing and in my fullfiling my oblegation Mr. Wallais was to give me one hundred Dollars Paper Currincy but if Head Quarters moved before I had finished it he was to Pay me for what I had Dun according to the argeament.

Apr. 22d. The French and Spanish Embasendor arived at Head Quarters and they was received with the selute of arms and Drumes and fifes and band of Musick and wellcomed by his Exelency.

The 30th. The army was revewed by the two Embasendors on the grand parrade.

May 2d. Both the French and Spanish Embasendors left Head Quarters at five in the morning for Philedelphia and as they past our army (they being on the grand parrade) they was seluted by the firing of thirteen Canon and a Desent selute of arms by our army and his Exelency accompanied them on there way.

The 6th. There was a farst ordered by Congress and

there was a Sermon Preached by Mr. Armstrong at Head Quarters.

The 12th. The King of the Ingens with five of his Nobles to attend him Come to Head Quarters to Congrattulate with his Exelency.

June 1st. I settels with Mr. Wallas and he gave me Eighty Dollars.

The 4th. The guard left Berington at twelve o'clock for New Winsor and after twenty miles march we Come to Mr. Kimballs in Morristown.

The 5th. We left Mr. Kimball's and after fourteen miles March we Come to Potewonick and piched our tents.

The 6th. We left Petwonick and after twenty miles march we Come to Gen. Arskell's at Kingwood and Come up with his Exelency.

The 7th. We left Kingwood and Come to Smith Clove at Head Quarters after a march of twenty-five miles and pitcht our tents and staid till

The 21st. We Left Smith's Clove and after fourteen miles march we Come to Mr. Ellis in New Winsor where the Gen. had his Quarters and picht our tents and staid there till.

The 27th. Was Sunday and there was a Sermon Preached at Head Quarters by Mr. Hitchcock and he took his text in the twenty-sevnth Chapter of Job at the fifth Varce you may find the words.

July 6th. There was one man killd and twenty wounded by thunder in Gen. Patteson Bregade.

THE COMMANDER-IN-CHIEF'S GUARD.

The 16th. At Night Gen. Wane with a party of the Infantry surprised the Enemy and took Stoney Point fort from them and betwixt five and six hundred Prisoners.

The 20th. After puting all the baggage aboard the sloop we left New Winsor at four in the afternoon and went by water to West Point and staid aboard that Night twelve miles.

The 21st. We onloded the baggage and Piched our tents at Morses folley at little Distant from West Point foart.

Aug. 6th. There was two more Deserted from the gard Viz. Timothy Smith and Levi Deen. Sarjt. Edwards was sent after them but found them not.

The 15th. We had a Sermon Preached at Head Quarters by Mr. Armstrong and he took his text in the one hundred and twenty-sixth pslam at the fifth varce you have these words—"they that sow in teers shall reep in joy."

The 29th. We had the Resolves of Congress of the Ninetenth Instant Read to us that the Solgers wages should be ten Dollars more added to there wages and what Clothes thay had not Receved that they should have them and Confirmed by General orders.

Sept. 15. His Exelency Gen. Washington and Gen. Green with there Addecamps went to New Winsor the honourable Chelevier LeDeLuzerne and Embasender from the Coart of France and accompened him to Head Quarters at West Point and When they arrived they was Receeved and wellcomed with the selutes of Drums and fifes and the gard present there arms. They arrived at three in the afternoon and at five there was thirteen Canon fired from the fourt on account of his arrival.

The 16. His Exelency and the Embasendor went and Vewd all the fourt and battery that were on West Point and Sarjt. Harris and ten of the guard went over the River to Gen. DePotales and carrys a markee and several other things and piched the markee and at five of the Clock in the afternoon Gen. Washington and the Embasendor and several other Gen. and offisers with them arrived there and Dined.

The 17th. The Embasender left West Point at eight of the Clock in the fournoon for Philedelphia and was accompened by his Excelency and addecamps as far as New Winsor and returned.

The 23d. Leut. Colefax and the part of the guard that left the guard at Barington for East town they arrived there the six Instant with the Baggage and left there the twentyth of Sept. and after the march of an hundred miles they Come to New Winsor the twenty-third and left the baggage and Come to West Point.

Oct. 1st. The North Carolina troops left West Point and Come to New Winsor and Incampt.

(Nov.) The 15th. One of the Guard, viz. John Piller Deserted from the guard at West Point.

The 19th. All the Carolina men that belonged to the guard jined there Ridgments and the Carolinian troops left West Point on there way to Gorja.

The 21st. There was three men to be hung for Robing

and one Whipt for Mr. King's house. Two of them had there repreave, the other two hung. They belonged to the Carolinia troops and five others Whipt.

The 30th. His Exelency and likewise the guard left West Point and Come to New Winsor and Encampt.

The 31st. We left New Winsor for Morristown and Come to Smith's Clove.

Dec. 1st. We left Smith's Clove and Come to Wingwood Eighteen miles.

The 3d. We left Wingwood and Come to Mr. Good's in Reading.

The 4th. We left Rocheway and Come to Morristown where Head Quarters was and Piched our tents.

The 6th. We begun to git the timber for our huts and to work on them.

The 9th. We finished our huts and left our tents and mooved into them.

The 23d. The man that was sent after our Clothes the seventeenth Instent returned.

The 31st. Lady Washington arrived at Head Quarters at Morristown.

1780

Jan. 7th. I had my Discharge from the Corps of Guards.

*   *   *   *

REVOLUTIONARY WAR.

The Commander-in-Chief's Guard.

REVOLUTIONARY WAR.

References to the Introduction

1 Lossing's Field Book of the Revolution, Vol. 1, 689.
2 Samuel Sherman's Pension Papers.
3 Caleb Gibbs' Pension Papers.
4 Custis' Recollections of Washington, 259.
5 Lossing's Field Book of the Revolution, Vol. 1, 688.
  Lodge's George Washington, Vol. 1, 160.
  The Historical Magazine (3rd Series), Vol. 1, 93.
6 Connecticut Men in the War of the Revolution, 299.
  Register of the Officers and Men of New Jersey in the Revolutionary War, 60.
7 Lossing's Field Book of the Revolution, Vol. 1, 688.
  Pennsylvania Archives (2nd Series), Vol. 11, 121.
8 Johnston's George Washington Day by Day, 71.
9 Lossing's Field Book of the Revolution, Vol. 1, 688.
  Connecticut Men in the War of the Revolution, 299.
  Register of the Officers and Men of New Jersey in the Revolutionary War, 60.
10 The men of this troop were from New England, principally Massachusetts.
11 Lossing's Field Book of the Revolution, Vol. 1, 687.
  Root's Chapter Sketches of the Connecticut Daughters of the American Revolution, 441.
12 Custis' Recollections of Washington, 262-3, n.
13 Lossing's Field Book of the Revolution, Vol. 1, 687.
14 Reid's Sketch of Enoch Long, 29.
15 Frontispiece "The Corporal's Musket," Music Department, Congressional Library.

References to the History of the Guard

* Washington's Orderly Book.
† Minutes of a Conspiracy against the Liberties of America.
‡ Elijah Fisher's Dairy.
1 Custis' Recollections of Washington, 259.
  Public Papers of George Clinton, Vol. 1, 584.
2 American Archives (4th Series), Vol. 6, 531.

3. Samuel Sherman's Pension Papers.
4. Sparks' Writings of Washington, Vol. 3, 354.
5. Lossing's Field Book of the Revolution, Vol. 2, 594.
6. Baker's Itinerary of General Washington, 16.
7. Lossing's Life of Washington, Vol. 2, 173.
8. American Archives (4th Series), Vol. 6, 1158.
9. Irving's Life of Washington, Vol. 2, 247, n.
10. Pennsylvania Journal, June 26, 1776.
11. Irving's Life of Washington, Vol. 2, 247, n.
12. Lossing's Life of Washington, Vol. 2, 176.
   Anthony Cherdaveyn's Pension Papers.
13. Journal of the New York Provincial Congress, Vol. 1, 495.
14. Journal of the New York Provincial Congess, Vol. 1, 496.
15. Mss., Congressional Library.
16. American Archives (4th Series), Vol. 6, 1109.
17. American Archives (4th Series), Vol. 6, 1119-20.
18. Lossing's Our Country, 863.
19. Lossing's Life of Washington, Vol. 2, 177.
20. New England Historical and Genealogical Register, Vol. 23, 208.
21. American Archives (4th Series), Vol. 6, 1120.
22. Mss., Tomlinson Collection, New York Mercantile Library.
23. Journal of the New York Provincial Congress, Vol. 1, 530.
24. Thatcher's Military Journal, 64.
25. The Historical Magazine, Vol. 2, 131.
26. Journal of the New York Provincial Congress, Vol. 1, 530.
27. Lossing's Life of Washington, Vol. 2, 177.
28. Thatcher's Military Journal, 222.
29. Baker's Itinerary of General Washington, 23-6.
30. Stryker's Battles of Trenton and Princeton, 30.
31. Pennsylvania Magazine, Vol. 4, 133.
32. Carswell Gardner's Pension Papers.
33. Ford's Writings of Washington, Vol. 7, 111.
34. Carswell Gardner and Samuel Sherman's Pension Papers.
35. Davis' History of Bucks County, 631.
36. Samuel Reid's Pension Papers.
    Ford's Writings of Washington, Vol. 5, 143.
37. Stryker's Battles of Trenton and Princeton, 246.
38. Mellick's Story of an Old Farm, 382.
39. The Historical Magazine, Vol. 19, 354.
40. Samuel Reid's Pension Papers.
41. Carswell Gardner and Samuel Sherman's Pension Papers.

REVOLUTIONARY WAR.

42 Samuel Sherman's Pension Papers.
43 Carswell Gardner's Pension Papers.
44 Historisch-genealogischer Calender, oder Jahrbuch der merkwurdigsten neuen Welt-Begebenheiten fur 1784, Leipzig zur Messe, bey Hande und Spener von Berlin (New York Mercantile Library).
45 Wiliam Colfax's Pension Papers.
46 Custis' Recollections of Washington, 258.
47 Sparks' Writings of Washington, Vol. 4, 407.
48 Custis' Recollections of Washington, 262.
49 Sparks' Writings of Washington, Vol. 4, 483-7.
50 Pickering's Journal.
51 Ford's Writings of Washington, Vol. 5, 513-4.
52 Pennsylvania Magazine, Vol. 16, 28-9.
53 Sparks' Writings of Washington, Vol. 5, 26.
54 Pennsylvania Magazine, Vol. 1, 275.
55 Ford's Writings of Washington, Vol. 6, 45-8.
56 Pennsylvania Magazine, Vol. 1, 283.
57 Pennsylvania Evening Post, August 28, 1777.
58 Scharf's History of Delaware, Vol. 1, 243.
59 Baker's Itinerary of General Washington, 45.
60 Pickering's Journal.
61 Baker's Itinerary of General Washington, 46-7.
62 Baker's Itinerary of General Washington, 48-50.
63 Sparks' Writings of Washington, Vol. 5, 78-9.
64 Baker's Itinerary of General Washington, 51-2.
65 Sparks' Writings of Washington, Vol. 5, 121-3.
66 Mss., Washington's Military Family, State Department.
67 Pennsylvania Magazine, Vol. 17, 418.
68 Baker's Itinerary of General Washington, 54-6.
69 Proceedings of New Jersey Historical Society, Vol. 7, 105.
70 Kapp's Life of Steuben, 118.
71 Ford's Writings of Washington, Vol. 7, 111.
72 Kapp's Life of Steuben, 129.
73 Kapp's Life of Steuben, 126-8.
74 Oaths of Allegiance, War Department.
75 Sparks' Writings of Washington, Vol. 5, 368.
76 Sparks' Writings of Washington, Vol. 5, 546-7.
77 Sanderson's Biography of the Signers to the Declaration of Independence (1846 Ed.), 203.
78 Laurens' Letters, Vol. 2, No. 13, 36-7, State Department.
79 Ford's Writings of Washington, Vol. 7, 111-2.

THE COMMANDER-IN-CHIEF'S GUARD.

80 Papers of Congress, No. 147, Vol. 2, 147, State Department.
81 Laurens' Letters, Vol. 2, No. 13, 36-7, State Department.
82 Mss., Chap. A, No. 78, Vol. 10, 109, State Department.
83 Letters to Washington, Vol. 91, 258, State Department.
84 Letters to Washington, Vol. 28, 258, State Department.
85 Mellick's Story of an Old Farm, 455.
86 Journals of Congress.
87 William Colfax's Pension Papers.
88 Mellick's Story of an Old Farm, 478.
Uniform of the Army of the United States, 1774 to 1889, Plate 2.
89 Gaines' New York Gazette, June 17, 1776.
90 Uniform Exhibit, War Department.
91 Historisch-genealogischer Calender, oder Jahrbuch der merkwurdigsten neuen Welt-Begebenheiten fur 1784, Leipzig zer Messe, bey Hande und Spener von Berlin. (New York Mercantile Library).
92 Magazine of American History, Vol. 24, 81.
93 Harper's Magazine, Vol. 18, 296-7.
94 Sparks' Writings of Washington, Vol. 6, 487.
95 Lamb's History of New York City, Vol. 2, 233.
96 The Historical Magazine, Vol. 19, 376.
97 Kapp's Life of Steuben, 277.
98 Letters to Washington, Vol. 38, 55, State Department.
99 Baker's Itinerary of General Washington, 181.
100 Ford's Writings of Washington, Vol. 8, 365.
101 Lossing's Field Book of the Revolution, Vol. 1, 737.
102 Baker's Itinerary of General Washington, 119-20.
103 David Severn's Pension Papers.
104 Nelsons' Historical Sketch of Passaic County, 34.
105 Mss., Washington's Military Family, State Department.
106 Sparks' Writings of Washington, Vol. 7, 313.
Heath's Memoirs.
107 Letters to Washington, Vol. 48, 272, State Department.
108 Mss., War Department.
109 Baker's Itinerary of General Washington, 156.
110 Baker's Itinerary of General Washington, 160-5.
111 Baker's Itinerary of General Washington, 166-8.
112 Carrington's Battles of the American Revolution, 647—map.
113 Johnston's Yorktown Campaign, 138, 151, 155.
114 Baker's Itinerary of General Washington, 176-80.
115 Jonathan Moore's Pension Papers.

REVOLUTIONARY WAR.

116 Freeman's Journal, March 27, 1782.
117 Heath's Memoirs.
118 Ruttenber's History of Orange County, N. Y., 145.
119 Levi Holden's Pension Papers.
120 Sparks' Writings of Washington, Vol. 8, 340, n.
121 Memoires de Rochambeau, Tom. 1, 309.
122 The Historical Magazine, Vol. 2, 132.
123 Thatcher's Military Journal, 385-6.
124 Heath's Memoirs.
125 Pennsylvania Packet, October 24, 1782.
126 Harper's Magazine, Vol. 67, 654.
   Ruttenber's History of Orange County, N. Y., 214-5.
127 Eager's History of Orange County, N. Y., 184.
128 Mss., Congressional Library.
129 Mss., Washington's Military Family, State Department.
130 Harper's Magazine, Vol. 67, 652.
131 Lossing's Field Book of the Revolution, Vol. 2, 668-70.
132 Heath's Memoirs.
133 Mss., War Department.
134 John Phillips' Pension Papers.
135 Journal of Congress, October 6, 1783.
136 Custis' Recollections of Washington, 257.
137 Lossing's Field Book of the Revolution, Vol. 2, 120.
138 Army Returns, Vol. 35, 52, War Department.
139 Sparks' Writings of Washington, Vol. 8, 465-8.
140 Baker's Itinerary of General Washington, 304.
141 Dunlap's History of Arts of Design, Vol. 1, 252.
142 Asa Redington's Reminiscences.
143 Dunlap's History of Arts of Design, Vol. 1, 254.
144 Mss., Howe Collection, New Jersey Historical Society.
145 Bezaleel Howe's Pension Papers.
146 Mss., Howe Collection, New Jersey Historical Society.
147 Joel Holt's Pension Papers.
148 Pennsylvania Magazine, Vol. 16, 166.
149 Mss., Howe Collection, New Jersey Historical Society.
150 Nehemiah Stratton's Pension Papers.
151 Abraham Currier's Pension Papers.

The Commander-in-Chief's Guard.

References to the Records of the Officers and Men

- * U. S. Pension Case.
- ‡ U. S. Land Warrant.
- 1 Mr. Charles W. Alban, St. Louis, Mo.
- 2 National Society, Sons of the American Revolution.
- 3 Mr. Eugene L. Baker, Groton, Conn.
- 4 Mr. Wendell Phillips, Kingston, Mass.
- 5 Mrs. Rhoda A. Trimmer, Pacific Grove, Cal.
- 6 Mr. John W. Berry, Gardiner, Me.
- 7 Mrs. Henry M. Qvay, Mill Village, Pa.
- 8 Mr. Samuel H. Blair, Newburgh, N. Y.
- 9 Mr. Samuel Blundin, Oxford Valley, Pa., et al.
- 10 Little's Passaic Valley, 46-7.
- 11 Mrs. Hannah M. Vincent, Oberlin, O., et al.
- 12 Mr. C. Fitch Cox, Groton, N. Y.
- 13 Mrs. Julia A. Hastings, Bristol, N. H.
- 14 Mrs. Mary E. Kendall, Albany, N. Y.
- 15 Mr. Charles C. Wheelwright, Boston, Mass.
- 16 Mr. H. J. Chapman, Bangor, Me., et al.
- 17 Mr. Thomas Ball, Hope Side, Va., et al.
- 18 Mr. John J. Currier, Newburyport, Mass.
- 19 Mr. Richard S. Colfax, Pompton, N. J.
- 20 Mr. James P. Fellows, Sanbornville, N. H.
- 21 Mr. Emory F. Skinner, Escambia, Fla., et al.
- 22 Hon. Ernest H. Crosby, New York.
- 23 Miss Fanny C. Allen, Leominster, Mass.
- 24 Mr. E. S. Crombie, Groveland, Mass., et al.
- 25 Mrs. Mary E. Gambold, Coatesville, Ind., et al.
- 26 Mrs. Addison S. Cressy, Bradford, N. H.
- 27 Mr. William H. Cutter, Meadville, Pa., et al.
- 28 Mr. Charles H. Duffer, St. Louis, Mo.
- 29 Mrs. Sarah B. Van Ness, East Lexington, Mass.
- 30 Dodge's Genealogy, Part 2, 522; Part 1, 124.
- 31 Mr. Francis Marvin, Port Jervis, N. Y.
- 32 Mr. Matthew Hale, Albany, N. Y., et al.
- 33 Mrs. Wilson C. Fitzgerald, Canaan, Me., et al.
- 34 Mr. Richard F. Everett, Watertown, N. Y.
- 35 Mr. A. W. Gilmore, St. Albans, Vt., et al.

Revolutionary War.

36 Miss Kate Deshler, New Brunswick, N. J.
37 Mr. Edward S. Fenton, Ovid, N. Y., et al.
38 Mr. Ransom N. Fisher, Livermore, Me.
39 Mr. James C. Flemister, Covington, Ga.
40 Mrs. Caroline E. Blagge, Galveston, Tex.
41 Mr. James A. Gill, Sheppards, Va., et al.
42 Mr. Samuel Dimock, Rocky Hill, Conn.
43 Miss Ellen E. Gordon, Rushford, N. Y., et al.
44 Mr. Benjamin R. Grymes, Weedonville, Va.
45 Mrs. Nancie L. Cornish, South Carver, Mass., et al.
46 Mr. Douglass H. Thomas, Baltimore, Md.
47 Rear Admiral Colby M. Chester, U. S. N., et al.
48 Rev. William Harris, Kapps Mills, N. C., et al.
49 Mrs. Thomas Vannevar, Roxbury, Mass.
50 Mr. S. C. Adamson, Waynesburg, Pa.
51 Mr. James C. Holden, Madison, N. J., et al.
52 Miss Eliza A. Holt, Milford, N. H., et al.
53 Mr. George R. Howe, East Orange, N. J.
54 Mrs. S. J. F. Barnett, Spartanburg, S. C., et al.
55 Hon. Stratton S. Knox, Cortland, N. Y., et al.
56 Mr. C. L. Landon, Granville Summit, Pa.
57 Mr. George Marks, Haydenville, Mass., et al.
58 Mr. Charles Lawrence, Waterloo, Quebec, Canada.
59 Mrs. Lucy L. Funsten, White Post, Va., et al.
60 Lathrop Family Memoir, 338, 354.
61 Mr. D. Ross Lovejoy, Niagara Falls, N. Y.,
62 Mr. William H. Manning, Ayer, Mass.
63 Mr. John D. Martin, Piermont, N. H., et al.
64 Mrs. Armilda Beatty, Poplar Grove, Ky.
65 Mr. Samuel Moore, Smith Center, Kan.
66 Mr. David H. Morrison, Alton, N. H., et al.
67 Mr. Henry F. Phillips, Newark, N. J.
68 Mr. Ned Pierce, Bellows Falls, N. H.
69 Hayley's Genealogy of the Hayley and Piper Families.
70 Mr. Augustus B. Cornell, Mansfield, O.
71 Dr. Daniel K. Pearsons, Chicago, Ill., et al.
72 Mrs. Landonia R. Minor, Richmond, Va., et al.
73 Mr. Aaron A. Plaisted, Waterville, Me.
74 Mr. Samuel R. Spencer, Suffield, Conn.
75 Mr. Alvah Spencer, Highland Station, Mich., et al.
76 Mrs. D. R. Fraser, Chicago, Ill.
77 Mrs. Thomas W. Williams, East Orange, N. J.

78 Miss Martha H. Shorey, Lynn, Mass., et al.
79 Mr. Charles P. Bliven, Providence, R. I.
80 Mrs. Alice P. Driggs, Jacksonville, Fla.
81 Miss Mariett Raymond, Niagara Falls, N. Y.
82 Mr. B. F. Smith, Holley, N. Y.
83 Mrs. R. W. Webster, Keene, N. H., et al.
84 Mr. John W. Sparks, Monterey, Ky., et al.
85 Mr. J. W. Stratton, Albion, Me., et al.
86 Mrs. Hariet B. Maxim, Hartford, Me.
87 Mr. Frank L. Shaw, Portland, Me., et al.
88 Mrs. W. J. Furlong, Rochelle, Ill., et al.
89 Mrs. Charles H. Brown, Newburyport, Mass., et al.
90 Mr. Charles Tubbs, Osceola, Pa.
91 Mr. Frank C. Vibbert, New Britain, Conn.
92 Mr. A. E. Wadsworth, Shinnston, W. Va., et al.
93 Mrs. E. W. Brady, Davenport, Ia.
94 Hon. J. R. Thornton, Alexandria, La.
95 Mr. Charles F. Wyman, Cambridge, Mass.

www.ingramcontent.com/pod-product-compliance
Lightning Source LLC
Chambersburg PA
CBHW022009300426
44117CB00005B/93